T0314141

FAST MONEY SCHEMES

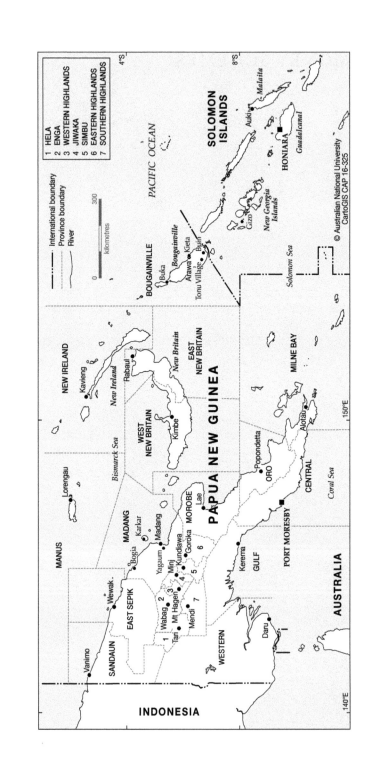

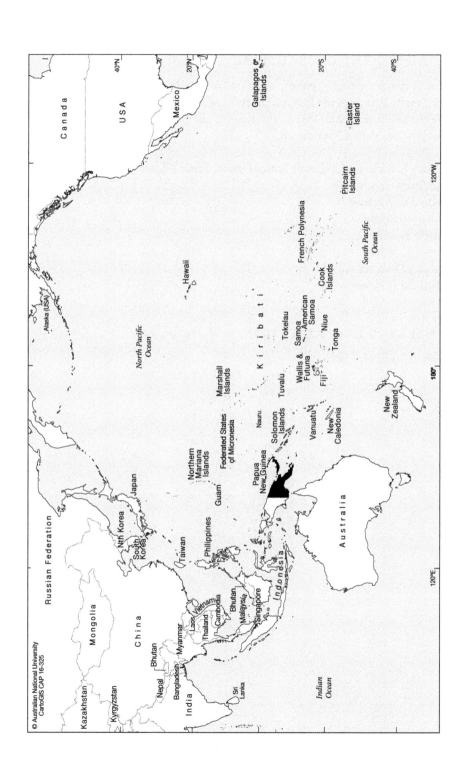

FRAMING THE GLOBAL SERIES

The Framing the Global project, an initiative of Indiana
University Press and the Indiana University Center
for the Study of Global Change, is funded by the
Andrew W. Mellon Foundation.

Hilary E. Kahn and Deborah Piston-Hatlen, *Series Editors*
Advisory Committee
Alfred C. Aman Jr.
Eduardo Brondizio
Maria Bucur
Bruce L. Jaffee
Patrick O'Meara
Radhika Parameswaran
Richard R. Wilk

TRACKING GLOBALIZATION

Robert J. Foster, *Editor*

FAST MONEY SCHEMES

Hope and Deception in
Papua New Guinea

John Cox

Indiana University Press

This book is a publication of

Indiana University Press
Office of Scholarly Publishing
Herman B Wells Library 350
1320 East 10th Street
Bloomington, Indiana 47405 USA

iupress.indiana.edu

The paper used in this publication meets the minimum requirements of
the American National Standard for Information Sciences—Permanence
of Paper for Printed Library Materials, ANSI Z39.48–1992.

Manufactured in the United States of America

Library of Congress Cataloging-in-Publication Data

Names: Cox, John (Anthropologist), author.
Title: Fast money schemes : hope and deception in Papua New Guinea / John Cox.
Description: Bloomington, Indiana : Indiana University Press, [2018] |
    Series: Framing the global | Includes bibliographical references and
    index.
Identifiers: LCCN 2018019381 (print) | LCCN 2018022039 (ebook) | ISBN
    9780253035639 (e-book) | ISBN 9780253025609 (cl : alk. paper) | ISBN
    9780253026118 (pb : alk. paper)
Subjects: LCSH: Ponzi schemes—Papua New Guinea—History. | Swindlers and
    swindling—Papua New Guinea—History.
Classification: LCC HV6699.P26 (ebook) | LCC HV6699.P26 C69 2018 (print) |
    DDC 364.16/309953—dc23
LC record available at https://lccn.loc.gov/2018019381

1 2 3 4 5   23 22 21 20 19 18

Contents

Acknowledgments

THIS MONOGRAPH IS the result of twelve years of research into scams in Papua New Guinea and Solomon Islands: a remarkable introduction to anthropology. There are many people and institutions to thank, so I will not acknowledge them all here but only those whose support and engagement was critical to the specific project of turning my doctoral research into this publication.

Martha Macintyre must head this list, not only for her role in initiating me into anthropology through the Australian Research Council Project Managing Modernity: Capitalism, Globalisation and Governance in Melanesia, but for her regular encouragement over the past five years. Her "How's your book going?" was invaluable if not always entirely welcome.

Bob Foster, one of my PhD examiners and the editor of this series, has been extremely patient with me during the writing and editing process. I thank him for having a vision of what the book could be that went well beyond my intellectual horizons and that has deepened my scholarly development greatly. Fred Errington also saw great potential in my doctoral work and I thank him for his generous comments as an examiner of my thesis. His and Bob's reports have opened many doors, and I am deeply grateful for their academic hospitality in nurturing junior scholars.

Let me also thank a large cohort of colleagues from my time at the Australian National University. Many, like myself, have now moved on to other institutions but I would like to acknowledge the superb camaraderie of Matthew Allen, Jon Altman, Chris Ballard, Chris Chevalier, Melissa Demian, Sinclair Dinnen, Miranda Forsyth, Chris Gregory, Melinda Hinkson, Margaret Jolly, Lia Kent, Kathy Lepani, Sarah Logan, Siobhan McDonnell, Kylie McKenna, Jenny Munro, Thiago Opperman, Gordon Peake, Pyone Myat Thu, Michelle Rooney, Carly Schuster, Tim Sharp, Ceridwen Spark, Graeme Smith, Matt Tomlinson, Grant Walton, and Terence Wood.

The book was completed in Fiji, during a two-month stay at the University of the South Pacific as a School Visitor with the School of Government, Development, and International Affairs. I thank Sandra Tarte, Head of School, for her welcome and I also acknowledge Glen Finau, Romitesh Kant, Jope Tarai, and Jason Titifanue, all productive junior scholars whose intellectual energy is inspiring.

I also express my gratitude to my new colleagues at La Trobe University, who have welcomed me into their ranks in a way that makes me feel deeply affirmed as a scholar and a member of a new team. Thanks to everyone at the Institute of Human Security and Social Change and to Helen Lee and Jack Taylor in Social Inquiry.

Finally, this project would not have been possible without the support of Georgina Phillips, the great love of my life. Her curiosity about the world first drew me into the Pacific more than twenty years ago. The formative experiences that we shared in Kiribati developed relationships and skills that have been the foundation for the various twists and turns of my career. Georgina's long commitment to improving health services in Papua New Guinea and other developing countries has given me access to many of the people interviewed in this book and a grounding and credibility there that I would not have been able to establish on my own.

The arguments in this book have been refined through processes of reflection and critical review that have taken place through Indiana University Press's reviewers and those of a number of other publications. Earlier versions of my work on fast money schemes have been explored (to date) in four edited volumes, two Australian National University discussion papers and four articles in the journal Oceania, often as contributions to special editions. I thank the editors and reviewers of each of these publications for their engagement with my work.

Abbreviations

ABC	Australian Broadcasting Corporation
ABG	Autonomous Bougainville Government
ANZ	Australia and New Zealand Banking Corporation
AOG	Assemblies of God
ASIC	Australian Securities and Investment Commission
AUD	Australian Dollar
AusAID	Australian Agency for International Development
BPNG	Bank of Papua New Guinea
BSP	Bank South Pacific
CBSI	Central Bank of Solomon Islands
CLC	Christian Life Centre
DWU	Divine Word University
FCF	Family Charity Fund
HRH	His/ Her Royal Highness
IBOM	International Bank of Me'ekamui
K	Papua New Guinea Kina
LLG	Local Level Government
NFF	National Federation of Foundations
NGO	Non-Government Organisation
NRI	National Research Institute
PM	Prime Minister
PNG	Papua New Guinea
PNGBC	Papua New Guinea Banking Corporation
POMSoX	Port Moresby Stock Exchange
PV	Personal Viability
RAMSI	Regional Assistance Mission to Solomon Islands
RAONK	Royal Assembly of Nations and Kingdoms
RKP	Royal Kingdom of Papala

SBD	Solomon Islands Dollar
SDA	Seventh-day Adventist
SIG	Solomon Islands Government
TP	Tok Pisin
UN	United Nations
UNDP	United Nations Development Programme
UNITECH	University of Technology, Lae
UPNG	University of Papua New Guinea
USD	United States Dollar

Interview Participants

Pseudonym	Age	Occupation	Province/ Regional Affiliation[1]	Chapter(s)	Interview[2]
Alphonse	38	Public servant	East Sepik (Rabaul)	5	Port Moresby
Ambrose	67	Retired tradesman	Madang-Bogia	5, 6, 8, 9	Madang
Andrew	24	NGO program manager	Sandaun	6	Madang
Anna	42	School Teacher	Madang	2, 5, 10	Madang
Balthasar	41	Public servant	Madang	1, 7, 8, 9, 10, 11	Madang
Cephas	46	Small business owner	Madang- Karkar	9	Karkar
Charlie	44	NGO program manager	East New Britain (ENB)	9	Madang
Christian	39	Doctor	Goroka	6	Port Moresby
Dorothy	51	Administrative assistant	ENB	6	Madang
Felix	48	Carpenter	East Sepik	2, 5	Madang
Francis	55	Journalist	East Sepik	5, 6	Madang
Geraldine	47	Accountant	Milne Bay	3, 5, 10	Madang
Isaac	37	Policeman	Mt Hagen	3, 8, 9, 11	Madang
Jack	35	Doctor	Bougainville	1, 2, 11	Port Moresby
Jackson	56	Public servant	ENB	6, 7	Port Moresby
Lindsay	45	Small businessperson	Madang-Karkar	5	Karkar
Marie	29	Teacher	Bougainville	2	Port Moresby
Martin	55	Academic services	Madang	5	Madang
Michael	31	Catechist	Chimbu	8	
Nancy	32	Housewife	Buka	11	Madang
Pastor Paul	42	Pastor	East Sepik	6, 10	
Pauline	47	Teacher	Buka	6, 9, 10	Madang
Rebecca	38	Teacher	Madang	1, 7, 8, 9, 10	Madang
Roga	40	Lecturer	Sandaun	4	Madang
Thomas	36	Laborer	Sepik- Angoram	4, 9	Madang
Victor	39	Doctor	Madang	5, 6, 7, 9, 10, 11	Madang

1. These are self-reported places of origin which I take to be typical of how people identify themselves in town. For this reason I do not seek to specify them further. The imprecision also assists in de-identifying individuals. Further descriptions on personal circumstances are found in the text.

2. All interviews were conducted between April and September 2009.

FAST MONEY SCHEMES

1 Studying Scams

It was just like a dream at that time. Now it's so obvious that it was a con but at that time it was like all your birthdays had come at once! It was like Christmas every day!

Jack, doctor and Bougainvillean investor

Port Moresby, the sprawling, dusty capital of Papua New Guinea (PNG), was the scene of a rush of Ponzi scams in 1999. Queues of people formed outside the offices of the "fast money schemes": some coming to make deposits, some to check their balances, others to roll over their earnings or even withdraw their rapidly growing balances. All had the hope of turning their deposits into huge sums of money with offers of 100 percent or even 200 percent interest per month. Rolling over K100 for a few months would produce returns in the thousands, or so they were told. *Money Rain*, *Windfall*, *Bonanza '99*, and *Millennium*: the very names of the schemes heightened expectations. The largest and longest lived is at the center of this drama and so of this book: *U-Vistract Financial Systems*, a Ponzi scam run by one Noah Musingku from the island of Bougainville. In a country with a population of some seven million people, as many as 300,000 people joined U-Vistract and the other fast money schemes, bringing with them their relatives, neighbors, and colleagues and losing millions of Kina, the national currency.[1]

Introductions were mostly made by word of mouth, but, as passersby saw the growing queues or heard stories of payouts, they were also drawn into the world of fast money:

"I went in just to see what was happening and they said it was a fast money scheme"

"I looked out of the bus window and I saw all these people and I asked what are they doing and people told me that it was U-Vistract"

"My uncle came to me and asked, 'Have you heard of Noah Musingku?'"

"Our staff were sitting at their desks with calculators working out how many thousands they would be paid"

"This scheme was offering 100 percent return in one month, that scheme was paying 200 percent, I was crazy to leave my money in the bank."

The Port Moresby "coconut wireless" buzzed with stories of instant wealth, and, as the schemes spread through the town, almost no one was immune from the excitement. Similar queues started forming at money scheme offices in provincial centers around the country.

Like Ponzi scams elsewhere, early investors were often paid large amounts—and publicly. This generated credibility for the schemes and attracted still more investors. The visibility of payments to prominent people—and even simply rumors of such payments (cf. Stewart and Strathern 2004)—provided evidence that the schemes' financial patter was true. Jack describes the conspicuous consumption of his cousin at the height of the fast money rush:

> There's a doctor who's from my area. He went off medical school for three months and was just investing. He got K10,000 from relatives and got a brand new K126,000 Toyota Prado. He used to drive us around and buy us drinks. For three months we never used to see him at school. He'd buy his classmates to take notes and make excuses for him. Every week, he'd go to invest. It must have been a lot of money because he was just playing around with money like it was nothing. Then he bought a brand new Toyota Celica. It was red. Probably worth K120,000, something like that. We used to call him a black tycoon. He had a lot of girlfriends, including an Australian lady who used to work for AusAID.

I was not there to see these queues of hopeful investors or the few successful "black tycoons" as I began research on this phenomenon with a visit to Port Moresby in 2005 and then conducted my main fieldwork during 2009. Nevertheless, many people, even those who ended up losing their money, have told me the same story in a similar tone recalling the heady excitement of the times. Indeed, the ability of fast money schemes to sustain the hopes of their investors long after the bubble had burst is remarkable. None were more successful in this regard than U-Vistract, the focus of this book. U-Vistract developed an elaborate cosmology of moral capitalism that it disseminated through well-produced newsletters, webpages, and its local organizers. More than fifteen years after the scheme was declared bankrupt by the PNG courts, U-Vistract continues to operate out of Bougainville and is even now drawing in small numbers of American and Australian investors through its internet presence as the International Bank of Meekamui (IBOM).

In this book I ask how this implausible scam has managed to persist over such a long period of time. Charles Ponzi's notorious scheme, after all, lasted less than a year before the authorities closed it down in August 1920. U-Vistract had a similar period of operations between its commencement in 1998 and the last payments to investors in 1999. However, it has managed to evade prosecution and, as its followers in PNG dwindle and lose hope of seeing their returns, is finding new dupes further afield. In the last few months of writing this book, I have given evidence to court cases in Sydney, Australia, and (via Skype) in Des Moines, Iowa. In both these cases, investors with no connections to PNG have been fooled into investing in U-Vistract. The scam is more global than I thought possible when conducting my initial fieldwork among middle-class Papua New Guineans, whose stories and experiences are the substance of this research.

In the following pages, I argue that U-Vistract's propaganda succeeded because it articulated far more than the material aspirations of middle-class Papua New Guineans. Through its financial patter, the scheme reengaged people in a moral vision of the nation and of themselves as catalysts of change. For both dupes and fraudsters the scheme was a locally staged performance of global ideas of financial investment, perhaps even ethical investment. As Foster (2008) has argued, global imaginings of share markets imply moral responsibilities and possibilities for individual investors, just as they resituate citizenship as a polity within market structures. As a type of "ethical investment" U-Vistract not only provided a means for people to deposit money into a financial scheme they believed to be good (and so make an ethical consumer choice), but it also represented an investment of individuals themselves in an ethical project of remaking themselves as prosperous global citizens. These good citizens prove their moral worth by exercising an appropriate mastery of financial disciplines, which now extend beyond saving and thrift within a household budget to calculation of risk and investment in a global market economy. This book shows how the "financial self" Zaloom (2006) is being created and reworked well beyond the financial centers of New York, Tokyo, Chicago, and London. Papua New Guinean financial selves are Christian moral actors who seek to harness the wealth of global stock markets for the purposes of fulfilling old hopes of egalitarian national development.

Scale-Making in "Economies of Appearances"

Stories of Ponzi schemes and mass pyramid scams are told everywhere, not least in the institutional centers of global finance, as New York's own Bernard Madoff demonstrated to the world. Indeed, Madoff's scam has become a metaphor for Wall Street's greed and deception. This book explores the fast money scheme experience of Papua New Guineans, but this is not a simple get rich quick story set in a quirky, out-of-the-way place. Nor is this a cautionary tale or a lament over the poor gullible victims of the scam, who in their out-of-the-way innocence could not have known any better. Rather, the fast money story reveals engagements with money and society that reconstitute middle-class Papua New Guineans as moral persons, citizens of a reformed Christian nation who have earned their right to join the cosmopolitan middle class in enjoying the prosperity of global share markets. Where other scholars (Hart and Ortiz 2008; Ho 2009, LiPuma and Lee 2004; Thrift 1998, 2001; Zaloom 2006; Miyazaki 2006) have studied finance as it is experienced and produced by the share traders and investment bankers working at the centers of powerful global networks, this book provides an ethnography of the reception of ideologies of investment by international consumers of financial products, albeit in the form of fraudulent mimicry. Local adaptations can provide new perspectives on global discourses, as Schuster (2015) has shown in her enthralling account of microfinance in Paraguay. This case comes from a country known as a primary producer of raw commodities such as gold, liquefied natural gas, tropical hardwoods, oil palm, coffee, and cocoa. PNG is rarely considered as a home to a growing middle class, and this places the aspirations of these distant investors into sharper relief than perhaps would be the case in a metropolitan example. Similarly, the fundamentalist Christianity that characterizes much of the public culture of PNG brings the moral dimensions of financial investment to the very fore.

Appadurai (1996) wrote of *financescapes*, referring to the flows of capital transforming the world on an unprecedented scale. PNG is very much part of such global financescapes. For the past decade, its economy has boomed with foreign investment in mining and associated services. The national capital, Port Moresby, has all the hallmarks of a boomtown, with new apartment towers going up quickly at prices few of the city's residents can afford. The spread of benefits from this economic development is highly uneven. Almost everywhere across the country, people complain of poverty, corruption, crime, ill health, and poor schooling. Yet, in this same moment, the middle classes are exposed to more possibilities of prosperity than ever before, even if these are simply experienced as images of distant and more modern people from elsewhere on television or the internet. For contemporary PNG, Appadurai's financescapes are "promissory notes of modernity" (Robbins 1998) that transform social relations through the power of anticipation. And this anticipation lies at the heart of any successful scam, or indeed of speculation more generally.

In her article "Inside: The Economy of Appearances" (Tsing 2000b; reprinted in Tsing 2005), Anna Tsing explores these themes of spectacle and promise, developing the idea of *scale-making projects*. Tsing analyses the case of Bre-X, a Canadian mining company that attracted millions of dollars of North American investment capital and high-level support from the Indonesian government, but on false pretenses.

Tsing's method of identifying scale-making projects translates well into the Papua New Guinean context. The scale-making done by PNG's fast money schemes draws on many of the same themes of investment, finance, and globalization. Yet what makes the Papua New Guinean fast money schemes so interesting is that they mark the emergence of a different kind of investor than the start-up capitalists who funded Bre-X. Bre-X was a fraud that mimicked mining ventures, but U-Vistract and its associated fast money schemes were frauds that mimicked financial investment itself. If Bre-X founded its deception on a well-known process of mineral exploration and production, U-Vistract's deceit was based on the idea that share markets produce wealth from their intrinsic processes that are abstracted from actual productive enterprises. Whether individual investors had a more elaborate rationale (and many did not), the scheme's appeal lay largely in repeating the financial patter of *trading, options, investments,* and so forth: a global language of money begetting money.

If this vision of global particle finance sounds intoxicating in its greed, one of the distinctive features of the Papua New Guinean fast money phenomenon was U-Vistract's efforts to create a moral foundation for the intersecting scale-making projects it fostered. This interplay of economic positioning and moral response lies at the heart of understanding fast money schemes because the shifting fields of money and morality provide opportunities for arbitrage (Guyer 2004; Miyazaki 2013). While global finance was understood as a money-making venture connecting Papua New Guineans to the wealth enjoyed by others, it was also joined to another global scale-making project: that of transnational Christianity, specifically in its neo-Pentecostal forms that emphasize the "prosperity gospel." As we shall see in the following chapters, Christian moral tropes were central to U-Vistract's conjunction of scale-making projects as it conjured images of the global, the national, and the personal. Christianity was fundamental to integrating these three scales and to girding them with a moral legitimacy that naked desire for money lacked.

U-Vistract's audacious claim to be a Christian reform of global financial systems was then true in a limited sense. The persons and their imagined communities that it fostered were not based on a morally and relationally hollow neoliberal *homo economicus.* Rather, they reflected a moral order that began with a disciplined Christian self. This self was "born again" into a more intimate relationship with God that presaged an affective self, finding fulfilment in its sentimental engagements with others and being moved by empathy for the sufferings of others into moral action. The later chapters of this book explain how these sentiments were merged into a distinctly Papua New Guinean modern social imaginary (Cox and Macintyre 2014; Taylor 2004) that included a critique of the national project of "development."

Fieldwork: Urban Papua New Guinea

Fast money scheme investors were clearly not the kind of discrete, geographically bounded community that has characterized the ethnographic traditions of studying Melanesia. While there were some apparent core constituencies of each scam (Bougainvilleans, Pentecostals), what was striking was how the scams spread out from these communities, cutting across the typical networks of church, family, affines, and kin to embrace friends, neighbors, and workmates as relationships that helped transmit the money schemes from individual to individual. These face-to-face transactions of information, forms, and account statements and the imaginings of wealth were also the flows of a global financescape, albeit heavily infused with Papua New Guinean national features.

To some extent this pattern of diffusion was characteristic of everyday life in the towns of PNG. However, the sharp distinction between town and village is proving hard to sustain in the face of increased mobility, the rise of peri-urban settlements, and now the advent of cheap mobile telecommunications that link urban wage earners to their rural subsistence kin in new ways (King 1998). Villagers have been seeking to be recognized as modern by their urban cousins for some time (Hirsch 1995, 2007; Knauft 2002). Moreover, the spread of schemes such as U-Vistract across various provinces has raised questions that are national in scale, suggesting that the study would need to be a multi-sited ethnography (Foster 1999a; Marcus 1995). In particular, I follow Foster (1995c; 2002a) in making considerable use of newspapers and other media through which fast money schemes were promoted and debated.

It became clear that middle-class investors were at the center of the dynamic flows of the scam across diverse networks of Papua New Guineans around the country. Indeed, Roeber (1999, 99) makes the claim that "fraud is a middle-class crime," intrinsically connected with city life and the uncertainties of living in the socially disembedded urban environment. He documents how fraudsters in Zambia played on middle-class competencies in negotiating city life. Fast money schemes were also a middle-class crime in PNG and certainly drew on middle-class ideas of "the desirable and the feasible" (Errington and Gewertz 2004).

The study is mainly urban based but does not seek to engage with a single geographically defined and locally bounded "community" of people within a particular urban locale. Rather the study begins with the phenomenon of fast money schemes and identifies relevant informants based on their involvement. Involvement is envisaged as occupying a very broad spectrum of activities and attitudes and so engages a variety of positionings. These may include direct promotion of money schemes; disillusioned investors, still hopeful investors, or past successful investors; authorities trying to close down the schemes; or microfinance operators trying to promote an alternative model of accessing money. These are the "chains, paths and threads" (Marcus 1995, 105) of fast money schemes.

Madang

Madang town is the provincial capital of Madang Province. Reliable figures on population are difficult to access, but Madang is usually regarded as the third or fourth largest city in PNG, after Port Moresby and Lae (the capital of Morobe Province and the nation's industrial and shipping hub) and sometimes Mount Hagen (capital of Western Highlands Province). The 2011 national census gives Madang a population of a mere 30,000, which seems a significant underestimation of the permanent residents, squatter settlers, and daily visitors who pass through this thriving port city. I chose Madang as my primary field site because it is a crossroads of many different groups of people: those indigenous to Madang Province, Sepik migrants who make up the greater population of the town and especially the peri-urban settlements,[2] New Guinea Islanders and Bougainvilleans—mostly skilled workers in town—and new populations of Highlanders drawn by the hope of working in various large-scale resource development projects (Stead 2016) or selling vegetables, *buai* (betel nut) (Sharp 2013, 2016) or handicrafts in Madang's several markets (Gewertz and Errington 2010). Smaller than Port Moresby or Lae, Madang also offered possibilities for the study that might give insight into the interactions of town and village (Street 2014). I already knew that Madang had an active U-Vistract agent, so I could expect to find some investors whose hopes had not gone cold.

During the fieldwork, Madang emerged as a site of national conflicts in relation to race and economic development. Tensions at the Chinese Ramu nickel mine erupted into public protests and even rioting in Madang, Port Moresby, and the major highlands centers of Goroka and Mount Hagen (Smith 2012). I witnessed some of the Madang rioting. This was minor by comparison with that in the Highlands towns. The windows of two "Asian" stores were smashed and some fifty-odd youths ran through town throwing stones. They were pursued by police who closed down the town market for several days (typically the informal economy takes the blame in these situations). A national debate about Asians and political corruption intensified, often taking an explicitly racist form (Chin 2008; Cox 2015; Wood 1995). These events form some of the background to the analysis in this book. Although they have no direct links with fast money scams, they speak of national anxieties about development, the global economy, corruption, and social inequality.

Port Moresby would have been a fruitful site, and many of the interviews with investors were conducted in Port Moresby or with people who had invested in Port Moresby during the height of the fast money rush. Yet too strong a focus on the national capital might have skewed results so as to imply that investment in fast money schemes was a vice of the profligate elite of the national capital, rather than illustrating the spread across the nation.

Being based in a village or town in Bougainville would have provided many interesting insights into U-Vistract in its homeland where the support is strongest. However, a focus on Bougainville would have also failed to capture the national spread and appeal of U-Vistract, particularly had I tried to engage with the U-Vistract–dominated community at Tonu, where Musingku has made his headquarters and exercises considerable control over his followers in perhaps a cultic manner (e.g., Kenneth 2005b). My former colleague at the Australian National University, Anthony Regan, has been working on a monograph studying U-Vistract's influence in Bougainville. Simon Kenema, a Bougainvillean anthropologist has also addressed elements of U-Vistract's life in Bougainville in a chapter of his PhD thesis (Kenema 2015). Therefore while I acknowledge the

Bougainvillean origins of U-Vistract (Cox 2013), the focus of this research is on how a Bougainvillean Ponzi scheme spread through PNG's national middle class, even among people without direct connections to Bougainville.

Divine Word University

While Madang appealed as a field site for the above reasons, in the end, pragmatic considerations made the decision inevitable. My partner, Dr. Georgina Phillips, who is an emergency physician, was planning to spend her sabbatical leave in PNG, where for some years she has been supporting the emergent specialist field of emergency medicine. Divine Word University (DWU) invited Georgina to conduct a comprehensive review of its health extension officer training program. DWU hosted us both for six months from April to September in 2009, the principal period of fieldwork undertaken for this study.

I have returned to Madang almost every year since then, the longest period being a six-week stay in 2010. Unlike earlier generations of Melanesianists, my relationships with people there have been maintained by email communication and now social media. PNG and Australia share a border, and the two countries are entwined in various ways. On several occasions I have enjoyed face-to-face contact with various key informants on their visits to Melbourne and Canberra and sometimes Brisbane. Indeed, as I completed this manuscript during a brief residency in Suva, Fiji, Georgina and I hosted two PNG friends who have contributed to this research in various ways.

While my principal period of research can be classified as short-term fieldwork, it has been foundational to the construction of an interactive network of contacts that has stretched out well beyond the initial time in-country. Short-term fieldwork of course has considerable limitations, but, like Douglas (2002), my short time in-country was compensated by my prior knowledge of fast money schemes gained from documentary archives and preliminary interviews collected during several previous visits to PNG (2005, 2006) and Solomon Islands (2007), and my cultural competence developed over two decades of working in the Pacific Islands. This began with the two formative years (1996–97) that Georgina and I spent living in Kiribati under the Australian Volunteers Abroad program and has continued in NGO program management, consulting work, and now into anthropological research. Indeed, an unlikely part of my fieldwork involved a (voluntary) consultancy through DWU where a Papua New Guinean academic and I delivered a course on strategic management to public servants in Honiara, Solomon Islands.

Fieldwork Activities and Morning Tea

Connections at DWU became the nucleus of an informal method for studying money scams. Talking to academic and other staff often became cause for more formal interviews. Perhaps mirroring the very ways that fast money scams spread through social networking, a conversation would lead to an introduction to some-one outside the university and so new connections would be made. This process is sometimes known as *chain referral* or *snowballing*, allowing organic networks of informants to develop through personal recommendations from existing con-tacts. It is often used by ethnographers wanting to investigate elites or those with something to hide (Bernard 2011).

Every day at 10 a.m., morning tea brings together all the DWU staff, together with visiting students doing short courses. Conversations at morning tea range far and wide but are often charged with current affairs and politics, including ongo-ing critiques of political corruption or the failures of the state. For me many of these conversations began at morning tea and continued well into the day. There was much interest in the topic of money schemes, and I have hardly met any Papua New Guineans without a story of some involvement with a scam either of them-selves, relatives, colleagues, or friends. Following the spread of this scam through these middle-class social networks became my principal mode of doing urban ethnographic research, an approach that foregrounded national interconnections over the local embeddedness that is found in more traditional village ethnography.

DWU itself is a self-conscious nation-making project, bringing together the myriad ethnic groups of the country for the purpose of modern education and the moral formation of Christian citizens. Its website proclaims, "DWU is a National University, open to all, serving society through its quality of research, teaching, learning and community service in a Christian environment" (www .dwu.ac.pg). The staff and students are drawn from almost all of the country's provinces and even come from diverse religious backgrounds, notwithstanding the university's founding by Divine Word missionaries. DWU puts considerable energy into celebrations of National Independence Day (Fig.1.1) and Cultural Day (Fig.1.2), a smaller version of the Goroka or Mount Hagen Cultural Shows. Students, too, organize themselves along provincial lines and present very enter-taining "cultural nights" where dancing in *bilas* (traditional costume) and other forms of culture are put on show, making the nation's cultural differences com-mensurable (cf. Errington and Gewertz 2004, 106ff.).

I was therefore introduced to the nation in microcosm, meeting Madangers, Sepiks, Islanders, Bougainvilleans, and Highlanders all under the one roof. All had their own *wantok* connections into Madang town and beyond. This was of great assistance to me in making connections in Port Moresby, Buka (the main town in Bougainville), and Goroka. DWU is a bounded yet porous national com-munity, located in one specific geographical place (I did not visit its Port Moresby or Wewak campuses) and yet giving rise to a temporal and spatial diversity of interconnections, including engagements with fast money schemes. Many of the stories were told of past investments when working in Port Moresby, Lae, or Wewak (the capital of East Sepik Province). Therefore, DWU emerges as a place

Figure 1.1. Independence celebrations at Divine Word University 2009.
Photograph courtesy of Dr. Georgina Phillips.

Figure 1.2. Chimbu dance group at Divine Word University Cultural Day 2009.
Photograph courtesy of Dr. Georgina Phillips.

of criss-crossing influences and people, of flow and friction that made it an excellent vantage point from which to explore the PNG fast money phenomenon.

While my interests were mostly in townsfolk, these new links also took me into the settlements and villages around Madang, observing the articulations between these different but interconnected settings where people live and interact. One dear friend took me on a bush walk through his village and the surrounding area in the hills just outside Madang with the express purpose of our meeting his cousin who had been an active investor in U-Vistract. Another took me into her settlement near Madang Airport where I met and interviewed local organizers of the Papalain scam.

Madang was my principal base where I lived and even had an office, courtesy of the university administration. My visits to Moresby and other places were useful but very brief, usually no more than a few days at a time. Another DWU connection took me to Buka town in Bougainville and then to a tiny islet in Buka's fringing lagoon where I was welcomed by a large bamboo band and then asked by my host to give a warning against money schemes. Village chiefs then sidled up to me with stories of thousands of Kina of *beche de mer* money lost in U-Vistract and newer scams, such as Questnet.

Sometimes the snowballing of these connections brought me suddenly into an unexpected intimacy with U-Vistract insiders. Late in my fieldwork, one confidant from morning tea arranged a meeting with "some people you should talk to." I thought I was meeting disgruntled investors still waiting for their money but ended up sitting down with Balthasar and Rebecca, two of the leaders of the U-Vistract organizing committee for Madang. They spoke with me for more than two hours, and I was surprised at their candor in explaining the scheme to me. They were not the shady manipulators one expects to be behind a national scam. Moreover, part of me found them convincing, and I shared many of their concerns regarding social inequality in PNG. I could understand why they thought those opposed to U-Vistract "had no heart for the people of PNG."

The fast money rush peaked in 1999–2000, but schemes like U-Vistract continue to operate and hold the loyalties of thousands of investors around the country and even beyond through the internet. Over time, more and more investors are becoming disillusioned and new recruits are few. Many of the interviews used in this book involve participants reflecting on their past behavior, which they now regard as foolish. In one case, my visit seemed to provide the occasion for a final renunciation of U-Vistract by one frustrated investor who handed me copies of U-Vistract propaganda dismissively as a way of acting out his rejection of the scheme's fantasies. Several of my sources have moved residence in the period under consideration: they may have invested in Port Moresby but now live in Madang, introducing a further temporal complication to the idea of a field site or an ethnographic present. PNG is not so far from Australia. A number of my informants were Papua New Guineans whom I had already met in Melbourne during their visits for study, training, or conferences, or whom I befriended in PNG and caught up with later in Australia.

Interviewing, Ethics, and Confidentiality

Primary data was obtained through in-depth interviews with a range of stakeholders. Most interviews were conducted in English with working-class people who typically have a very high fluency in English.[3] Key stakeholders included the following:

- Investors in fast money schemes
- Regulatory authorities such as the Bank of Papua New Guinea
- Other financial sector actors, including commercial banks and microfinance institutions
- Clergy and active members of churches, especially the United Church and Pentecostal churches in PNG
- Nongovernment organizations and donor agencies involved in community development and microfinance
- Journalists
- Local academics, researchers, and social commentators
- Provincial and local-level government officials
- Private businesses

There are some specific constraints in studying money scams. The schemes under consideration are deliberate and criminal attempts to defraud people. They use a range of ingenious measures to legitimate their claims and activities, and these are extremely adaptable and ready to coopt current events into the story of the scheme. Participant observation, for example, is highly problematic for a foreign anthropologist in a context where the involvement of white people is routinely used by a scam to validate itself. I elected not to attend U-Vistract meetings to prevent any possibility that my being seen at such a meeting could be reinterpreted by the scam's leaders as evidence that the scheme's claims were true.

Similarly, I did not seek out Noah Musingku in his "Royal Palace" at Tonu in South Bougainville. While such a meeting would have been intriguing, Musingku's views are widely available on the internet and in published U-Vistract propaganda. Besides, experienced swindlers rarely give away revealing material. Visiting Musingku would no doubt have given rise to a new round of payment stories. My discretion in not seeking out Musingku was validated for me in a recent trip to Buka, when a highly respected Bougainvillean journalist told me his own story of keeping a close eye on U-Vistract but never publishing a story on the scheme for fear of giving it publicity and generating new stories of payouts. Musingku himself (2011b) seems to believe that even adverse publicity helps spread his scheme and claims that 10 million new clients have joined from reading critical comment on the internet.[4]

Within this context, where the very appearance of a white foreigner could give validation to a scam, the foundational ethnographic approach of participant observation became problematic in my view. Unlike Verdery (1995, 626; also Bainton 2010), I did not join a pyramid scheme nor attend meetings. Unlike Peter Lawrence (1964, 2–3; see also Leavitt 2000 and Tuzin 1997), I did not want to risk becoming part of the story and its accompanying expectations. However, I admit that I have not been entirely successful in this regard as the "U-Vistract" and "Musingku" entries in Wikipedia (Wikipedia 2011a and 2011b), which are clearly edited by U-Vistract insiders, now quote some of my earlier published material (Bainton and Cox 2009), albeit to give the misleading impression of academic support for the scheme.

To avoid giving undue publicity or contributing to any possible inadvertent validation of the scams, interviews were conducted privately, mostly with individuals, although sometimes in small groups. Interviews typically lasted for one to two hours and were recorded with the permission of the participants, either by hand in notebooks or on a digital voice recorder.

To my surprise, most people were very happy to speak quite openly and at length about their experiences of investing in fast money schemes, even those who had lost substantial amounts of money. However, to avoid possible embarrassment, I took the precaution of using pseudonyms and some other means of disguising the specific identities of interview participants. Transcripts of interviews are used with the permission of the participants on the understanding of anonymity. I very much see the candor of my informants' accounts as providing the richness of ethnographic detail that was not available to me through participant observation. Their accounts are a strength of this book, in the vividness of their descriptions of the fast money rush and their reflections on the state of the nation that have pushed my own analysis of fast money schemes beyond a simple narrative of greed and gullibility toward what I hope is a more satisfying account of a complex phenomenon. Holmes and Marcus (2005) have made a similar argument about the value of elite informant perspectives as "para-ethnography."

While the purpose of this research was not to warn against fraud, I did feel some responsibility to explain how pyramid schemes work to those who were confused about where money had come from or who expected that their money would come through eventually. At the end of interviews with investors who still held out hopes of being paid, I politely explained that I believed the money schemes they had invested in were fraudulent and that they had lost their money with no realistic prospect of recovering it. I also explained that any money they saw being paid to successful investors had come from the contributions of later investors and had not been generated by foreign banks or the like. These explanations were politely accepted but did not seem to alter the views of the true believers.

Media and Other Written Sources

The fast money schemes in PNG were a very public phenomenon and attracted considerable attention in the mass media, particularly the country's two English language daily newspapers: the *Post-Courier* and the *National*. Mass media became a battleground for testing the claims of fast money schemes against official attempts to warn the public and close the schemes down. Both newspapers covered money scheme rallies and court cases, ran editorials criticizing U-Vistract and other schemes, and printed letters to the editor condemning and supporting the schemes. Both published advertising propaganda from U-Vistract (usually with a disclaimer), as well as official warnings from the Bank of Papua New Guinea naming U-Vistract, Money Rain, and other fast money schemes as scams.

While editors of the newspapers have told me that they see themselves as staunch opponents of the scams, the role of the media in giving attention to U-Vistract has had unintended effects that complicate this self-image. For example, the story of U-Vistract's "Jesus Money" (Gridneff 2009; see chap. 2) led to widespread condemnation of the scheme but also publicized the scheme's claims to be issuing a new currency. For at least some of the followers I interviewed, the media coverage confirmed what the scheme was telling them and gave them a common reference point in discussing the scheme's claims with skeptical outsiders. The Bougainvillean journalist referred to above was the only media professional I encountered who seemed to have reflected critically on the role and responsibilities of the PNG media in relation to reporting fraud. His decision was to not publish stories that could unintentionally promote U-Vistract. In his mind, any attention given to the scam would reconfirm its influence and importance to the remaining followers.

As U-Vistract began to lose access to the daily newspapers, it stepped up production of its own propaganda and distributed copies of *U-Vistract News* to its clients, offering alternative explanations of official attacks on the scheme. Once Musingku returned to Bougainville, this continued through a new magazine, the *Papala Chronicles*, which presented news of payments to investors, attacks on government authorities, warnings about security, and Christian homilies and injunctions about the use of money. These newsletters and magazines are well produced and even mimic the style of media reports by reporting the scheme's propaganda as news and in the third person to indicate objectivity and distance. Articles in the *Papala Chronicles* end with the initials "pc," suggesting perhaps that the source is the *Post-Courier*, or is at least as reliable as the *Post-Courier*. Quotations from U-Vistract propaganda are used liberally throughout the book to provide some of the scheme's character and indicate its rhetorical strategies in communicating with its supporters. They are also used knowing that the *Papala Chronicles* has had a fairly wide readership and that many U-Vistract investors did read the *Papala Chronicles* as they would a newspaper, namely as a source of information about current and forthcoming events.

The daily newspapers also provide a significant representation of PNG's civil society and public discourse (Foster 2002a). While limited circulation and low literacy rates mean that circulation of the daily newspapers may reach as little as 10 percent of PNG's population, even allowing for multiple readers of each edition (Media Council of Papua New Guinea 2007, 19–20), newspapers are avidly read by PNG's urban middle class and provide much of the content of people's understandings of current events, including questions of morality and broader social change. Letters to the editor may not be representative of the country as a whole but they do certainly provide an arena for public debate among those who identify themselves as elites and grassroots alike (Filer 1985). I am more confident than Filer that letters to newspapers do reflect middle-class opinion, and I am sure that the circulation of national newspapers into even remote villages has progressed well beyond Kulick and Stroud's (1990, 288) observation that the *Sydney Morning Herald* was the only regular literature entering their Sepik village. Lipset and Halvaksz (2009) argue that newspaper discourses on marijuana are reflected in rural communities in PNG. Bashkow (2006, 224) also notes the national discourses on "whitemen" that circulate between villages and urban centers. Foster's claim (2002a, 88) that commercial media and advertising "constitute a vibrant arena within PNG's emergent public culture" can surely be applied to newspapers more generally.

This book uses quotations from newspapers and other public sources extensively to show the broader national resonance of various themes. These include debates over fast money schemes, ideas of investment and finance, and perceptions of government, politicians, and banks. Written sources such as newspapers augment interview transcripts and demonstrate the public nature of ideas and experiences that might otherwise have been seen as idiosyncratic or even esoteric. One of the central points of the book is that fast money schemes were a mainstream national event, not only because they drew in thousands of investors but also because they appealed to mainstream ideas of money, finance, development, and critiques of the nation. Newspaper articles and letters provide evidence of that broader national discussion, even if their readership is confined largely to the PNG working class (Foster 2002a).[5] Indeed, this is the very point that the same conceptions of finance, banks, corruption, and nation are found in middle-class discourse and in propaganda from fast money schemes. Both are often argued out in the pages of newspapers and increasingly in social media, including by the Bank of Papua New Guinea (Stopim Pyramid Schemes & Scams Lo PNG 2016).

Biersack (2005) argues against Appadurai's (1996) claims for the centrality of electronic media in circulating global images, at least as far as PNG is concerned. While use of the electronic media in PNG is growing rapidly (Logan 2012), newspapers and radio still occupy a central place in forming "imagined communities" (Anderson 1983; Foster 2002a). Nevertheless, U-Vistract continues to produce blogs and Wikipedia entries and maintains its own website (Musingku 2011b) and Facebook page. Its mastery of computer technology is often mentioned as a factor influencing investors (Regan 2010).

While public expressions of exasperation recollect popular accusations of "cargo cult," the fast money schemes spread in broad daylight: they were public and involved hundreds of thousands of people. "Everyone was in it!" as I have been told over and again, demonstrating that these were not the activities of a secretive and confined cult but a very public performance of mainstream PNG values and aspirations. It was also a case of fraud, but fraud by its nature cannot succeed unless it appears to be something comprehensible and desirable. That is what makes U-Vistract and the other fast money schemes a fascinating vantage point from which to observe Papua New Guinean visions of "the desirable and the feasible" (Errington and Gewertz 2004).

Papua New Guinea and Its "Working Class"

PNG is not often thought of as a place where the middle class earn and spend money, amass savings, and make calculations about where best to invest them. More frequently it is viewed as a country where the people are a rural, "innocent population" who practice intact culture and make their humble livelihoods through subsistence horticulture (Golub 2014), perhaps augmented by agricultural commodities such as coffee (West 2012). The innocent population narrative is shared by Papua New Guineans and foreigners alike. When the global economy interrupts this idyll, it brings large-scale resource extraction to pillage the pristine natural resources and corrupts local officials and indigenous culture alike. Despite the best efforts of anthropologists, it is a place where the agency of contemporary Papua New Guineans is usually overshadowed by narratives of victimhood or the primitive (Golub 2016; West 2012). The latter type swings between exotic stories of cultural diversity and the violent disorder of tribal fighting, sorcery-related violence, or urban crime.

None of these characterizations allow much space for a middle-class PNG. Nevertheless, it is clear that there is a sizeable middle class that has been "emerging" for some time (Gewertz and Errington 1999; for other countries in the Pacific region see Barbara, Cox, and Leach 2015; Besnier 2009). This book explores their moral and economic values and how they intersect with familiar global expectations of lifestyle and personal development (Spark 2014, 2015). It does so acknowledging that in PNG social and economic inequalities are severe: there are some very wealthy members of the elite and some very poor "grassroots." Amarshi, Good, and Mortimer (1979, 158) labeled the emerging bourgeoisie of PNG the "parasitic group" because they "act as if the control of the state for administrative purposes was an end in itself" and monopolize access to education. Despite a decade when a resources boom has contributed extraordinary levels of international investment into the national economy, the state remains the primary center of wealth creation for local elites (cf. Hameiri 2007 on neighboring Solomon Islands). The corruption, incompetence, and mismanagement overseen by these elites are severe obstacles to the delivery of services and ensure that those outside their patronage networks are locked out of access to education, employment, and other prerequisites of social advancement (Standish 2007).

Turner (1990, 72–75) gives a brief discussion of the problems of class terminology in PNG but notes that Papua New Guineans regularly divide the country into grassroots and elites. Where urban wage earners were once regarded as straightforwardly elite, increasingly, middle-class budgets are coming under strain, even at the higher end of incomes (Gewertz and Errington 2010, 108–109). There is a growing middle class in PNG of urban salaried people who often refer to themselves as the working class and distinguish themselves from subsistence grassroots workers who do not work in the sense of receiving salaries or regular payments for services (Reed 2003, 63). Town-dwellers and often children of town-dwellers, the working class, are little studied by anthropologists, partly because their lives are not constituted by the village as the center of meaning, unless as "ideological commitments, sometimes romanticised, but constrained by the demands of working" (Macintyre 2011, 93).

The working class are hardly elite when compared with senior public servants, powerful politicians, and landowner rentier millionaires who capture the benefits of resource development. Indeed, part of the discourse of the working class in PNG is complaints about the cost of living in towns and the inadequacy of ordinary wages to meet basic costs (Monsell-Davis 1993, 57–58). The high cost of living in Port Moresby and PNG generally is a regular lament of middle-class Papua New Guineans (e.g., Kowa 2011). Women have particular challenges in urban areas, especially when they choose to live independently (Demian 2017; Macintyre 2011).

Where previous generations of public servants and other professional workers could expect to have a reasonably high standard of living, including access to formal housing in the urban centers, now there is a pervasive feeling that PNG's working class are missing out on the nation's economic prosperity. The working class may be better described as the *working poor*. Of course the working class enjoy privileges that set them well apart from their rural relatives, but to maintain a paradigmatic opposition between elites and grassroots is to obscure the plentiful interactions and interdependence between these groups within PNG (Kelly 1995, 260–261). This book shows how some of these relationships are being reconfigured by discourses of Christian citizenship, development, and financialization.

In the face of rising costs of living, deteriorating housing stock, and faltering services, discourses of nation and citizenship that previously included the working class are becoming embittering. Koim's (2009) letter to the *Post-Courier* articulates a common complaint that ordinary workers are losing out as politicians and high-level public servants capture the nation's wealth in generous pay rises and other perks. While elites prosper, desperation drives lower-level public servants into debt, corruption, bribery, and fraud. Koim is one of many Papua New Guineans who feel that the egalitarian ideals of the independence era have been betrayed: "Is this what the Preamble to the Constitution of Papua New Guinea speaks about … 'our national wealth, won by honest, hard work be shared equitably by all'? A simple public servant who earns around K500 (net) pay finds it very hard to survive with his family in a city like Port Moresby and reach another payday." (Koim 2009).

While the powerful elites of Waigani (the center of political and government activity in Port Moresby) were heavily involved in fast money schemes and were the principal beneficiaries of early payouts,[6] ordinary investors were not "elite" in the sense of being politically powerful or very wealthy (Gewertz and Errington 1999, 7–8, 25). Most of the people interviewed for this research are educated and have regular work, but they are teachers, low-level public servants, maintenance staff, and so forth. The highest status people I spoke with were academics and doctors, but with one or two exceptions none of these people were particularly wealthy and few had robust political connections.[7]

The people interviewed for this research may not be particularly politically or economically powerful but they do fit Roeber's definition of the middle class as having "the set of cultural skills that allow individuals and groups to interpret the disembedded social relationships of the [urban] ether" (Roeber 1999, 104). Indeed, as we shall see, it is these very skills of negotiating modern urban life (such as prudent management of money) that were mimicked by U-Vistract to defraud the working class.

Guide to the Chapters

The book comprises ten chapters and a conclusion. The first includes the introduction, background to the research project, sources, and fieldwork details. Chapter 2 provides background information important for understanding the spread of fast money schemes in PNG and so tells the long story of U-Vistract in some detail, following the scheme from Port Moresby to Honiara in neighboring Solomon Islands and back to Bougainville. Newspaper articles are used to indicate the public visibility of this story as a national scandal.

Chapter 3 explains how Ponzi schemes and pyramid scams work and provides a grounding in how popular fraud works elsewhere, particularly modes of affinity fraud such as Ponzi scams. This includes surveys of the relevant academic literature, including work on mass pyramid schemes in Eastern Europe, Africa, and Latin America. Some discussion of the Madoff Ponzi scheme is also included to show that such scams are not simply the province of societies with transitional or developing economies. The chapter closes by considering the relevance of Tsing's analysis of scale-making projects, developed in her article on a gold-mining fraud (2000b), for understanding how fast money schemes engaged the public of PNG so successfully.

Chapter 4 considers the legacy and limitations of the cargo cult literature for studying fast money schemes in Melanesia. Because of the powerful influence of cargo cult narratives in defining Melanesia (Lindstrom 1993) and in their application to money schemes by Melanesians, it is important to point out what features of anthropological thought are most relevant in this particular case. Moral equivalence has been a central theme in anthropological treatments of cargo cults, and the chapter introduces some of the concerns with inequality that are found in contemporary PNG.

Chapter 5 explores some of the techniques that U-Vistract and other fast money schemes used to lure their investors. Some of these were relatively straightforward and simply involved the clever use of printed materials, computers, or mimicry of official-sounding bank discourse. Giddens's (1990) work on abstract systems and entry points provides a useful way to analyze how the scheme operated. The chapter includes a range of ethnographic material that considers people's motivations for investing in fast money schemes: their doubts, calculations, and some of the social pressures on them to join in the scheme. This chapter focuses on the ambiguous and skeptical dispositions of investors (or would-be investors), showing a range of individual positionings and the underlying ideas and social concerns that shape their responses. These investors are diffident and deliberating rather than greedy and gullible. Their understandings of the risks posed by the scheme reflect ideas of money and disciplines of personal finance and make it difficult to sustain the popular view of a blind rush of uncontrolled, desperate cargoistic desire.

In Chapter 6, I explore the connections between U-Vistract and Pentecostal Christianity both in terms of organizational networks and also the prosperity gospel ideology. One of Verdery's (1995) useful insights is that pyramid schemes usually have an inside track: a network of beneficiaries that does not simply reflect the popular understanding of first come, first served but is composed of insiders who know in advance that the proceeds of the scheme will be redistributed in their favor. U-Vistract was very successful at infiltrating the political elite of Port Moresby, particularly during the prime ministership of Bill Skate (1997–1999). Another important inside track was the Christian churches, particularly neo-Pentecostals. As Comaroff and Comaroff (2000, 313) put it, "The line between Ponzi schemes and evangelical prosperity gospels is very thin indeed." The moral engagements of individual Christian investors with U-Vistract are explored. Providence and prosperity stand in tension with doubt, fraud, and hypocrisy.

Chapter 7 considers the construction of a national scale by U-Vistract, responding to "negative nationalist" (Robbins 1998) sentiment. Popular disillusionment with the nation of PNG, centered on questions of corruption and inequality, provided a fruitful resource for U-Vistract to draw on in constructing its virtual world as a critique of the national development project. The chapter shows how the scam incorporated Pentecostal moral critiques of the nation-state to imagine a reformed nation led by faithful Christian citizens (O'Neill 2010).

Chapter 8 focuses on the processes by which U-Vistract engaged its investors ethically and channeled their moral sensibilities to the benefit of the scheme, positioning themselves as proprietors of "development." Contemporary anxieties about social inequality and corruption are used as an introduction to revisit patronage systems in PNG. The personalized largesse of politicians is identified as a key paradigm that shapes popular views of development and particularly ideas of state delivery of services that might mitigate and address social inequality. U-Vistract's vision of Christian citizenship involved the assumption of a leadership role where investors were encouraged to see themselves as having the resources to act where the PNG state had failed. In doing so they would displace the corrupt and morally failed political leadership of the nation by acting out a fantasy of how PNG's patronage politics should work. Middle-class investors were groomed to see themselves as Christian patrons, disbursing their resources generously and to good developmental effect.

Chapter 9 takes its inspiration from an interview with two U-Vistract insiders, one of whom exclaimed, "Some of us are fed up of banks!" Their dissatisfaction with the banking system is echoed by many Papua New Guineans. Nevertheless, ideals of how the banking system should work are employed as a critique of the current banks, and the chapter explores how U-Vistract was able to position itself as a credible alternative to legitimate PNG banking and financial operations.

Chapter 10 brings the global financial system and its ideas of wealth into focus. U-Vistract offered a critique of national systems by connecting investors with an imagined global world of other nations that had become prosperous because of their access to financial markets. It then positioned itself as the leader of a Christian reform of international finance, thereby linking two global scale-making projects: finance and Christianity. This conjunction of scale-making projects also has implications for the kinds of persons being created within and beyond the scam. Both Pentecostal prosperity Christianity and global practices of investment constitute disciplines of the self and entail moral commitments. This study of the PNG fast money scheme experience makes these processes explicit within a particular context, but, in doing so, a new purchase is gained on the global transformations that follow the introduction of neoliberal practices and ideas.

Chapter 10 considers how U-Vistract investors invested in the global. Financially, they were led to believe that through the scheme they would be able to access global circuits of wealth previously unavailable to them. As Christian citizens, they also invested in a more global outlook on themselves and on the project of national development in PNG. Papua New Guineans are frustrated that their "rich country" remains in a disadvantaged position within a global community of nations and powerful transnational organizations such as the United Nations and the World Bank. Yet this position of comparative disadvantage also implies sufficient transnational connections that can be worked to raise national fortunes to global standards of prosperity. As noted earlier, this includes not only mechanisms of personal financial investment but also a Christian moral dimension.

The conclusion reflects on the interactions of local, national, and global tropes in the U-Vistract scam and the infiltration of financialization and its moral justifications into all aspects of life in PNG and beyond. While this book draws on intriguing and often exasperating material from PNG, it is the local interactions with global myths of finance, investment, money, and the economy that are of principal interest. This book both is not and is a cargo cult story. It is not a cargo cult story in that the fast money schemes were not powered by indigenous Melanesian cosmologies in the ways documented in the classic ethnographies of Lawrence (1964) and Burridge (1969). I do not mean to diminish the importance of the work of these great scholars. Indeed, Burridge's stress on moral equivalence has shaped my interpretation of fast money schemes in a profound way. The book is a cargo cult story in a sense that Lindstrom (1993) would appreciate. The mix of finance, religion, and nation-making documented here of U-Vistract has its peculiarities, but capitalism has its own mystifications, rituals, and secret knowledge and its own headlong rushes in the pursuit of wealth. Yet deception does not emerge only from the moral failing of greed, as the logic of popular accounts of fraud often imply. As the cargo literature reminds us, there is always a moral and relational dimension to these desires. In the U-Vistract case, hope for a better nation and a better world were as much a part of the scam's success as mere individualistic greed.

This book then makes a modest contribution to anthropology's ongoing contestation of separations of morality and economics and of the ways in which those conceptual divisions produce a rather atrophied ideal "rational choice" person—*homo economicus*—and a truncated view of society as the working out of impersonal market forces. Here I reveal a moral middle class of Christian citizens led astray by promises of prosperity but still engaged in the work of developing their nation. This book reveals aspirations for a global moral economy where existing structures of privilege are reformed, even as individuals are reformed by Christian devotion and discipline, in order that all may share in the prosperity that the global community is believed to enjoy. This vision may sound reactionary to some and neoliberal to others, and I do not believe that U-Vistract or other scams are in any way emancipatory. However, at the core of the moral plausibility of this Ponzi scheme is a pressing concern with inequalities global and national that may yet have find a more satisfactory political program among a new generation of Melanesians.

Notes

1. The Papua New Guinea Kina was worth approximately 33 US cents in 1999.
2. Forty years ago, Morauta noted (1974, 56) the presence of numbers of Sepik workers in the villages around Madang.
3. English is the language of bureaucracy in Papua New Guinea and arguably is the language of U-Vistract, as all of the scheme's forms, newsletters, and so on were written in English.
4. "You are all aware of how the conventional media has endeavored to fabricate and publicize every negative reports about me and our system over the past decade. The PNG Media Fraternal for instance, made a formal decision in 2000 AD following a National Court decision, to fight the U-Vistract system head-on right to the end. They linked up with Australian Media and did a very good job spreading all kinds of negative reports about the U-Vistract system. Little did they know that they were being used within God's Mysteries to spread our fame all over the world, totally free of charge! At the appointed time now God is using those negative reports to our advantage. Every single day people are reading those negative reports from the internet, debating and discussing them, and finally making informed decisions to invest with us. Without those negative reports it would be very difficult to attract new clients/investors worldwide.

"This was how we got another 10 million new clients/investors recently. All they did was to go on the internet, read about our reports, then have a debate or two within their networks and finally made an informed decision to invest with us. It's very clear that without those negative reports spread free of charge by the media, no one would have known us. The world would not have a clue of what we are all about and what we were doing. The UV system has now taken the world by storm. The new system is now taking over and replacing the old/conventional system all over the world, thanks to the enemy especially the PNG Media Fraternal for the decision to spread our fame at the right time. The Mysteries of God are beyond grasp of the enemy. God only reveals it to whom He appoints" (Musingku 2011b).
5. The working class may also overlap with those in the postindependence generation, who, according to Kavanamur, Yala, and Clements (2003a, 5), have a "strong nation-building ethos."
6. Cf. Verdery's (1995) "inside tracks" and "unruly coalitions" within the Romanian pyramid scheme Caritas.
7. Fife writes about the privilege of "indigenous teachers who play a fundamental role in implementing a largely externally defined model of rationalism and morality that creates pressures for a bureaucratization of consciousness in the urban areas of Papua New Guinea" (1995, 129).

2 The Story of U-Vistract

Once upon a Time, There Was U-Vistract . . .

HOW much longer will Mr Noah Musingku be allowed to openly flout the laws of Papua New Guinea? The renegade financier, who has successfully gulled millions from his unwary fellow countrymen, is reportedly behind yet another fantasy, this time in Bougainville. There are arrest warrants unfulfilled for Mr Musingku, who appears to find no difficulty in accessing anyone and everyone he wishes. Bougainville remains an integral part of PNG.

How is it possible that this fantastic figure can continue to thumb his nose at both the leadership and the ordinary people of PNG with complete impunity? And where were the government officials when Mr Musingku first started his fiendishly simple pyramid scheme, U-Vistract, in Port Moresby?

Today the Bank of PNG can take action, send in police and bank officials, and comb through the books of another pyramid scheme, known as the Papalain Association. But it is the original investors in U-Vistract who have been ignored and treated with contempt. Apart from the first handful of investors, who received considerable sums of money back from the scheme, many thousands of ordinary Papua New Guineans have received not one toea back from U-Vistract. In the meantime Mr Musingku and his henchmen have travelled overseas widely, attempted to create a new currency through the Singapore Mint, promised the equivalent of tens of millions of kina to the Solomon Islands government, and continued to lie to all and sundry about dates for the repayment of invested funds.

The PNG Government should long ago have arrested Mr Musingku and brought him before the courts of this country. There is no lack of aggrieved people to give evidence against this man or his organisation. Does the Government not realise that Mr Musingku and other members of his organisation have inflicted a terrible level of hardship on hundreds of PNG families?

If public gossip is to be believed, the iniquitous U-Vistract net not only enmeshed ordinary families, but dozens of institutional investors, the boards of management of schools, the elders of churches, and perhaps most significantly, a considerable number of members of Parliament. It seems possible that it is these elected or appointed leaders who are the most unwilling to reveal their exposure to U-Vistract. For how will they explain their action in "investing" public money in U-Vistract, fully aware that the same funding was ear-marked for projects and electoral advancement? They cannot.

So these experienced and well-educated people are consumed with shame and embarrassment as a result of their actions. Above all, they do not want their involvement with U-Vistract to come to light, and they will give only the most lukewarm response to responsible attempts to bring Mr Musingku to account. In the process, successive governments have been made to look incapable of policing their own territory, and of acting against forces that pose a potential threat of social destabilisation on a national scale.

Government after government has emphasised the desirability of political stability, and The National has supported their concerns. But strangely, it does not seem to occur to our leaders that a social movement like U-Vistract or its descendants could utterly destroy the fragile social fabric of PNG. And if it does, could the disruption of political stability be far behind? The re-appearance of Mr Musingku in Bougainville, this time with even more inflated and fantastic fairy stories, underlines the point. We warmly applaud the statement from Mr John Momis, the Bougainville Governor, describing the latest Musingku web-spinning as "bullshit."

But we doubt that this forthright condemnation will either deter Mr Musingku, or convince those who are determined to believe his fabrications. The prospect of a Bougainville so recently at peace being disrupted by a wildfire social movement of this kind is most disturbing, and one which we are certain Mr Momis recognises. The National Government can no longer put this issue on the back-burner. To continue to pussy-foot around Mr Musingku demeans the Government, confuses the people, and leaves the way open for the rapid growth of a hugely destructive social disease, one compounded of equal parts of greed and ignorance. We call upon the Government to take immediate action to kill-off this pyramid menace once and for all, and to bring its perpetrators before the courts.

This lengthy editorial from the *National* newspaper (May 25, 2004) captures the public spectacle of U-Vistract. Schemes like U-Vistract were a national scandal, and the press played a role in documenting their activities and hosting debates about their authenticity. The *National* repeatedly called for government action against them (e.g., *National* 2004b; 2005; 2006c; 2009). The spectacle, scale, and longevity of U-Vistract make it an interesting window into contemporary Papua New Guinean experiences and imaginings of social and economic change. Here I follow Verdery (1995), who has made a similar case about pyramid scams in Romania being a window into social and economic changes in that country.

The editor of the *National* expresses the frustration that, despite its illegality, U-Vistract and its principal director, Noah Musingku, have not been brought to justice. The scheme threatens not only the project of reconciliation in post-conflict Bougainville but also the social order of PNG itself. There is a note of moral panic about the "social disease ... compounded of equal parts of greed and ignorance." Indeed, it is the "experienced and well-educated" leaders of PNG who have shown a lack of courage in acting against the scheme. In fact, they have sought to gain from U-Vistract and so involved institutions such as churches and schools, the very fabric of civil society.

There is a tension here between "greed and ignorance" and the education and social standing of those seen as responsible for the extraordinary spread of the scheme. Were it simply the uneducated, "financially illiterate" rural poor, then U-Vistract could be dismissed as another cargo cult: a product of protean backwardness, superstition and traditionalism, gullibility, and, above all, unrestrainable desire. However, it is the urban elite, the schools and churches, families—in short, respectable modern PNG society—that have joined this scheme. This is why U-Vistract represents such a threat to the National's idea of social order: it unsettles common sense views of progress and prosperity and even the "reasonability" underpinning the class hierarchy that constitutes the modern nation of PNG (Gewertz and Errington 1999). These tensions of class inequality and the ethics of prosperity are the core themes explored in this research through the eyes of participants in U-Vistract: its "investors," skeptics, and opponents.

Names and Rationales

In 1999, the Bank of Papua New Guinea (BPNG) took action against twelve major fast money schemes including Bonanza '99, Money Rain, U-Vistract Finance Corporation Limited, Gold Money Investment Ltd., Windfall, Millenium Corporation Ltd., and the National Federation of Foundations. Other large schemes included KVDC Gold Ltd. (Minikula 2005), Papalain, and Hosava (McLeod 2004), which also promised high and rapid investment returns. Since 1999, BPNG has warned against these schemes in public notices placed in newspapers, and senior BPNG officials routinely give warnings against fast money schemes at public events (e.g., Matbob 2010).

The fast money schemes were all run by Melanesians and targeted Papua New Guinean investors. There is no evidence of foreigners being involved in the establishment or ongoing management of any of the scams. However, this may have happened behind the scenes.

U-Vistract Financial Systems Ltd.

The largest and most enduring of the fast money schemes was U-Vistract. Its size, extent, and longevity make it the focus of this book. U-Vistract also produced highly sophisticated newsletters and websites. U-Vistract began operating in Port Moresby some time during 1998 when it was formally registered with the PNG Investment Promotion Authority. By 2000, U-Vistract claimed to have 70,000 investors and K580 million of their money (*National*, March 28, 2000). This is probably an underestimation, particularly when feeder schemes are taken into account.

The meaning and origins of the name U-Vistract are obscure, although the full version, U-Vistract Finance Corporation Ltd., or sometimes U-Vistract Financial Systems Ltd., is clearly intended to present a certain corporate image perhaps lacking in more descriptive names such as *Money Rain* or *Windfall*. Propaganda from the scheme has tried to create an aura of mystery around the name: "The "U" in the name "U-Vistract" stands for "Universe," what the other part means is kept as a secret by HM King David Peii II, because people have to figure that out by themselves (Ambassador to Bougainville 2012, 11). Taking up the challenge of "figuring out" the name U-Vistract, I presume that Vistract is a combination of the first letters of vision, strategy, and action, reflecting the rubric of many participatory planning exercises in Papua New Guinea and the scheme's claims to a grand corporate plan for transforming global finance.

While presenting itself as a financial institution, U-Vistract's organizational structure is that of an informal network centered on the Bougainvillean founder, Noah Musingku. Initially Musingku operated with a handful of henchmen, including his brother Meshach Autahe, and worked from hotels or by visiting influential people at home. As the scheme grew, they opened offices in Port Moresby, Buka, and other towns around the country. One Madang landlord I spoke to had rented out her property to the fast money scheme but was only paid one month's rent and failed to recover the arrears. These offices usually had computers but are more often remembered for the queues of people waiting to deposit their money. Many remember seeing others walking out with bags of cash after being paid.

When U-Vistract was declared bankrupt, these offices were closed, but Musingku and his cronies maintained connections with investors through local "clients' committees." These were run by an "agent" of the scheme, usually a Bougainvillean, who claimed to be working towards retrieving clients' monies. Agents were in regular phone contact with Musingku and circulated U-Vistract propaganda magazines, such as the *Papala Chronicles*, among the local members. The agents would gather clients together and hold meetings at church halls or in public places such as Tusbab Beach in Madang. Some still do. At these meetings, investors would be reassured that their money was coming, be told of the latest efforts of the government to thwart the scheme, or be asked to make new contributions towards special programs or expenses.

As the scheme's promises have failed to be realized, fewer and fewer people respond to these invitations. One retired tradesman who lived in a village outside of Madang told me he goes along every other month "just to keep up with the news," implying that he was not convinced by the updates but found them entertaining. Like some of the ambivalent investors profiled in chapter 4, he had almost, but not quite, given up on actually being paid.

With the establishment of the U-Vistract headquarters at Tonu in Bougainville, staff with banking or telecommunications experience were employed to establish the money scheme's new systems. Yet according to the *Post-Courier* (Kenneth 2005a), they were paid only a fraction of the entitlements promised to them, and most left disillusioned after a few months. U-Vistract also nominated dozens of high-level people, including a number of politicians, as "governors" for jurisdictions corresponding to PNG provinces or other countries such as Fiji and Solomon Islands. The role of governor seems to have been purely honorific, without any organizational responsibilities. These governors included Pentecostal pastors such as Bob Lutu and Suckling Tamanabae, who was appointed as "Global Spiritual Governor." Tamanabae was later elected into the National Parliament and became the actual governor of Oro Province.

Noah Musingku

U-Vistract was founded by Noah Musingku from Tonu village in Siwai District, southern Bougainville. Musingku was educated at Buin and Kerevat High Schools, Unitech, and the University of Papua New Guinea (UPNG). He also served for a brief time in the Papua New Guinea Defence Force. Now Musingku is notorious as a conman and even runs a personal blog titled "Most Wanted Man," the title ironically taking up media characterizations of him (Musingku 2009). In 1998–99, however, as U-Vistract captured the imagination of the nation, he was best known as the former president of the National Union of Students.

Musingku came from a United Church background but joined a Pentecostal group (Christian Life Centre, or CLC) as an adult and was known as a deeply religious person: a "God-fearing man," a "*lotu*" man." Those who know him speak of him as a rather introverted personality: a thoughtful and humble person, exemplifying Christian virtues in his demeanor, never raising his voice in anger, and speaking softly and respectfully. Musingku before U-Vistract was also known for his strange personal habits such as wearing long sleeves and walking distances in the heat across town to save paying bus fares. Musingku has a kind of anticharismatic charisma, perhaps not unlike the lisp of the infamous swindler Bernie Madoff. Some speak of Musingku as having special powers of persuasion and even attribute this to use of "black magic." His abilities to persuade and to generate a sense of mystery about himself are indeed amply demonstrated in the spread and persistence of U-Vistract.

The "Bank for Bougainvilleans"

U-Vistract emerged initially as the "Bank for Bougainvilleans" and claimed to be for the poor people of Bougainville, the island province where ten years of civil war had come to a close. The war had begun in 1989 as a protest against the Panguna copper mine, then the single greatest revenue generator within the PNG economy. The prolonged civil war and blockade by the PNG government forces had left Bougainville economically and socially devastated. Many better-educated Bougainvilleans escaped to Port Moresby and established themselves in careers there. This was especially true of former employees of the Panguna copper mine, at least some of whom had used redundancy payments from the company to educate their children in Australian boarding schools. U-Vistract started within the Bougainvillean diaspora of Port Moresby. Regan (2009) estimates that this community numbered some 15,000 people in 1999, a substantial and relatively well-to-do minority of the national capital's population. Presenting the scheme as the "Bank for Bougainvilleans" was an attempt to exploit the feelings of disenfranchisement among Bougainvilleans following the war. U-Vistract offered Bougainvilleans a pathway of prosperous economic development (*Post-Courier* 1999b).

For some of these early investors, U-Vistract provided money they could not have accessed elsewhere and seemed a credible way for Bougainvilleans to support each other. Tertiary students arriving in Port Moresby from Bougainville were often met by U-Vistract agents and offered financial support. The following reminiscence from Jack expresses the intense atmosphere of excitement, fascination, and doubt, as well as the closeness of the Bougainvillean community:

> It was in 1999. I was a third year student at UPNG [University of Papua New Guinea] and I had an uncle in fourth year. He was much older than me. He came one time to my room and asked, "Do you know about Noah Musingku's U-Vistract?" I said I didn't, I hadn't heard of it. He said, "If you put some money in, you can get 100 percent profit in a week." I didn't believe him, so he asked me to give him K100 so he could show me how it worked but I didn't have that much money then as a student. So I only gave him K30. One week later, he came back and gave me K60 and so that's how I got interested in this scheme. So he said, "You can invest yourself. Go and see him [Noah Musingku] directly. He is staying at the Islander Hotel (now it's the Holiday Inn). He told me it's free for Bougainvilleans and he [Musingku] wouldn't have any trouble accepting my money.
>
> Noah was at the Islander.... In the foyer, I saw some Bougainvilleans, so I thought, "This must be true." So I asked one of them that I wanted to put some money in Noah Musingku's money scheme. So he gave me the room number and told me to go up.
>
> There was a queue stretching five or six meters from the door of the room. They were all Bougainvilleans. When it came to my turn, I came in and Noah

was there sitting on a chair, collecting the money. Initially he was the one collecting the money himself but then he had helpers. They'd give you a form to sign and a receipt for the money you put in. The forms had Christian sayings on them at the bottom....

It must have been hundreds of people I knew who were involved. Among my personal friends and the Bougainvilleans I knew, most of them invested. All of my immediate family—every one of my immediate family members was in it. In the village, my Mum's brother put K50,000 and he said, "Roll it over" and he never got anything from it.

In 1999, Musingku hosted his wedding in Port Moresby with some fanfare, chartering flights from Bougainville and paying for an extravagant reception at the Lamana Hotel. This highly conspicuous display of consumption publicly demonstrated his command of money. The event is said to have been formative in establishing Musingku's credibility as a financier for many Bougainvilleans such that it sustains their faith in him today, even after a decade of unfulfilled promises. Marie, a relative of Musingku now working in Port Moresby, describes the impact of the wedding:

Noah got married in January 1999. He chartered a F28 and brought people from Bougainville—people from the village. Everyone just talked about it and that convinced a lot of people. They stayed in hotels, not with *wantoks*. They were fed in hotels. Eventually they went round after that and told people all about it, "Wow! That's the biggest wedding! We stayed in the hotel!" So from that people believed it was true.

His only living aunt came and she was all excited. When she went back she made people in the village believe. Those people who were flown here were the old people. They are still strong believers in him. It was an amazing stay for them: they had never been to Port Moresby before.

Back in Bougainville, there were thousands of small contributions to the scheme. Microfinance programs noted the impact of U-Vistract on the savings-based programs they were trying to establish. The AusAID-funded *Bougainville Haus Moni* microfinance scheme noted a loss of at least half of its deposits to U-Vistract and other related fast money schemes (Newsom 2002).

"Our Window of Hope"—Kabui

Fast money schemes were risky businesses but provided a "window of hope" for investors, especially simple villagers, according to the Bougainville People's Congress president Joseph Kabui. Mr. Kabui said Prime Minister Sir Mekere Morauta's announcement on the establishment of a committee to look into the operations of the schemes is a move in the right direction. He stressed a need to exempt U-Vistract, Money Link, Millennium and Nekong from paying tax to the Government in their Bougainvillle operations.

"While investors know that there are risks involved, they are also aware of the benefits provided by the schemes," he said. "By investing in the schemes, small investors in Bougainville have planned to rebuild houses destroyed during the crisis, pay for children's school fees and meet costs for other basic needs and services. The schemes, do provide a window of hope and opportunities to a simple villager who has placed his/her trust in the operations of the schemes by investing." He sympathized with the owners of the schemes who were being pressured by clients to pay out their money.

The Government through the central bank is also exerting pressure on the schemes to comply with the country's finance Acts.

He called for understanding from the Government when dealing with the fast money making schemes on Bougainville. (*Post-Courier*, August 26, 1999)

Musingku was initially hailed by the Bougainvillean elite as a source of collective pride, being Bougainville's first "international financier." Prominent Bougainvillean leaders, such as Joseph Kabui, publicly supported U-Vistract. While the scheme's initial rhetoric was about serving the rural poor of Bougainville, in Port Moresby "high-level" Bougainvilleans were purposefully targeted by the scheme. For those slow to join, pressure mounted, and a sense of disloyalty to other Bougainvilleans was created. This is apparently what induced the then-ombudsman, a prominent and highly respected Bougainvillean, to join U-Vistract. At a time when his office was investigating possible misuse of politicians' Rural Development Funds as investments in fast money schemes, the ombudsman was discovered to have invested his own money in U-Vistract. Unlike many, he made an extremely good return on his investments. When called on to account for himself, he explained that "he had been made to feel that he was staying out of something that many Bougainvilleans had been backing. 'By not joining in, you felt that in a way you are not one of them. This is a common thing in PNG'" (O'Callaghan 2000b).

One "high-level" Bougainvillean spoke of being courted by Musingku, who badgered him over a period of months, even coming to see him at his home in Port Moresby with a briefcase full of money. Musingku seemed eager that all should join the scheme. Although this person had grave doubts about the scheme, he sensed the opportunity to outsmart Musingku, who was desperate to attract someone of his standing. The two agreed on a deal where Musingku would pay within two weeks, not the full month required of ordinary investors. On this occasion, Musingku paid, and the high-level Bougainvillean was K40,000 the richer. The price, however, was in having his name and reputation publicly used to legitimate U-Vistract against the actions of BPNG.

Broadening the Base of the Pyramid

News of U-Vistract filtered out to the broader community through those who had married Bougainvilleans, their friends, neighbors, and workmates and particularly through church networks. Non-Bougainvilleans initially invested under the name of a Bougainvillean colleague, friend, or *tambu* (in-law). Their Bougainvillean contact would collect money and invest on their behalf. Some informants speak of Bougainvilleans as standing out, not only because of their dark skin color but also because of their comparative wealth or success in the modern economy. "Bougainvillean students at my school always had pocket money, they always wore nice clothes that we couldn't afford" was a typical sentiment expressed, indicating that Bougainvilleans themselves could be seen as successful people and even a credible source of money. Certainly Bougainvilleans cultivated a vision of themselves as a distinct and more modern people who did not really belong within the PNG nation (Nash and Ogan 1990).

Nash and Ogan (1990) outline Bougainvillean attitudes to other "red skin" Papua New Guineans, but it is difficult to chart how Bougainvilleans are perceived by other groups across the country. The Bougainville crisis created animosity between Bougainvilleans and other Papua New Guineans, but many also admire Bougainvilleans for asserting their own desires for autonomy. The Bougainville conflict is a symbol of what happens when the claims of customary landowners over mineral rights are not given due consideration, affirming a national ideology of land ownership (Filer 2006).

Thousands of non-Bougainvilleans invested in U-Vistract through Bougainvillean colleagues, friends, and in-laws, indicating multiple intersections and close relationships between Bougainvilleans and other Papua New Guineans. Isaac, a Mount Hagen policeman (see chap. 8), describes how his relationship with a Bougainvillean colleague drew him into U-Vistract: "I joined U-Vistract, that's a fast money scheme. I was introduced by one Buka fellow. A Buka fellow, he introduced me to the system. He even explained to me that if you put in K100, after a month another K100 will be added on to your K100. That's what he explained to me. So he explained it to me, so I went ahead. For a start, I invested K1000. That's my own money."

There is a significant Bougainvillean diaspora in Port Moresby and in many provincial centers of PNG. However, urban Bougainvilleans proudly pointed out to me that, while they live in the major cities of PNG, there are no Bougainvillean informal settlements because Bougainvilleans come to town for skilled work or study, "not just to hang around." In the colonial period, many "Bukas" had access to work and education that saw them well placed into the early days of independence (Griffin, Nelson, and Firth, 1979, 210), particularly through Catholic educational systems (Ghai and Regan 2000). Nash and Ogan (1990, 5) describe how Siwais became favorites of colonial patrol officers, being perceived as more modern than other Bougainvilleans. These attitudes reappeared in Bougainvillean interpretations of plantation and mining experiences where other Melanesians, particularly Highlanders, were derided as "primitive" and fit only for menial labor whereas "coastals" and "islanders" were seen as capable of professional work (Nash and Ogan 1990, 10–11).

With the opening of Panguna mine, Bougainville became the single most important source of income for the country, and many educated Bougainvilleans took on work with the mine. The mine created a remarkable escalation of economic activities and educational opportunities for Bougainvilleans well in advance of other sites of intensive development in PNG at the time. Anna draws on this view of Bougainvilleans as more prosperous than other Papua New Guineans as she reflects on her first contact with U-Vistract through a Bougainvillean in-law:

> At that time I didn't read anything about it in the papers, so the only infor-
> mation I had was from my sister-in-law. But I didn't know anyone else in the
> scheme. When I came to study in Madang in 1984–85, there were students
> from Bougainville and they seemed to be wealthy. They had a lot of money
> and I used to think that was because of the BCL [Bougainville Copper Ltd.]
> but later they said it was this investment in this money scheme. So I thought
> maybe they invested in that.

For those who share these perceptions of Bougainville as a place of wealth and development, Bougainville becomes as likely a source of the beginnings of a new financial system as anywhere else in PNG.

As U-Vistract grew, membership opened up to non-Bougainvilleans, who could only invest if they provided character references from pastors or other religious leaders. Pentecostal churches were particularly active in the scheme's spread for reasons discussed in depth in chapter 5. Members of these churches were not required to authenticate themselves. Police officers were also welcome to invest and were apparently considered to be of good character by virtue of their employment.

The various schemes competed with each other in offering higher returns. Money Rain offered a 200 percent return to U-Vistract's 100 percent, while others promised 300 percent. This competition muddied the waters and generated great excitement at the possibilities of ever-higher returns. In Port Moresby at least, the presence of so many apparently independent and competing schemes made windfall gains seem possible, and people rushed to invest so as not to miss out on the opportunity of making their fortune.

Money Rain was the next largest scheme after U-Vistract. The relation-ship between the two schemes was close but never formally disclosed. Although publicly presenting itself as a separate company, Money Rain was an agency of U-Vistract. Money Rain initially provided a pathway for non-Bougainvilleans to invest in a fast money scheme, as they were not then eligible for U-Vistract membership. Like U-Vistract, Money Rain presented itself as a Christian scheme and was successful in attracting leaders from the United Church, particularly well-to-do members with high positions within government. It was run by a

Solomon Islander, Flitz Lloyd Sanau, who had married a woman from a United Church area of Central Province. In the words of one NGO director, "Money Rain was Gulf people but Nekong and Millennium were Bougainvillean schemes. They were smaller pyramids that used to feed off the big one: U-Vistract. Money Rain was under U-Vistract. I also put money into Millennium but I never got anything out of it."

Government Patronage

Initially, U-Vistract and the other fast money schemes were not illegal. They enjoyed close relationships with Prime Minister Bill Skate and his treasurer, Iairo Lasaro, who exempted ten fast money schemes from the requirements of the Financial Institutions Act. Coral Pacific (Windfall) was the first of these, granted an exemption in June 1999, while U-Vistract, Nekong, and Millennium had their exemptions gazetted a month later (*National* August 5, 1999). Lasaro[1] had granted a three-year licence without conditions to U-Vistract and pressured the then-governor of BPNG, Morea Vele, to facilitate their operations, particularly in relation to ensuring that the scheme was accepted as a legitimate business by mainstream financial institutions. Vele admitted to succumbing to this political pressure, as well as to pressure from "Bougainvillean parents who wanted money for school fees and other necessities" (*National* August 5, 1999).

The treasurer's support formalized relationships between high-level politicians and public servants who were also involved in the schemes as investors and even promoters. The Clerk of Parliament was said to be the agent for Money Rain among parliamentarians and parliamentary staff. In 1999, he allegedly invested K300,000 of parliamentary money into Money Rain. According to this story, his investment was successful and he kept the 200 percent interest while returning the principal to the parliamentary fund (Korimbao 2000a). This was a breach of the Public Finances Act, yet an investigation by the speaker, Bernard Narokobi, denied that such an abuse had occurred. The *National* stuck to its story (Korimbao, 2000b).

Returning to the Christian theme, the chief political figures involved in supporting the schemes, Prime Minister Bill Skate and Treasurer Iairo Lasaro, publicly identified themselves as born-again Christians and embraced prosperity theology, a theme developed in chapter 5 of this book. Some years earlier, Lasaro had expressed the prosperity gospel view in Parliament that if PNG committed "ten per cent of its budget to God ... God himself will open the windows of heaven and pour out more blessings in this nation." This included protection from a range of troubles including natural disasters and law and order problems (*Hansard* November 20, 1987, quoted in Gibbs 2005a). Lasaro was an elder with the CLC, the Pentecostal church Musingku attended. Skate had previously sponsored a visit of the prosperity gospel televangelist Benny Hinn (Gibbs 2005).

The Crash and Government Reaction

As more and more people joined the schemes, liabilities mounted and the money dried up late in 1999. Soon payments were delayed and investors wanting their money were given excuses. One informant was told that there was simply not enough cash in the system to pay everyone, so they would have to return next month to be paid. Many investors opted to roll their money over each month, notionally accruing huge sums in "compound interest" so did not immediately realize that they had lost their investment. U-Vistract started to question the moral caliber of its investors and announced that only born again Christians would be paid. This was a clever way of relegitimating the scheme to members while withholding payments. By asserting a moral claim over investors, it was up to the participants to authenticate themselves to the scam as genuine, not the other way around. This inversion is typical of many types of fraud (Kich 2005).

Inevitably, pyramid schemes create bubbles that must burst. It is impossible to keep finding enough new investors to finance the payments promised to existing customers. At the very peak of their influence and public presence, pyramid schemes are at their most vulnerable.

The PNG fast money schemes were no exception. Their collapse coincided with action from BPNG to rein them in. The Skate government had fallen and Sir Mekere Morauta, a former BPNG governor, was sworn in as the new prime minister in July 1999. Morauta immediately canceled the exemptions from the Financial Institutions Act. In September 1999, BPNG required the schemes to produce their financial records and demanded that depositors be repaid within three months. The schemes were forbidden from taking further deposits and required to open new bank accounts for the purpose of repaying investors in the event that the promised funds from overseas materialized.

This change of policy caught the scams by surprise and caused a flurry of public meetings in Port Moresby placating angry investors. These meetings were often full of religious language and prayer and characterized the banks and government as greedy and corrupt. Two MPs criticized the prime minister and requested that the government support the fast money schemes and protect ordinary people's investments. They saw the fast money schemes as threatening the interests of commercial banks by "helping small people in a big way with better returns" (*Post-Courier*, August 13, 1999).

This claim that BPNG was destroying a legitimate business was soon echoed by all the schemes. As well as blaming BPNG, attention turned to the commercial banks that were accused of withholding depositors' funds and of freezing the accounts of the money schemes. BPNG and the Papua New Guinea Banking Corporation (PNGBC) published public notices explaining their actions and refuting the promoters' claims.

Several of the scam promoters wanted to travel overseas on the pretext of needing to collect the money due to investors (Pamba 1999). Musingku had his three passports confiscated. All the while, he made public pleas for more time to allow the transfer of money into PNG and begged to be allowed to travel overseas to arrange these transactions, even volunteering to be accompanied by officials from BPNG.

In April 2000, Parliament passed amendments to the Banking and Financial Act that strengthened the powers of BPNG and introduced stronger penalties for fast money schemes. The bank announced its intention to prosecute eleven scams for breaching the act by taking illegal deposits. The new BPNG governor attacked the schemes, renewing public warnings (Government of Papua New Guinea 2000).

In giving the schemes deadlines to repay depositors, BPNG set up the pre-conditions under which it could declare the schemes insolvent. In March 2000, it published another public notice, explaining bankruptcy provisions in relation to U-Vistract. Musingku and the other directors of U-Vistract were declared insolvent in April 2000 with provisions lasting until April 2005 (*National*, June 15, 2000). U-Vistract was liquidated. The liquidator found no assets registered with any bank in PNG, making it impossible to recover the costs of the liquidation process, although it appears that Musingku had transferred some K700,000 out of company accounts into his own bank account, claiming this was to pay investors.

In a public notice in the *National* (May 12, 2000), the liquidator explained the reasons for requesting a release from the appointment as liquidator and noted the lack of cooperation of the directors and the difficulty in convincing investors that the liquidator was acting in their interests. Lawyers for the liquidator and the petitioning creditor were assaulted by U-Vistract investors, the suspicion being that the company's directors had encouraged this at a public meeting. Musingku and his assistant Noah Ariku continued to take deposits from investors and so were charged with contempt of court. Musingku did not attend the 2002 hearing and a warrant for his arrest was issued and remains in force (*National* September 2002).

Delays and Excuses

As promises went unmet, investors demanded answers from the promoters and their agents. Agents of each scam became adept at repeating explanations. Some were so persuasive as to elicit further contributions. For example, U-Vistract's provincial agents would ask clients for money to travel to Lae or Moresby so they could "sort things out." New Papalain collections were justified in terms of the legal costs required to fight "the compensation case," which when resolved would result in monies being released to members of the scheme.

In explaining their failure to pay, the fast money schemes went on the offensive, blaming government officials and agencies. BPNG was accused of holding up payments, refusing to release funds, and even of being jealous of the success of the fast money schemes. Alternatively, BPNG figures would be claimed by the schemes as supporters, either through simple lies or more elaborate forgery of signatures and use of bank letterhead.

While each scheme has its long-suffering true believers, the explanations are being greeted with increasing skepticism. Some schemes are being lampooned as "the next week bank" (because of their reiteration that the money is coming "next week" or "next month"). Many investors do not accept the loss of their savings and intend to get their money back. However, they have little alternative but to keep at the promoters, as giving up would entail acceptance of the fraud and permanent loss of money. While some investors still hang on to dreams of tremendous wealth, others simply want their money refunded and feel they have a right to the return of their initial investment, regardless of how long they have to wait.

U-Vistract beyond Port Moresby

U-Vistract established provincial offices in Buka, Lae, Madang, Goroka, and Rabaul. According to a 1999 U-Vistract report to the prime minister, the Buka office had 60,000 clients, Port Moresby 5,857, Lae 700, Goroka and Madang 350 each, and 300 in Rabaul, for a total of 67,557 investors. The same document claimed that investment receipts totaled K297 million for Port Moresby, K30 million for Buka, K2 million for Lae, K1 million for Rabaul, and K500,000 each for Goroka and Madang. This reported total of K331 million was supposedly due to earn K662 million interest. Lae, Rabaul, Buka, and Goroka are also named in addition to Port Moresby in a letter to the editor condemning U-Vistract (Sympathizer, November 20, 2003). The list of towns seems to accurately represent the principal U-Vistract centers, although the scheme certainly spread to other places as well, including New Ireland. A warning was issued against the "Meekamui Bank" on Manus Island in February 2006 (*National* February 6, 2006).

The above figures represent an attempt to demonstrate the importance of U-Vistract in order to save the scheme from government intervention, but the numbers of members seem very modest for the areas outside Bougainville. Sixty thousand for Bougainville may seem fanciful, but some think that as many as 50 percent of Bougainville's 180,000 people were involved in the scheme (Regan 2009). Stories are told of long lines of people outside the Buka office, forming at 3 a.m., and of officials writing receipts as they threw the money deposited over their shoulders into a huge pile on the floor. In another example, men from one of the northern islets of Buka explained to me how they had invested K5,000 in the scheme, the takings from that year's *beche de mer* harvest.

In May 2000, Musingku traveled around the country reassuring investors. A newspaper article (Metta 2000) reported on his visit to Kavieng and intentions to fly to Rabaul, supposedly paying the Islands region first and then the Eastern Highlands. At a public meeting in 2003, the scheme admitted that it owed K48million to 2,700 members in Madang (Gare 2003). This is a much larger figure than the one given in the U-Vistract report above, indicating that the scheme continued to grow rapidly, even after it ceased payments and was declared bankrupt. Madang investors speak of thousands of members joining the scheme from Madang town, the North Coast, Rai Coast, and other areas of the province. Villagers often pooled small contributions of K10 or K20, and members often continued their contributions for years.

Felix, a Sepik worker at Modillon Hospital in Madang, captures the scale of U-Vistract in Madang as well as the continuing small contributions:

> There's a lady called Susie, she's a North Solomon lady. She's living near Divine Word University. She came here about '92–93 and during that time, she advertised all these schemes. So many people invested! All the Madangs, Bogia, Rai Coast, Karkar—all of Madang Province invested to Susie. She was the leader of the U-Vistract Madang Branch. From Rai Coast and Bogia, all of Madang must have had 10,000 people. It was strong among Sepiks—all the people in town and the settlements. There were some big shots too—all the government leaders!
>
> So many people! Like me, my family. We invested a total of K775 from 1992 to 2009. It's because she was looking for people to invest, sort of a friend-to-friend system. Many people from the bush came.
>
> Some invested with K100, some put in K2,000 or K3,000, some hospital members put in K3,000 or K4,000. In the end, we're still waiting. When we have a meeting at Tusbab Beach, that lady, Susie, we're having a meeting over there, and she's telling us what is happening. We always contribute K10 or K20 every meeting, some pay K10 but she'll say K20. Then the other month it was K100. That's what we do, so until today.

The provincial membership of U-Vistract continued expanding long after the collapse of payments in Port Moresby and subsequent actions to outlaw the scheme by BPNG and the national government. U-Vistract was still receiving substantial amounts of money from depositors as late as 2003, when the chairman, Musingku's brother Meshach Autahe, collected K30,000 from investors in East New Britain telling them that he needed their money for a "clearance fee," which could be used to release millions of dollars from Vanuatu (*Post-Courier* May 6, 2003).

One investor from a rural area outside Madang town told me in 2009 that the government should seize U-Vistract's bank accounts and make them pay up or shut them down. Of course, this is what had been done ten years earlier (and reported thoroughly in the press at the time), but this investor was quite oblivious to these actions on the part of the responsible authorities.

In Madang and presumably elsewhere, the spread of the scheme to new investors has halted. Increasing numbers of old investors have given up hope of receiving their money. Nevertheless, small collections continue to be taken up within the network of supporters. These are often on the pretext of some technological upgrade to U-Vistract's infrastructure, such as broadband or e-commerce. Madang organizers of the scam distinguish between *investors* and *contributors*. Investors are those who put money in before 2005 and will receive 100 percent interest per month as promised. Contributors will also have a share of the money but with a lower return as they have only contributed to specific expenses, such as the broadband infrastructure to be installed at Musingku's headquarters in Tonu. Musingku certainly has internet access, so these collections may actually have been used for the stated purposes. Other collections were not so straightforward: Felix, quoted above, explained to me that he had sent money to U-Vistract in both 2008 and 2009 as "stamp duty" to allow U-Vistract to pay his yearly school fees. The stamp duty costs were K10 per child. This process required him to provide school bank account details for the transfers to be made directly, but of course no such payments were made.

U-Vistract Abroad

U-Vistract also spread to Australia, Fiji, and Solomon Islands. In Australia, a small number of Queensland investors contributed some AUD500,000 between July and October 1999. Some were Bougainvilleans working or studying abroad, and it is likely that all of them had close personal links to PNG. Money was also collected from church groups in Kempsey and Brisbane. These activities drew the attention of the Australian Securities and Investments Commission (ASIC), which stopped the further spread of the scheme and required U-Vistract to return the money to its investors (ASIC 1999).

Regan (2009) discusses U-Vistract's role in Fiji, where some three thousand Fijians invested in the scheme, mostly through Pentecostal church connections. The number of investors in the Solomon Islands was not large and was probably limited to the Bougainvillean diaspora there. During the Bougainville crisis, thousands fled across the border, settling mainly in Gizo, Honiara, and Guadalcanal. Musingku returned to the Solomon Islands in 2002 and courted the Solomon Islands government. U-Vistract seems not to have had a public profile in Vanuatu, but I have spoken to ni-Vanuatu people whose relatives invested considerable sums in the scam.

"A Christian Ministry"

> "The organization is not a money scheme aimed at cheating people or making overnight millionaires. The organization is here to promote Christianity, peace, justice and equality."
>
> *U-Vistract News*, "The U-Vistract Vision"

As I discuss in depth later in the book, Christianity featured heavily in the way U-Vistract, Money Rain, and other schemes were promoted, with various churches and their pastors being drawn into the schemes (Gibbs 2005a). Many church leaders, congregations, and other church bodies invested in the schemes and some even acted as active promoters. The best-known story was of a United Church women's group being stranded in Port Moresby en route to a regional conference in Samoa. The women could not complete their journey because a bishop had invested their funding in Money Rain (*Post-Courier*, August 23, 1999). In another incident, a United Church bishop invested K50,000 of church funds in U-Vistract, losing the whole amount. Salaries for church executives were not paid for a year, but no disciplinary action was taken.

The United Church was not the only mainline church to become involved in the schemes. However, other churches responded more decisively at an institutional level. A Lutheran congregation in Lae was drawn into the scheme by a former pastor, but because of these activities, he was subsequently expelled from the church. Catholic and Anglican clergy were quick to warn against the schemes, although this did not stop individuals from investing. Perhaps the congregational governance and funding structures of the United Church and various Pentecostal churches made them more vulnerable to fraud than more hierarchical churches.

Pentecostal networks openly supported U-Vistract (Gibbs 2005a). Three Pentecostal pastors gave written character witnesses for Musingku during his trial for contempt of court. Pastor Bob Lutu, Deputy Senior Pastor for the CLC, stated that Musingku was "a Born Again Christian … who faithfully attends Christian Life Centre … It has been our experience that the Church income was at a high level when members of the church were receiving returns on their investments under the programme" (Lutu 2000). Many members invested in the scheme and donated this income to the church, funding a new building, social programs, and the pastor's own vehicle. Pastor Lutu was even said to be on the board of U-Vistract. He and other pastors endorsed U-Vistract at Sunday worship and promoted the scheme to members. Their preaching also denounced BPNG and those within the church who opposed fast money schemes.

U-Vistract's Christian moral credentials were impeccable, drowning out more sober warnings from BPNG. Many believed U-Vistract's claims that BPNG was "jealous" of U-Vistract, or that a corrupt government wanted to appropriate U-Vistract's investments. U-Vistract's forms and newsletters carried Bible verses and devotional materials. Meetings would begin with prayer and sometimes whole worship services supported by choirs from local churches. Christian motifs also became part of the scheme's rationales: U-Vistract itself repeatedly claimed not to be a money scheme but a "Christian ministry" (*U-Vistract News*

2001a; *Papala Chronicles* 18, October 21, 2005b). Prosperity gospel teachings were adapted by Musingku to legitimate U-Vistract. The scheme developed an elaborate cosmology of itself as a Christian reform of the global financial system that would guarantee prosperity for the world's poor.

As money from new investors faltered, making payments impossible, U-Vistract intensified its Christian moral demands. Under the headline of "U-Vistract—Change and Get Paid" (*Post-Courier*, May 31, 2001a), the *Post-Courier* reported on a meeting of U-Vistract investors. There, one of the U-Vistract promoters, Noah Ariku, addressed the scheme's members and gave them a homily on the evils of money. Ariku stated that "U-Vistract will not pay its investors until they become born again Christians" and would screen clients on the basis of their personal morality, excluding smokers, womanisers, and gamblers. As with the return of Christ and other eschatological events, payments would be made "soon" but the timing of the payments was according to "God's will and timing." These techniques of inserting the scheme into a Christian moral universe are discussed at length in chapters 5 and 6.

Musingku on the Run

In 2002, Musingku attempted to reestablish U-Vistract in Port Moresby as the "Royal Reserve Bank of Papala." "The Kingdom of Papala" had already been introduced into U-Vistract's rhetoric in 2000 as an attempt to subvert and replace the sovereign authority of the PNG state (Cox 2013). Musingku addressed U-Vistract investors claiming that "[U-Vistract] is ... incorporated under seal of government and constitutional laws of the Independent State of the Kingdom of Papala" (*Post-Courier* April 25, 2000a). In the 2002 incident, Musingku occupied a building in downtown Port Moresby previously used by the Bank of Hawaii and went so far as to set up automatic teller machines in the lobby, according to one informant.[2] Within days, police and BPNG officials raided the new pseudo-bank and closed it down (Krau and Daia Bore 2002).

Musingku fled Port Moresby for Bougainville and then the Solomon Islands. He was now a wanted man, and PNG police tried to organize for his extradition once they became aware of his activities in Solomon Islands. In Honiara, Musingku set up the "Royal Assembly of Nations and Kingdoms" (RAONK)—a supposed alternative to the United Nations—and the "RAONK Money Centre" (Kone 2003) and offered assistance to the Solomon Islands government. The deal would have paid Musingku USD10 million for settling government debts of SBD1.7 billion (USD350 million). Musingku would pay in "U-V Dollars" (Fraenkel 2004, 154). This absurd transaction was nearly approved but for the opposition of Central Bank governor Rick Hou, who refused to issue a banking license to the scheme. Musingku's time in Honiara was limited. He again fled, before the arrival of the Regional Assistance Mission to Solomon Islands (RAMSI) in

July 2003. Back in PNG, Musingku unsuccessfully made approaches to the new prime minister, Michael Somare (Kenneth 2003).

Returning to Bougainville, Musingku courted separatist leader Francis Ona, setting up camp with him in Guava village, Ona's base in the "No-Go Zone" within the "Republic of Meekamui." Having proclaimed independence in 1989 and appointed himself president, Ona did not acknowledge the sovereignty of the PNG government or the Bougainville Transitional Government/Bougainville Interim Provincial Government and opposed the peace process (Hermkens 2013). He therefore offered a sanctuary where Musingku could not be pursued by PNG authorities. Musingku's promises of money were no doubt important in building a relationship with Ona, who was already an investor and had collected money from his supporters, which was invested in U-Vistract (Regan 2010). The funds were substantial enough for U-Vistract to charter a helicopter to fly into the No-Go Zone to receive them (O'Callaghan 2000a). Musingku linked his own self-proclaimed Royal Kingdom of Papala with Ona's Meekamui. This proceeded as far as transforming Ona's Republic of Me'ekamui into a kingdom with Musingku overseeing Ona's coronation. Ona appears to have seen Musingku as a means of reinvigorating his legitimacy in the face of the advancing peace process. However, being associated with Musingku actually discredited Ona further (Regan 2010). Bougainvillean veteran politicians Joseph Kabui and John Momis responded to Ona's coronation with a joint press release condemning Musingku (*National* May 23, 2004a).

While still resident with Ona, Musingku again attracted headlines because of the visit of two Australian expatriates of dubious repute. In September 2004, "Prince" Jeffrey Richards and "Lord" Rex Nesbitt of the "Independent Principality of Mogilno" (a self-proclaimed pseudo-state in Queensland) flew into the disused Aropa Airport on a small charter plane. Their entry into Bougainville was illegal and resulted in the arrest of the pilot and the owner of the aircraft but not the passengers. Richards and Nesbitt are suspected of trading arms for alluvial gold, but nothing clear has emerged about their activities (Gomez 2004). They may also have provided satellite and internet services to Musingku through a New Zealander, Simon O'Keefe, who was also implicated in illegal gold-buying (Vulum 2005). Richards and Nesbitt claimed to be assisting with rural health care and remained at Guava until after the death of Francis Ona in July 2005, finally leaving in March 2006.

The Royal Kingdom of Papala

As Musingku's promises of wealth failed to materialize, his relationship with Ona broke down (Regan 2010). By November 2004, Musingku had retreated to his own village, Tonu, where he crowned himself King David Pei II of the Kingdom of Papala, supposedly drawing on Bougainvillean tradition. The Kingdom of

Papala had initially been spoken of as a concept "like the Kingdom of God" but "not a claim to physical territory" (O'Callaghan 2000a). With his return to Tonu, the Kingdom of Papala began to take on a much more embodied territorial character, destabilizing the politics of South Bougainville (Regan 2009 and 2010; Wolfers 2006).

Initial relationships with the Tonu community were not entirely welcoming, with the scammers running out of food and money. Two disillusioned Bougainvilleans who had gone to Tonu to work on a U-Vistract database left and denounced the scheme as a fraud to the *Post-Courier* (October 5, 2005). More than five years after the scheme had been declared bankrupt, this still earned the headline "U-Vistract Broke" (Kenneth October 5, 2005a).

Later, lack of food again emerged as a problem, and Musingku was asked to leave United Church premises (Kinna 2006a). Nevertheless, Musingku overcame these difficulties and reportedly bought pigs at well above market prices, paying only with the promise of high returns "when the money comes." He also set about paying local trade stores with U-V Dollars, allegedly to the benefit of his "Royal Guards" (Regan 2009) and to the detriment of the cash flow of Tonu businesses. In addition to small collections and money collected at roadblocks, he has recently initiated a revenue-raising venture based on selling phone cards. Serial numbers from Telekom cards are reprinted as Papala Telekom and sold for double the price. Marie told me: "People think he's making his own telecards for public telephones. I spoke to a lady last week [and she said]: "You know he makes them himself! They're just like the ones Telekom makes but they make it here in Tonu." They're not educated. They can be easily convinced. He just takes the number from a K5 card, prints it on a piece of paper and sells it for K10."

From Tonu, Musingku produced his regular newsletter, the *Papala Chronicles*, and several blogs that detail his plans to bring in a new global financial and political order. These materials have been circulated among U-Vistract investors around the country. Felix, a disillusioned Madang investor handed me a pile of photocopied *Papala Chronicles* saying, "Take them away, I don't believe it any more."

Musingku has also staged various events in Tonu to confirm his importance, often using visiting foreigners on whom he bestows grandiose titles. The initial edition of the *Papala Chronicles* carried stories and photographs of a ceremony marking the issuing of "Custodial Safe Keeping Receipts" confirming the immediate availability of USD1,111,000,000,000 in investors' funds. "Roving Ambassador Wolfgang Kasser" received a certificate on behalf of "overseas investors" and told the assembled crowd that he had "lined up big investors around the world who are ready to use the royal international banking system." He went on to open a personal bank account saying, "It's a privilege to be one of the first white men to open a major account at your royal bank" (Miikaii 2005).

It is not unlikely that many of these people are criminals who assist in smuggling gold, scrap metal, and oil (stolen from Bougainville Copper Ltd. [BCL] stores in Kieta) out of Bougainville. There are fears in Buka that Musingku has provided a haven for criminals, a physical location beyond the law comparable to the networks of money launderers and fraudsters drawn together by the pseudo-state of Melchizedek (Van Fossen 2002).

Musingku's reinvention as King David Pei II of the Kingdom of Papala represents a rejection of PNG sovereignty and a claim to the means of creating money (see below regarding the fictitious Bougainville Kina). While many within Bougainville (Tanis 2005) and beyond have found these claims ridiculous, many middle-class investors were relatively uninterested in Musingku's pretensions and saw them as simply a particularistic expression of Bougainvillean *kastom*. I have addressed these issues in a separate article (Cox 2013, also Cox 2016) and do not consider them further in this book.

Fijian Mercenaries

Without Ona's protection, Musingku felt increasingly vulnerable to several still-armed groups of South Bougainville. His fiction of the Twin Kingdoms of Me'ekamui and Papala failed to convince many of Ona's followers, and after Ona's death,[3] Musingku was seen as a rival by Meekamui Defence Force leaders (Regan 2010). In October 2005, Musingku recruited five Fijian mercenaries for his protection, provoking the headline "U-Vistract Plots War" (Masiu 2006), not to mention a diplomatic incident involving the governments of Fiji, PNG, and Solomon Islands (whence the mercenaries had entered Bougainville). The Fijians had been recruited through Christian networks in Fiji and entered PNG supposedly as "missionaries," as they told PNG immigration officials. They were promised USD1.5 million each for their services (Regan 2010; Maclellan 2007).

The presence of the Fijian mercenaries further destabilized Musingku's position. Other Bougainvilleans saw recruitment of foreign soldiers as a provocation, and rumors spread that the Fijians would train hundreds of Siwai youth as militants loyal to Musingku. The reality of the situation was quite different, with the Fijians dismayed at the young men they were asked to train, regarding them as slovenly and lacking discipline. The Fijians' training role was also predicated on promises of large payments and provision of equipment, such as uniforms, which Musingku could not deliver (Regan 2009).

Despite the ramshackle arrangements for the Fijians, fears of Musingku developing a military capability were taken seriously by other militias and the Autonomous Bougainville Government (ABG). Indeed *Papala Chronicles*, in characteristic exaggeration, boasted that 800 Fijian soldiers would be joining the group (Jagui 2005d). However, at the 2006 meeting of the Melanesian Spearhead Group in Vanuatu, serious fears were raised by the Fijian government that 300 Fijians were preparing to move to Bougainville ("Fiji Stops 300 Bound for Bougainville," *National* March 21, 2006). Violence between U-Vistract forces and police erupted as a gang associated with U-Vistract attacked three police stations ("Policeman Hurt in Bougainville Shoot Out," *Post-Courier* May 11, 2006).

In November 2006, a newly formed militant group going by the name of the Bougainville Freedom Fighters attacked Musingku's camp, wounding some of his followers and injuring Musingku himself. Musingku and the Fijians escaped and made camp in the mountains outside of Tonu. It is suspected that this militant group acted with the tacit approval of the ABG (Kinna 2006b) and, specifically, Buin police (Regan 2009; 2010). The national government backed the ABG and Bougainville Affairs Minister Sir Peter Barter visited Bougainville Freedom Fighters militants in hospital. The whole incident renewed fears about security in South Bougainville and was seen to have jeopardized the peace process (Masono 2006).

The attack on Musingku's camp confirmed the Fijians' doubts about working in Bougainville. Four of the five Fijians left Tonu and were jailed in Buka for a year over immigration offenses ("Fijians Found Guilty," *Post-Courier* April 12, 2007). They have now returned to Fiji (without being paid), but the remaining Fijian is still close to Musingku and is the head of his security forces.

U-Vistract Today

U-Vistract has acted as a "spoiler" (Momis 2006; Regan 2010; Wolfers 2006) of the Bougainville peace process. Since 2008, the political situation in South Bougainville has stabilized with the ABG's reconciliation process expanding and garnering more support, although there are still concerns about former militants being armed. After Joseph Kabui's death in June 2008, James Tanis, a former Bougainville Revolutionary Army commander, became president of the ABG and met with Musingku in Tonu to discuss weapons disposal and other matters. There is talk of offering Musingku a pardon, something bitterly resented by those among the Bougainvillean diaspora, who regard Musingku as a conman who should be brought to justice (Regan 2010). Musingku is now trying to represent himself as a peacemaker, "I'm not here to destroy the Peace Process but to give life to it." (Musingku 2011b).

Soon after meeting with Tanis, Musingku launched his pseudo-currency, the Bougainville Kina (BVK) (Gridneff 2009; Cox 2014b). Provocatively, the K50 note is said to have the face of Jesus Christ on it, while other notes apparently feature Musingku, his brother Meshach Autahe, Francis Ona, and Joseph Kabui. The latter two are the only images I have seen in circulation. The politics of this announcement are unclear. Tanis, wary of this event being associated with his talk of pardon but also not wanting to confront Musingku, confirmed that the ABG did not recognize the new U-Vistract currency. Many Bougainvilleans have been outraged at the use of Ona's and Kabui's images without permission and the Catholic archbishop condemned the use of the face of Christ as blasphemous. Nevertheless, the incident attracted attention for Musingku and reengaged his latent supporters around the country, many of whom traveled to Tonu after the announcement of the new currency, anticipating their long-awaited payments.

After more than a decade of the scheme, Bougainville finally seems to be tiring of Musingku. A 2010 U-Vistract–organized commemoration of the Unilateral Declaration of Independence for Meekamui in Arawa was dispersed in summary fashion by a former Bougainville Revolutionary Army leader. One of the MPs for South Bougainville has constructed a new road to allow travel between Arawa and Buin without going through U-Vistract roadblocks, depriving the Kingdom of Papala of an important revenue stream. Musingku has been reported as very unwell, withdrawn, and intensely fearful of being murdered (Kenneth 2010a). Some say he is kept a virtual prisoner by his brother. Nevertheless, in October 2013 the scheme overhauled its website and is now emphasizing matters that relate to the Bougainville autonomy process, such as questions of constitutional reform.

More recently, U-Vistract has made the headlines due to its connections with international scammers (Cox 2014b, 2016). On February 16, 2014, Barry Webb, an American citizen, was detained as he entered Port Moresby from the Philippines. He was traveling to Bougainville to deliver a briefcase full of newly minted BVK, the U-Vistract pseudo-currency. When questioned by PNG authorities, Webb claimed to represent the International Organisation of Economic Development (IOED), a fictitious organization with a name clearly intended to recall the Organisation for Economic Co-operation and Development, or OECD. Webb produced a letter from Noah Musingku. According to the letter, Webb had been appointed as the Kingdom of Papala's "Minister for International Monetary Relations" (*Post-Courier* February 17, 2014).

Webb's arrest in Port Moresby raises the question of what international connections the U-Vistract scam might have. Webb appears to have a criminal record in the United States and is closely associated with Frank Mezias, who has attempted to defraud Native Americans while posing as a representative of UNESCO. Mezias apparently runs the IOED website and a number of other fake companies.

Van Fossen (2002) has described a similar scam network based around a pseudo-state, the "Kingdom of Melchizedek." This elaborate scam was run by the convicted swindler Mark Pedley. Pedley targeted separatist groups in the Pacific and used their aspirations for sovereignty to reinforce Melchizedek's claims. Pedley invented more than 300 fake banks, with names that recall the World Bank and other international lenders. In 2000, he entered Fiji on a Kingdom of Melchizedek "diplomatic passport." Melchizedek offers close parallels to Mezias and his associate Webb, not to mention Musingku himself.

U-Vistract has attracted several dubious foreigners to its Bougainville headquarters. They are usually represented in U-Vistract propaganda with royal titles or other official-sounding terms, such as "Governor." Barry Webb seems to be the latest of these. They suggest broader connections that corroborate other evidence of the scam being used to defraud people in the United States and possibly other countries.

It is likely that these international connections are interested in the gold produced by small-scale miners in South Bougainville. Musingku certainly buys and sells this gold, which may give some plausibility, at least among some Bougainvilleans, to his claims that the U-Vistract "monetary system" and the BVK are backed by gold resources. Musingku has been involved in conflicts over small-scale gold mining between local armed groups (Regan 2010).

There are also local impacts of the BVK scam. U-Vistract agents are taking "deposits" of PNG Kina and giving Bougainville Kina in exchange as if it were legal tender. This is already having an impact on small businesses in South Bougainville (Toreas 2014).

This then is the remarkable and continuing story of U-Vistract. For nearly twenty years, the scheme has sustained a network of investors across Papua New Guinea and well beyond but has changed its focus several times: from a Bougainvillean welfare society to the heights of conspicuous consumption by Port Moresby's elite; from a so-called Christian ministry to a separatist kingdom (Cox 2016). Musingku's activities on Bougainville have been covered thoroughly and accurately by Anthony Regan (2009, 2010), so I will not develop this aspect of the U-Vistract story. The central questions of interest for this book relate to the spread of the scheme across PNG, beyond the core Bougainvillean constituency, particularly the ways in which the experiences of middle-class investors reflect broader ideas of money, wealth, Christianity, and national development. My particular focus is on how Musingku and his cronies were able to reassemble familiar notions of global finance and investment into a compelling narrative that fooled a nation.

Notes

1. Lasaro's connection with U-Vistract extended for several years beyond his parliamentary term, and he was appointed "governor general" by Musingku.

2. Rebecca makes mention of this event in chapter 9.

3. Regan (2010) suggests that Ona's death was partly attributable to the stress of realizing that he had been deceived by Musingku.

3 Money Schemes in Melanesia

In 2005, when I first visited PNG to conduct preliminary research on fast money schemes, I was surprised at some of the responses to my questions. Many people replied, "Microfinance!" (something I had thought of as being rather "slow" money) and then launched into stories of the get rich quick schemes that I was investigating. Others spoke of pyramid selling schemes, and almost everyone assured me that fast money schemes were a result of the "cargo cult mentality" that supposedly cripples PNG's development (see chap. 4). This chapter marks out some of the distinctions and the similarities between these various phenomena and gives a model of how Melanesian fast money schemes typically have operated.

In making these distinctions, I also recognize that the conflation of fast money and microfinance is not simply a conceptual confusion but points to a contemporary PNG financescape of low salaries, bribes, competing demands, payday lenders or "loan sharks" (Monsell-Davis 1993; Goddard 2005, 121–148; Sharp et al. 2015), and banks that "do not have a heart for the people," as one fast money scheme promoter put it. Even well-salaried Papua New Guineans supplement their income with subsistence contributions from their own gardens or from rural kin. Many try to set up family members in small enterprises to expand household income. Others try their luck in card games or poker machines (see the collection edited by Pickles 2014a) In this daily effort to manage money, the lines between licit and illicit blur, and fast money schemes become one of many possibilities of accessing more money (Bainton 2011; Krige 2012).[1]

Fast Money Schemes, Pyramid Scams, or Ponzi Schemes?

Fast money, quick money, and *easy money* are all commonly used terms for these fraudulent investment schemes in PNG. In Tok Pisin the common terms are *isi moni* (easy money), *kwik moni* (quick money), and *winmoni* (win money; sometimes with the double entendre of wind money [Macintyre 2013] and also simply meaning profit or interest on a loan). Andrew Strathern (1980, 164–165) links cargo expectations, gambling, and shares as *winmoni*. All imply money gained without labor, opposed to *wokmoni* (Bainton 2011; Macintyre 2013; Stevenson 1984).

In PNG, the term *money scheme* has now acquired the connotation of fraud, although at the height of the fast money rush, it was still possible for people to wonder whether fast money schemes were legitimate or not. I suspect that *scheme* and *scam* sound sufficiently close to each other that many Tok Pisin speakers elide the distinction between the two English terms. It has become commonplace for the scams to deny that they are money schemes or pyramid schemes. U-Vistract, for instance, repeatedly states that it is a "Christian Ministry, not a money scheme" (e.g., *U-Vistract News* 2001a; *Papala Chronicles* 2005c).

Most PNG fast money schemes are variants of the Ponzi scam. Ponzi scams are named for the infamous Italian American swindler Charles Ponzi, who ran an investment scheme in Boston in 1919–20. Ponzi sold international postage coupons and promised 50 percent returns on capital per quarter. Payments to many of the early investors generated a great rush of new participants who, at the peak of the scheme, contributed some USD200,000 per day (Bhattacharya 1998; Zuckoff 2005). This pattern of high returns followed by a rush of thousands of investors and then an inevitable crash is common to Ponzi's scheme in the United States, the Eastern European examples below, and to Melanesian fast money schemes. Writing of scams in the Caribbean, Carvajal, Monroe, Pattillo, and Wynter (2009, 31) argue that, "Ponzi and pyramid schemes are phenomena that can occur in any financial market, industrialized or developing."

I have not heard the term *Ponzi scheme* being used in PNG or Solomon Islands; the only exception to this being the U-Vistract Wikipedia site (Wikipedia 2011b), which acknowledges that outsiders see U-Vistract as a Ponzi scheme. As is common elsewhere, *pyramid scheme* is used as a blanket term for a variety of money scams.[2] Technically, a pyramid scheme is explicitly set up to reward participants as they recruit new members. Participants graduate through various ranks of the pyramid scheme and only receive payment once enough new members have recruited in the same way.[3] The larger the pyramid grows, the more difficult it becomes to sustain the expansion, and the collapse of the scheme becomes inevitable after a year or so of operations.

Ponzi schemes also lure investors on the promise of high returns but without formal hierarchical recruitment structures. Initially attracting large deposits, they then authenticate themselves by paying out early depositors.[4] News of these payments spreads quickly by word of mouth (or other media such as television; Borenstein 1999) and draws in a new round of investors. Of the Melanesian schemes, U-Vistract and Money Rain both demonstrated their effectiveness with lavish payments to early investors, including handpicked people of renown or high status. As we shall see in chapters 4 and 5, these high-profile witnesses to the effectiveness of the schemes overwhelmed many people's initial skepticism. The infamous Ponzi scam run by New York financier Bernard Madoff also generated a strong and lasting following within networks of very wealthy people, creating an exclusive atmosphere around the scheme (F. Smith 2010, 229–230). Ponzi schemes make high returns appear plausible. This is done through a mix of personal contacts, propaganda, and through demonstrating that the scheme really works by paying benefits to early investors. This is true of Madoff, Charles Ponzi himself, mass pyramid schemes in Albania, Russia, and Romania, and popular fraud in Southern Africa (Krige 2012).

Most Melanesian fast money scams worked in this way, demonstrating results by paying out a few insiders. However, there were other large scams that operated without ever making payments to investors. Examples include PNG's Papalain, a long-running scheme based on the premise of compensation for Wau and Bulolo forestry workers made redundant during the colonial period, and the Solomon Islands Family Charity Fund (FCF), which promised millions of dollars left to the world's poor by Princess Diana. These schemes typically had lower entry-level contributions for "membership" (K50 for Papalain and SBD250 for FCF). They also promised a set payment (K50,000 for Papalain, SBD1.2 million for FCF), rather than accruing monthly interest on deposits. Low entry fees made joining more like buying a lottery ticket than putting one's savings into a risky investment. Papalain and FCF also differed from U-Vistract or Money Rain (or the AM scheme in Solomon Islands) in that they targeted the urban poor: Sepik migrants in the Momase region of PNG (Papalain) or North Malaitans in Honiara and Auki (FCF).

Multilevel Marketing Schemes

Pyramid or Ponzi schemes should be distinguished from pyramid selling (multilevel marketing, or MLM) schemes, such as Amway (Koehn 2001). Pyramid selling is not an investment scam as such but a structure for selling actual goods. Each vendor recruits new "downliners," who then contribute a percentage of their sales back to the vendor. This type of scheme is fairly new to Melanesia, although has been tried by Proma Products, an Australian MLM that sells cosmetics and health products. Gewertz and Errington (1998, 355–358) document another Australian network marketing scheme that claimed to buy local products and invest in "blue chip companies."

Another global scam, Questnet, has recently begun operations in PNG, Solomon Islands, and other Pacific Islands countries. Questnet uses MLM techniques and internet merchandising to sell the "Biodisc," a transparent disc claimed to have healing powers. Biodisc allegedly purifies water, imparting it with properties that will cure almost any ailment. Questnet infiltrated the Lae Urban Local-Level Government where officials were investigated for promoting the scam (*National*, August 14, 2006). In Solomon Islands, a senior medical specialist has been using his professional standing to promote Biodisc. In Madang, I have met health professionals who have also purchased the disc, even using hospital premises as a site from which to promote and sell it (Cox and Phillips 2015). The scheme is still active in PNG, as are other MLMs such as HopRocket.

The Bank of Papua New Guinea recently put out a warning on the Facebook page Stopim Pyramid Schemes & Scams Lo PNG ("Stop pyramid schemes and scams in PNG") against fraudulent MLM schemes, naming the latter.

Contrary to the previous example, however, multilevel marketing schemes are not inherently illegal or even fraudulent. Nevertheless, they do operate in ways that resemble scams. These include utilization of personal networks for economic transactions and promises of great wealth without the burden of paid employment or subordination to an employer. Koehn (2001, 160) believes that MLMs are inherently unsustainable because they rely on an appeal to greed. Certainly they promise benefits well in excess of their capacity to deliver and also target economically vulnerable people as those most likely to be recruited as marketers.

Schemes such as Amway embody the desires of their American promoters who see Asian markets in terms of limitless opportunity. Cahn (2006, 2008) has argued that Mexican MLMs also appeal to the logic of neoliberalism, including consumerism, and even provide a means through which disciplined neoliberal subjects can be created. Blaming unsuccessful marketers for their predicament and then inducing them to blame themselves is an effective strategy for sustaining the logic of the scheme in the face of the marketers' actual experience. Cahn (2008) also gives examples of the fusion of these ideas with conventional Mexican Christian piety. Gewertz and Errington (1998) conclude that such schemes perform a "sleight of hand," transforming the "less fortunate" into entrepreneurial subjects who can be blamed for their business failures. MLMs then also resemble the small enterprises expected of participants in microfinance programs.

Microfinance and Popular Economies

Microfinance is a means of providing financial services to the world's poor, largely through the programs of NGOs such as the Bangladeshi Grameen Bank. Microfinance programs vary greatly in their structures but are usually based on membership in a local group that encourages savings and makes small loans to eligible participants (Conroy 2000). While microfinance programs may have a role in providing a structure for rural savings, and even postconflict reconciliation activities in Bougainville (Shaw and Clarke 2004), they have not been as successful in the Pacific region as is often claimed for Asia (Donaghue 2004; Gregory 1999). Indeed, many question whether Grameen-style programs work at all for the interests of the poor, even in their homeland of Bangladesh. (Karim 2011; cf. Elyachar 2005). Schuster's study of microfinance in Paraguay (2015) shows how microfinance programs financialize women's social ties and create unsustainable expectations of entrepreneurial success at the bottom of the economic pyramid. These of course are then fertile grounds for Ponzi schemes, as indeed Schuster discovered in her fieldwork, noting the intertwining of the Ponzi scheme Elite

Activity and the microfinance NGO she studied (Schuster 2015, 18). Distinctions between legitimate and illegitimate financial spheres are notoriously difficult to sustain.

Microfinance programs were established in Bougainville in 1996 but were severely affected by U-Vistract and its feeder schemes (Conroy 2000; Newsom 2002; Shaw and Clarke 2004).[5] As noted of MLMs above, the implicit promises of prosperity that microfinance programs bring may lead to heightened expectations (hence the conflation of microfinance and fast money schemes among many of my informants) and ultimately disappointment and self-blame (cf. Gewertz and Errington 1998). Both fast money scams and microfinance schemes draw on similar visions of prosperity and present themselves as a reliable route out of poverty. The Bank of Papua New Guinea seems to recognize this affinity and gives warnings against fast money schemes when launching microfinance initiatives (e.g., Kamit 2006; Matbob 2010).

Bainton (2010, 2011) has argued a similar case for the self-help/micro-entrepreneurship course "Personal Viability" (PV), active in PNG and Solomon Islands. PV uses a pyramid as its logo and participants graduate through three levels of membership. Personal Viability cultivates personal discipline as the means by which individuals achieve their economic goals. U-Vistract acted similarly, as we shall see in later chapters. Indeed, both U-Vistract and Personal Viability claimed the title of *Grasruts Benk* (Grassroots Bank), in the latter case a reference to a savings-based microfinance scheme (Bainton 2010, 148). Much of PV's grassroots entrepreneurship is based on participation in microfinance programs where the disciplines of saving and responsible spending are taught with the expectation that participants will be able to use their savings to generate income from micro entrepreneurial activities, even to "inculcate a culture of saving," as another microfinance program in Madang Province described its aims (Matbob 2010). Such disciplining processes are characteristic of most microfinance programs (Schuster 2015; Sexton 1982, 1986), and similar disciplines were taken up by U-Vistract but targeted at middle-class investors rather than the poor.

Krige (2011, 2012) also shows how licit and illicit finance overlap in South Africa. Krige follows the activities of Sowetans as they engage in a variety of economic practices that he describes as "popular economies." These include less legitimate activities such as pyramid scams and gambling but also multi-level marketing schemes, microfinance, and other forms of micro entrepreneurship. Comaroff and Comaroff (1999) saw pyramid scams as "occult economies": magical attempts at generating money without apparent agency and a subaltern response to the utopian promises of contemporary capitalism. However, Krige's popular economies are less millennial and reflect both fatalism and opportunism in people caught between their aspirations for fulfilment as global consumers and economic circumstances that provide insufficient opportunities for living out such lifestyles (cf. Wardlow 2002, 156). Like the microcredit borrowers who service old debts with new loans—Schuster's (2015, 6–7) bicycling debt (pedalling endlessly simply to survive)—those caught in popular economies are simply trying every means to make ends meet (cf. Sharp et al. 2015). Krige argues that, at the popular level, there is little concern with the legality of various money-making schemes and so illegal pyramid schemes and legal multilevel marketing schemes occupy the same social, discursive, and performative space.

For South African popular economies and Melanesian fast money schemes alike, this local space is a mix of pragmatic opportunism engagement with global economic cosmologies. Sowetan and Papua New Guinean households take opportunities as they come and juggle money by whatever means is available, be it payday loans, help from kin, bets, card games, Ponzi schemes, projects of becoming entrepreneurial through microfinance programs, pyramid marketing, or refashioning the self through prosperity gospel Pentecostalism (chapter 6; Piot 2010).

Nigerian "419" Scams

Perhaps the best-known example of international fraud are Nigerian email scams, or 419 fraud (named for the relevant clause of Nigeria's antifraud legislation and now a vernacular term for all fraud in Nigeria [D. J. Smith 2007]). Based in Nigeria, millions of emails are spammed across the globe on the assumption that, even if only a tiny proportion of those contacted respond, the returns to the promoters will be substantial. Because these scams rely on email contact with individuals, they do not need to make use of localized social networks in order to proliferate (Kich 2005). This mode of operating is then quite distinct from Madoff, Eastern European pyramid scams, or Melanesian fast money schemes— all of which spread by word of mouth and personal networks. Annually, Nigerian 419 scams make millions of dollars, so they are remarkably effective, even to the point of representing a high proportion of Nigerian foreign exchange revenue. Australians, for example, remit some AUD10 million a year to Nigeria, according to a study of fraud by Queensland Police (Commonwealth of Australia 2010).[6]

Notwithstanding their imperfect English expression, Nigerian email scams show high levels of rhetorical sophistication, demonstrated in their capacity to persuade millions of people around the globe to part with their money on fraudulent grounds (Kich 2005). Dyrud (2005, 10) explains that this success comes from appealing to people's aspirations: "it is not stupidity that Nigerian scammers prey upon: it is hope." As I shall explore for Melanesia, this hope rests within a global culture of neoliberal capitalism and its promises of unfettered growth.

Rather than being driven by millennial hopes that capitalism will bring prosperity and more, Nigerian 419 scams represent a deep and often ruthless pessimism. As Daniel Jordan Smith demonstrates, the very rationales behind Nigerian email scam letters offer a window into popular ideas of power, corruption, and access to wealth (Smith 2007, 39– 52). The scenarios involve oil tycoons, wealthy foreigners, and even charities as actors. The pretexts of the scams reveal how many Nigerians imagine the world operates. These disillusioned Nigerian views converge with the ways in which their (Western) dupes imagine global flows of money through circuits of corrupt "third world" officials. While they may prey upon the hopes of their victims (Dyrud 2005), 419 scams actually emerge from a context of despair and disenchantment. Rather bleakly, their imagined world is characterized by organized crime and corruption, which typifies local elites and international financial mechanisms. Resentment against these elites and inequalities can infuse an element of moral justification into the fraud perpetrated against (presumed) wealthy foreigners (Apter 2005; cf. Musingku's 2001 diatribe against "globalism" in chap. 8).

The postcolonial Nigerian context explored by Apter (1999; 2005) and Smith offers opportunities for comparisons with PNG. The questions of the "resource curse," economic marginality, injustice, and corruption raised in the Nigerian studies are similarly pressing in PNG.[7] Africans and Melanesians alike suffer widespread disillusionment with the modern state and the project of development. If Eastern European pyramid schemes were generated within the transition from planned to market economies, Nigerian 419 scams have emerged from a context of failing oil revenues, structural adjustment, and corruption.

Smith's argument that Nigerians see themselves as having a "culture of corruption" has echoes in Melanesian ambivalence about the nation, dubbed "negative nationalism" by Robbins (2004a, 171–172; chap. 7). However, where Robbins sees negative nationalism as a factor driving Urapmin (PNG Highlands) people toward transnational Christian identities, Smith (2007, 210–220) regards Christianity as also permeated with the corruption typical of other Nigerian spheres of life (cf. Piot 2010). This concern with the national scale is also characteristic of other mass Ponzi fraud in Eastern Europe and beyond (Berdahl 2010; Verdery 1995).

The Promises of Development

Nelson (2012a; 2012b) has documented the El Millonario scam in the Mayan highlands of Guatemala. Like Bougainville, the context she describes is "postconflict" and characterized by a recent history of state violence followed by humanitarian and development assistance. Nelson argues that the flows of money into poor Guatemalan villages set the scene for "El Millonario" to swindle thousands of dollars from poor villagers on the pretext of being a humanitarian NGO working for the good of indigenous communities. Like U-Vistract, the scheme developed a religious rationale and co-opted local authorities, but the force of its persuasiveness came from "mixing development culture with 'traditional' beliefs in ways that morphed human connections ('social capital') into money" (Nelson 2012a, 216). This made the scam a credible vehicle of collective action, embodying the utopian hopes of liberation theology, indigenous beliefs, and the development project itself. While the Papua New Guinean context imbues U-Vistract with its own ideological and organizational characteristics, Nelson's analysis prefigures many of the arguments that I develop in this book in relation to the spread and persistence of fast money schemes. In particular, her recognition of the centrality of "development" as a driver of the aspirations of scams is also common to the PNG environment, as will become apparent in later chapters.

Eastern European Pyramid Schemes: Unruly Coalitions and Inside Tracks

The 1990s mass pyramid schemes in Romania, Russia, and Albania drew considerable attention from economists (Jarvis 2000; Bezemer 2001) because of their size and disruptive impact on the "transition" to market capitalism. Anthropological studies include Verdery's work (1995; 1996) on the Romanian Caritas scheme, Borenstein's (1999) study of MMM in Russia, and Musaraj's (2011) article on VEFA and other Albanian schemes. Berdahl (2010) has also written about an East German real estate scam that operated as a Ponzi scheme. Each of these pyramid schemes inserted themselves into postsocialist national narratives of the new possibilities under capitalism.

Verdery (1995) examines Caritas, a very large Romanian pyramid scam. Caritas was linked to the nationalist political party Romanian National Unity Party (PUNR), which in turn gained significant political advantages from publicly backing Caritas. Caritas used PUNR to expand beyond its home region to become a national scheme. For a time, this made it difficult for authorities to act against Caritas. However, the political value of being associated with the scheme eventually reversed as Caritas collapsed (Verdery 1995, 659ff.; cf. Musaraj 2011).

In addition to political capital, Verdery also speculates on the mobilization and redistribution of wealth facilitated by pyramid schemes.[8] She posits that Caritas was used by "unruly coalitions" (informal regionally based networks of minor bureaucrats, secret police, and ex-party officials, among others) to further their interests in the new Romania. These lower-level officials lacked access to the wealth of government enterprises, which was controlled by the economic and former political elite. However, through the pyramid schemes, "unruly coalitions" mobilized small-holder wealth and redistributed it to their members, some of whom made great profits, even when the scheme collapsed within months. Members of the unruly coalitions ("the inside track") were guaranteed a payout in the first round of investments, thus rewarding key relationships and establishing an economic base to allow pursuit of other business or political ends. These payments may also have laundered money from illegal enterprises (Verdery 1995, 662–664).

Verdery examines how Romanian attitudes to wealth, money, and the economy were changing and what the implications of these changes were for broader values and ethics. Caritas mediated ideas of prosperity that were seen as foreign and Western and allowed Romanians to appropriate these imaginings as a new national project. This required moral reevaluations of money, work, and capital. Similar processes are noted by Berdahl (2010) and Musaraj (2011). Musaraj (2011) sees Albanian pyramid schemes as active forces in translating the neoliberal economic model into particular economic and political manifestations. She is careful to avoid explaining pyramid schemes as mania or ignorance, or as the inevitable result of postsocialist transformation.

Borenstein's (1999) chapter on pyramid schemes in Russia shows how the multimillion rouble scam MMM used innovative television advertising to market itself as a story of the nation's struggles and fortunes. This use of technology sets MMM apart from the Romanian Caritas, which was based on face-to-face networking. Melanesian fast money schemes did not have access to television and operated more like the Romanian scam, although U-Vistract's production of propaganda leaflets and internet sites also makes it a technological innovator within PNG.

There are other points of comparison: the content of MMM's advertising, although mediated by television, generated an intimacy with viewers by using everyman figures whose aspirations and struggles were easy for ordinary Russians to identify with and targeted various types of Russians, old and young. The advertisements were based on Russian realist propaganda and recognizable figures from folklore (Borenstein 1999, 56–61). These narratives were full of melodrama that engaged millions of members around these representations of daily struggle for the deserving poor (compare Black's 2009 study of sentimentality and the KIVA microfinance program—chap. 6).

Like U-Vistract, MMM even mimicked the authority of statehood and attacked the banking system as corrupt and fraudulent (Borenstein 1999, 51; Cox 2013). When the government tried to close down MMM, the scheme mobilized its popular following using rhetoric and imagery that the state apparatus simply could not engage with, leaving MMM on an equivalent standing to the government in terms of its popular support and legitimacy. The soap opera characters, while fictional, became much-loved defenders of the scheme against the anonymous and distrusted authorities (Borenstein 1999, 62). Letters to newspapers urged that the scheme take over more government functions, particularly in relation to welfare (Borenstein 1999, 63).

Like Verdery, I see fast money schemes as a window into ideas, ethics, and aspirations of investors. Verdery's description of Caritas does not transfer exactly to U-Vistract, but there are many similarities that suggest ways of interpreting the Melanesian data. For example, the political implications of pyramid schemes are relevant in both cases, particularly their role in mobilizing resources for the benefit of informal patronage networks or "unruly coalitions." Patronage and clientelism are gaining importance as concepts for exploring Melanesian political and social systems (Cox 2009; Fraenkel 2004; Foster 2002b; Hameiri 2007).

Madoff: "The Greatest Swindler of All Time"

In December 2008, New York financier Bernard Madoff was arrested for fraud and subsequently jailed for 150 years, the most severe penalty available to the courts. Madoff was a highly respected financial trader and stockbroker who had helped found NASDAQ and was its nonexecutive chair. Alongside a legitimate securities trading business, he had run a Ponzi scheme for more than twenty years. His clients were owed some USD65 billion, very little of which is recoverable.

To date, accounts of the Madoff fraud are mostly by journalists (Arvedlund 2009; Kirtzman 2009) or by legal experts concerned about the implications of the Madoff fraud for broader financial regulatory reform (Gregoriou and L'Habitant 2009). Madoff's success in perpetrating a fraud of such longevity and on such a large scale is unprecedented. His success lay in a number of strategies, including running a legitimate trading firm as a cover for the fraud. Madoff cultivated an aura of exclusivity[9] and turned away many investors or initially discouraged investors from investing too much until they had seen the returns. This built high levels of trust, making investors feel that he did not need their money.

Madoff's scam was a classic instance of affinity fraud, the exploitation of trust within social networks for illegitimate financial gain. He made a point of targeting those within his own community (wealthy New York Jewry) and participating actively in the life of the community, particularly in philanthropy. Many prominent members of the Jewish community invested with Madoff, as did Jewish institutions such as the prestigious Yeshiva University and various philanthropic trusts (Kirtzmann 2009).

Madoff was also phenomenally successful in keeping authorities at bay (Kirtzman 2009). His personal reputation as an eminent financier, including membership in industry bodies responsible for oversight, use of complex feeder schemes, and his ability to confuse investigators with jargon and evasion all combined to ensure that the scam passed undetected until it eventually ran out of new investor funds during the 2008 global financial crisis. Madoff claimed that he had a unique "commercial in confidence" technique of investing, which he called split-strike conversion. This fictitious method claimed to place futures options on shares to avoid losses in trading. The few investigators who had questioned Madoff's credibility had had their suspicions raised by the high rates of return and the apparent impossibility of replicating Madoff's strategy. Remarkably, these suspicions were not investigated with any rigor by the Securities and Exchange Commission, which in November 2007 found no evidence of fraud in Madoff's operations (Kirtzman 2009, 209). Krugman (2008, A45) attributes the lack of rigor in these investigations to similarities between the "Madoff economy" and the finance economy and an "innate tendency on the part of even the elite to idolize men who are making a lot of money, and assume that they know what they're doing." Millennial capitalism seems able to produce "occult economies" even in the world cities that are the centers of capital and financial power. Ponzi fraud cannot simply be explained as a matter for peripheries characterized by "transition," "development," or "financial illiteracy," nor as a phenomenon caused by maladapted individuals on the fringes of market economies.[10]

Trust in Abstract Systems

Madoff played on greed and ignorance, but his scam also revealed the importance of personal trust in supposedly rational and dispassionate investment decisions, both for individuals and institutions, even those entrusted with regulatory oversight. It is hard to judge whether the American media are more scandalized by the failure of regulators to arrest Madoff earlier or by his betrayal of investors, particularly those with whom he was on intimate terms. Madoff's betrayal of his investors' trust is a cause of public outrage because trust and sentiment are so fundamental to market speculation.

Giddens's (1990) analysis of trust in modern institutions provides some insights useful for understanding how Ponzi schemes operate. He distinguishes between "facework commitments" based on personalized trust and "faceless commitments," which are relationships of trust in abstract systems or expert systems, such as banks. However, he also allows that most abstract systems have access points where the personal and the abstract systems interact (Giddens 1990, 83). Madoff and U-Vistract's Noah Musingku both presented their scams as expert systems of finance that demanded popular trust. Moreover, they used existing social networks, including religious communities, as ways of creating access points to this expert system so that the intimacy of their facework commitments concealed the fraudulent nature of the supposed expert system. In PNG, trust in government systems is very low and understandings of how those systems operate are highly personalized. As Geraldine, an accountant from Port Moresby (chap. 5), put it: "It was all about trust. Trust in people in power and people of faith so that way you saw the genuineness of the scheme, although it's pyramid based. The chairperson was influential. Not only the church but individuals put in a lot of money. They invested their own funds, trusting their leader because you have a lot of trust in that person."

There are several parallels between Madoff and Musingku: affinity fraud, the building of a respectable reputation within a religious community, and claims to new ways of providing access to the benefits of global share markets. Melanesian investors were fooled by U-Vistract on very much the same terms as Americans were swindled by Madoff. Both U-Vistract and Madoff investors were introduced to the scheme through relatives, close friends, or trusted colleagues. Both believed they were getting a better deal from the burgeoning global financial system. Yet Madoff's respectable and wealthy investors are not predefined as being financially illiterate or somehow new to or unfamiliar with how money "really works;" nor are affluent New York Jews (or petty Romanian bureaucrats) seen as having a cargo cult mentality, as Melanesians are often rendered even by themselves. As I explain in the next chapter, Melanesians often stereotype themselves using these very tropes of ignorance, naïveté, and magical thinking. Keesing (1979, 59) warned against the "ethnocentric cynicism" of those who attribute inherent ("native") credulity to participants in Maasina rule, a postwar political movement in Solomon Islands, amplifying supernatural elements of the movement to the exclusion of the prevailing natural and political features. This warning is also well taken in relation to Melanesian fast money schemes. Thinking about PNG fast money schemes through the Madoff story or through Verdery's work on Caritas, as well as the other examples above, shows Ponzi fraud to be a global phenomenon,[11] indeed as a product of the global economy and its cosmology.

Millennial Capitalism

Millennial capitalism is useful term coined by Comaroff and Comaroff (2000) to indicate the triumphalism of neoliberalism, the enchantment of its utopian promises, the conjuring necessary for the mobilization of finance capital (Tsing 2000b), and even the irrationality and magic that is constitutive of modernity itself (Sutcliffe 2011). Millennial capitalism also owes a debt to earlier analyses of an epochal shift in value away from production to consumption and speculation (Strange's "casino capitalism" [1986]). Investors become more like gamblers, and gambling is absorbed as powerful service industry and de facto source of taxation revenue (Comaroff and Comaroff 2000).

The Comaroffs (1999, 2000) understand pyramid schemes as a global phenomenon that is proliferating in reaction to the predominance of neoliberal capitalism. Alongside intensifications of sorcery, trading in body parts, and proliferation of prosperity gospels, pyramid schemes are occult economies: all distinct but related responses from those in the shadows of millennial capitalism whose position in the global economy brings the desires of consumerism without the means to achieve these dreams.

Millennial capitalism remains a useful overarching concept because it draws attention to the utopian promises of the contemporary economic system and connects ideologies of finance, whether they take the form of "legitimate" forms of investment or occult economies. These connections are perhaps most apparent in the case of Bernard Madoff. Madoff's case demonstrates that Ponzi schemes can also occur amongst the wealthy and respectable at the centers of global financial ideology and activity and are not simply the province of the poor and uneducated, or naïve citizens of developing countries presumed to have a cargo cult mentality.

Scale-Making and Spectacle: Economies of Appearances

Tsing (2000a, 2000b) provides an example of how understanding scale can assist in understanding fraud and processes of globalization. Tsing's model is useful for explaining aspects of U-Vistract's success in PNG. In her investigation of the Bre-X gold mining fraud in Indonesia, Tsing develops the idea of scale-making projects (2000b). Bre-X was a Canadian mining company that attracted millions of dollars of North American investment and high-level support from the Indonesian government. However, its claims to have discovered huge reserves of gold in Kalimantan were false. By 1997, after three years of prospecting, promotion, and listings on various Canadian and American stock exchanges, the project was exposed as a fraud, with no commercial gold deposits at all.

For Tsing, the Bre-X fraud was not primarily a question of individual greed or gullibility on the part of investors. Rather, it was generated by the interaction of three distinct scale-making projects: global finance, national franchise cronyism, and regional frontier-making. Her intention in developing the idea of scale-making is to avoid simplistic dualisms pitting the global against the local. Each of her three scale-making projects involves different participants who pursue their interests through creating a narrative of scale in which to operate, the scale being determined by the ambitions of the various actors. North American investors, stockbrokers, and financiers combined to create a narrative wherein their investment activities offshore become part of the expansion of global capital. Indonesian bureaucrats and political cronies legitimized their profiteering from international businesses through a competing story of nation-building and the culture of the frontier in Kalimantan, where thousands of migrant workers have come to work on resource extraction projects of different sizes, often beyond the reach of the state's capacity to enforce the law. Simultaneously, the language of the frontier rendered the place a wilderness waiting to be developed, thus emptying out the claims of indigenous landowners.

Each of these narratives creates space for the various interests of the scale-makers to flourish, yet it is their convergence and interaction that gives each of them their efficacy. Tsing recognizes not only the coexistence of the various scales but also the desirability of moving between scales. It is the interaction of global finance, national crony capitalism, and regional frontier-making that together created the Bre-X fraud. "The links among them cross scales and strengthen each project's ability to remake the world" (Tsing 2005, 60). The coming together of these three sets of ideological viewpoints created a certain momentum that drove the story of a huge gold discovery to a point where due diligence was set to one side and all participants were convinced of the legitimacy of the project.

The articulations between the various scales create a story of "spectacular accumulation" that is spectacular not only in its promises of great wealth but also spectacular in the sense of creating a public spectacle, drawing the attention of international investors, Indonesian officials, and other participants (c.f. Debord 1994). As Tsing observes, "the self-conscious making of a spectacle is a necessary aid to gathering investment funds" (2005, 57). Thus her term the *economy of appearances* refers to the art of conjuring images of spectacular success that underpin so much of contemporary capitalism, not least in relation to fraud and scams. It is these appearances or spectacles that not only draw disparate actors together but that also reshape or articulate their interests into common projects such as Bre-X. As Tsing notes of "contracts of work," permits issued by Indonesian officials to allow foreign mineral exploration, "they remake the identities of both giver and receiver, vitalising the miracle nation and its globalist speculators" (2005, 74).

Positioning the Desirable and the Feasible in Papua New Guinea

Tsing's ideas about the interaction of different systems of imagining the world and economic development resemble the framework developed by Errington and Gewertz, who also argue strongly against deterministic evolutionary understandings of globalization and foreground local and historical contingencies. In their 2004 ethnography of Ramu Sugar Limited, PNG's largest sugar producing enterprise, Errington and Gewertz discuss narratives of "the desirable and the feasible" in relation to the industrial project of growing and refining sugarcane for national consumption. Ramu Sugar is a more sober enterprise than the spectacular accumulation modeled in Tsing's account of Bre-X generating venture capital for mining projects. Nevertheless, reading Errington and Gewertz's work with Tsing in mind, the story of Ramu Sugar can be seen as an example of the convergence of various Papua New Guinean scale-making projects.

Errington and Gewertz identify several different stances which each contain variant understandings of the desirable and the feasible. These range from the traditional villager and landowner to workers who create new communities within the Ramu Sugar compound that attenuate, displace, and augment kinship ties to the modernizing company executive, to economic nationalists, and finally to international neoliberal institutions that now threaten the very existence of this nation-building economic project. Ramu Sugar has been constructed out of these disparate narratives, which sometimes coexist alongside each other, even in the experience of individual workers and other stakeholders of the sugar company. Each player has an important role in shaping the story of Ramu Sugar, but each also provides a convenient set of positioned starting points for discussing common social narratives of economic change and aspiration across Papua New Guinea. Errington and Gewertz document a changing PNG that is moving out of village life to engage with towns, company compounds, higher levels of government, and international agencies. The positionings they describe for Ramu Sugar therefore also serve as a way of exploring the class differences and tensions that are becoming more and more pronounced across the country as well as the various criss-crossing scales from village to town to nation and globe.

As Tsing argues, we should not assume that, "scales ought to fit neatly inside each other, the small inside the large, each neutral and fully encompassed by the next scale up" (Tsing 2005, 104). Similarly, the various viewpoints identified by Errington and Gewertz do not fit neatly inside each other but overlap. Participants face dilemmas as they move between scales in different social situations. Workers at Ramu Sugar, for instance, may collect funds to support their colleagues in cases of funeral costs, cutting across ethnic or regional identities and kinship links (Errington and Gewertz 2004, 91ff). Similarly, there are overlaps and tensions as people envisage the nation or the province or the global economy in ways that do not allow the larger scales to encompass the smaller.

U-Vistract, Scale-Making, Spectacular Accumulation, and the Desirable and the Feasible

Melanesian fast money schemes have adapted to these various positionings of the desirable and the feasible as they spread around the country, from town to village, across provincial, ethnic, and class divisions. This extraordinary spread is often explained in moral terms by reference to the greed and gullibility of individual participants, yet the experience of investors implies a more complex combination of motives and influences that do indeed reflect wider ideas of the economically (and ethically) desirable and feasible and the interaction of different scale-making projects. There may still be greedy and gullible individuals who invested in U-Vistract, but identifying (and, by implication, making moral judgements about) their motives does not explain what it was about U-Vistract that made the scheme plausible to hundreds of thousands of investors. Even the greediest and the most gullible of dupes require some convincing.

The desire of Papua New Guinean urban elites and villagers alike to unlock the investment secrets of the global world of finance underpins the success of U-Vistract. The scam's success is not adequately framed by reference to tradition or a culture-bound ignorance of how finance and money really work. U-Vistract's ability to engage with the desires of local leaders and to appear as a credible conduit for accessing global wealth was crucial to its expansion.

Looked at in Tsing's terms, U-Vistract was highly successful as a scale-making project based on ideas of global speculative financial markets and spectacular accumulation. These are not merely Papua New Guinean misconceptions of how finance really works. Rather, they are global ideas, not merely in content, but also in their extent and power, as many scholars of globalization have noted (e.g., Carrier and Miller 1998). With long-term shifts in value away from production of physical goods to trading in finance and speculation and marketing of brands and other images, economic activity has become increasingly concerned with appearance and spectacle (Coronil 2001; Kaplan 2003; Tsing 2005).

When considering U-Vistract and other fast money schemes, global and local views of the economy and the state interact in interesting and not altogether clear ways. On the one hand, U-Vistract conjured a vision of wealth generated by global financial institutions and transactions that were much the same as those imagined by investors in financial markets everywhere. Yet it was Papua New Guineans who entered into this relationship of imagination with U-Vistract, and they brought their own visions of the desirable and the feasible into the scheme. The view of the global economy that the scheme appealed to was not simply an extraneous view[12] imposed on Papua New Guineans by outsiders. Rather, U-Vistract produced a global financial scale using existing Papua New Guinean expositions and appropriations of the very global economy that they were already embedded in and highly conscious of. Therefore, the broader frameworks that U-Vistract used to promote itself cannot be dismissed as thin, deceptive artifice. In order to make sense to other Papua New Guineans, the fraudulent claims of U-Vistract had to emerge from Papua New Guinean interpretations of the economy, nation, and society within which they already live, work, and consume. Moreover, U-Vistract proved adept at articulating the failings of the system to the extent that thousands parted with their money and many wait patiently to be paid, sometimes for years on end. As will become clear in the following chapters, U-Vistract conjured a global scale but did so on the national stage and in the national idiom. Berdahl (2010, 111) observes, "Thus, while there may be moments where processes and institutions we consider to be global, such as capitalism, mass consumption, finance capital, and investment banks, displace and replace national ones, we should also remain alert to those instances when the salience of the national in relation to these processes and institutions may be observed in particularly bold relief."

This is not to suggest that U-Vistract flourished because it somehow cracked the code of the PNG understanding of the global economy. Guyer's work on money in West Africa can also add to our understanding here. Writing of commodity exchanges between different "value registers," she argues that "when one scale is not exactly reducible to the terms of another, a margin for gain lies in the negotiation of situational matching" (2004, 51). It is the lack of clarity and commensurability between scales that creates this arbitrage from the need to negotiate and reconcile different viewpoints.[13] Applying this insight to the Melanesian context, U-Vistract was successful in manipulating "margin for gain" as people negotiated various scale-making projects. This was possible precisely because of the competing and inchoate versions of what is desirable and feasible in relation to PNG's economies, be they local or global, financial or moral, cash or subsistence, gift or commodity. How U-Vistract reworked dreams of abundance into moral concerns with inequality and aspirations for full participation in a prosperous transnational community will emerge with greater clarity in later chapters.

Notes

1. Loan sharks and banks are discussed in chapter 9.

2. "The labels Ponzi scheme and pyramid scheme are often used interchangeably to describe specific forms of investment fraud where sustainability depends on the influx of new "investors" to the scheme" (Carvajal, Monroe, Pattillo, and Wynter 2009, 6).

3. An Italian scheme, Pentagono, worked with a pyramidal recruitment structure and spread through Melanesian towns in the early 1990s, often utilizing Catholic clergy.

4. Pozza, Cox, and Morad (2010, 13 n23) provide several American legal definitions of Ponzi scheme.

5. I pay tribute to my former colleague Gwen Gibbon who worked on the Bougainville Microfinance Program with great passion. Gwen died in 2005, just as I began work on the Australian Research Council project that introduced me to the world of Melanesian fast money schemes.

6. According to the head of Queensland Police's fraud squad, Detective Superintendent Brian Hay, "Many did not realise that they were victims of a scam. Many thought they were involved in legitimate investments. In fact, 76 per cent of people that were involved in the largest loss category, which was business investment scams, continued to send money after we spoke to them and told them they were victims of a scam. We are talking about people over the age of 45 who are professionally qualified and tertiary educated, and who have been successful in life. In fact, they were people who had, in many circumstances, large amounts of disposable income to send to the crooks" (Commonwealth of Australia 2010).

7. While there are no known links between U-Vistract and Nigerian scams, the acronym of the International Bank of Me'ekamui (IBOM), may be an in-joke for Nigerians familiar with Akwa Ibom State (c.f. Smith 2007, 3).

8. Korovilas (1999) argues that pyramid schemes mobilized remittances from Albanians working abroad and so were responsible for rapid economic growth in Albania.

9. Tennant (2011) compares his Jamaican data with the Madoff scheme and identifies "exclusivity" as a significant success factor.

10. Compare Parenteau's (2005, 120) observations of the 1990s US equity bubble: "Few individual investors make equity investments on the basis of sophisticated analytical tools

like the varieties of discounted cash flow models understood by professional investors. More frequently, trend-following behavior is adopted by less informed ... as a way to piggy-back on the bets of what are believed to be better-informed investors.... From such simple shifts in investor behavior, massive financial manias can be perpetrated."

11. "Such schemes are pervasive and persistent phenomena and emerge on a regular basis even in developed countries with strong regulatory frameworks, as shown by the recent experience in the United States with an USD 50 billion alleged Ponzi scheme run by Bernard Madoff" (Carvajal, Monroe, Pattillo and Wynter 2009, 3).

12. Nor perhaps could there be such a view, as Ho (2005, 2009), Miyazaki (2006), and Zaloom (2003 and 2009) argue in their studies of financiers and share traders.

13. Berdahl (2010) shows this type of arbitrage in her treatment of the German swindler "Doc Schneider," who used his status as a West German businessman to finance East German real estate projects. He was convicted of fraud in 1996 and is remembered as a national crook in Germany but as a local hero in Leipzig.

4 Cargo Cult Mentality

Pyramid Schemes as Cargo Cults

The term *cargo cult* hearkens back to the popular movements that challenged inequalities of wealth and racialized power in colonial Melanesia, particularly after the Second World War. In some areas, these movements have persisted into (or recurred in) the present. Madang Province, for example, is famous as the home of the Yali cult (P. Lawrence 1964) and more recently of a small-scale "Black Jesus" cult, whose leader claimed to be the son of Yali. In the rendering of cargo cults most common in the popular imagination of Melanesia and the mass media, cultists do not properly understand capitalist production. They imagine Western material goods as being unfairly withheld from them by capricious whites and believed that this unjust situation could be redressed by mimetic rituals. Practices such as building airstrips or wharves for cargo planes and ships or marching with wooden rifles in mimicry of US soldiers have lingered in the popular memory, and cargo cultists are caricatured as simply waiting for cargo to come.

Yet as decades of anthropological research have demonstrated, the practices of such movements were not simply about the unknowing anticipation of material goods to be delivered through magical means. They were rituals for harnessing the power of dead ancestors to bring not only cargo in abundance but also to transform social relationships. Along the north coast of PNG, legends of two alienated brothers have a very wide precolonial dispersion (Burridge 1995; P. Lawrence 1964). In some cargo myths these two brothers have come to represent the racial divide that has made Melanesians poor and subject to rich and powerful whites. These myths then are a powerful way to reinterpret, resist, and reimagine the transformation of the unjust social relations and material circumstances introduced by colonial forms of alienation.

Anthropological studies of Melanesian cargo cults provide some of the best precedents for critiquing simplistic accounts of apparently "irrational" phenomena. Since Worsley's 1957 classic *The Trumpet Shall Sound* (Worsley, [1957] 1968), anthropologists have attempted to show the political, social, and cultural logics undergirding various movements labeled cargo cult. The subsequent debates have been voluminous, even to the point of arguments that the term should be abandoned altogether as an analytical tool (see Otto 2009; Lattas 2007; Jebens 2004;

Lindstrom 1993; Hermann 1992). McDowell (1988) has warned that cargo cult studies achieve little beyond privileging the categories of analysis in ways that invariably characterize the objects of study as radically other, indeed primitive. Lindstrom's work has been particularly influential in arguing the case that the desire for material possessions is an obsession of Western society that is reflected in both academic studies and popular accounts of cargo cults.

This is not to say that cargo cults are a mere projection of Western preoccupations. There is also a long record of ethnographic studies of cargo cults. Peter Lawrence's (1964) account of the Yali movement or Burridge's *Mambu* ([1960] 1995) have become the classic ethnographic accounts. Their work has been augmented by many subsequent anthropologists including Lattas (1998, 2010) and Otto (2009), who study contemporary cargo cults in PNG.

Cargo cults are a phenomenon distinct from Ponzi schemes, yet there are many overlaps and similarities. Both make promises of transformative abundance that often draw on widespread anxieties about inequality or being left behind as others prosper. Both assume secret knowledge that is to be revealed by an expert and accessed through the appropriate mimetic rituals and even moral surveillance of cultists/investors. Perhaps the same characterization could be found in Pentecostal Christianity or in entrepreneurial self-help courses such as the Personal Viability movement or even in microfinance programs.

The cargo cult trope has become part of the culture of pyramid scams in Melanesia in a way that does not characterize fraud in other regions of the world.[1] The same themes of irrationality, mania, contagion, superstition, and ignorance—in short, the same fears of unbounded hopes and unrequited desire (Lindstrom 1993)—also characterize accounts of Eastern European pyramid schemes (Musaraj 2011). However, no one seriously analyzes Eastern European scams as cargo cults.[2] "Economic transition" is the preferred explanation there, but this too is highly problematic, as Musaraj argues (2011, 86), because it presumes an evolutionary development from socialism to capitalism and ignores continuities between pyramid schemes and "legitimate" financial practices and ideologies (Bezemer 2001).[3] In the process, the local texture of engagements with money and changing social values is obscured. Anthropological studies of these local textures reveal that notionally rational and legitimate financial systems are infused with sentiment and even superstition. They emerge as far less rational than their driving ideologies would admit (Kaplan 2003; Ho 2005; Miyazaki 2006; Zaloom 2003, 2009; Patterson and Macintyre 2011a). Indeed, as noted above, Comaroff and Comaroff (2000) argue that global capitalism is itself millennial.

U-Vistract was first and foremost a scam, concocted by its founder and his cronies for the purpose of defrauding investors. It was not the search for truth that Burridge (1995) saw in cargo cults. While the scheme drew on a broad range of ideas about money and prosperity to appeal to investors across the nation, it was not the earnest construction of meaning that Lattas describes as the "poetic logic that seized upon metaphors and metonyms, that exploited chance resemblances and associations, to create mimetic channels and magical gateways between bush Kaliai culture and Western culture" (Lattas 1998, xxiv).

This is not to argue that the mimesis of cargo cults was entirely free from deception. Peter Lawrence (1964, 182) describes Yali being fooled by a coin trick during a cargo séance near Madang, but such mimetic ritual was directed at cosmological ends. If a cargo cult was a means of seeking the truth for both its leaders and followers (Burridge 1995), albeit in an idiosyncratic manner (Dalton 2000b), then fast money schemes had rather different mimetic intentions: they deployed known falsehoods in order to profit from deception.

It is even possible that a scam can turn into a cult. Arguably, Musingku's core followers in Tonu have their lives comprehensively encompassed by the scheme and are directly regulated by the leaders of the Kingdom of Papala, in very much a cultic fashion.[4] I have not been to Tonu myself, but life there includes regular worship services and moral surveillance. It also involves economic activities, such as the purchase of goods from U-Vistract stores using U-Vistract currency or identity cards, communal labor, and the contribution of pigs to feasts on the promise of riches to come. The Tonu headquarters may then have a stronger claim to being a cult than is true of U-Vistract followers who live in other parts of PNG and whose relationship to the scheme is that of patient, doubting, or frustrated investors. At Tonu, the Kingdom of Papala is acted out in daily rituals but it is never questioned or identified as a scam. Rather, the connections to Bougainvillean *kastom* stories are emphasized in acts of local place-making (Kenema 2015).

By contrast, U-Vistract investors living throughout the rest of PNG are subject to ridicule from relatives and friends and hold on to their hopes in a context where the scheme is now widely known to be fraudulent. Many prefer to keep quiet about U-Vistract to avoid such arguments. As the years go by, with more and more promises unmet, the numbers of investors who come to meetings steadily drop away and most move out of reach of the scam leaders who might reinvigorate their hopes. Meanwhile U-Vistract has reoriented its activities online to link up with global networks of fraudsters in the United States, and this has included at least one recent visit to PNG of an American citizen who was attempting to deliver newly minted Bougainville Kina notes (Cox 2014b).

In exploring the cargo cult tradition for what it might say about contemporary Melanesian fast money schemes (or even Ponzi schemes elsewhere), I want to mark out some distinctions and draw out some common themes. The distinctions relate to questions of cosmology and the gendered moral implications of such cosmologies. Put simply, the cosmologies that underpin cargo cults are drawn from indigenous traditions, whereas Ponzi schemes reproduce global ideologies of finance and investment. This is not an absolute difference. Ponzi schemes may also draw on local traditions and cargo cults represent an attempt to integrate the disruptions and humiliations of colonial or global capitalism into traditional value systems. I do not take the myths and rituals of finance that underpin Ponzi schemes as straightforwardly modern, rational, and calculative as opposed to the traditional, superstitious, and credulous cosmologies of cargo cults. Rather, I see cargo cults and modern finance as having much in common as utopian millennial projects. Nevertheless, their mythologies stem from differ-ent historical sources and so produce different forms of social organization and distinct subjectivities.

Macintyre (2013) has contextualized the influence of the Personal Viability self-help scheme on Lihir Island in PNG, the site of the Newcrest gold mine. Macintyre explores the continuities between the 1960s Johnson cult, a social movement that began in nearby New Hanover and spread through New Ireland Province, including Lihir. The various manifestations of the Johnson cult wanted to attract President Lyndon Johnson himself to come and run the local govern-ment, bringing prosperity that Australian colonialism was seen as having failed to deliver. Macintyre shows that in the Lihirian context, cargo cults, fast money schemes, Personal Viability, and other forms of organization for "development," including the mining project itself, all draw on ideas of *winmoni*, understood explicitly as money that does not require hard work and that represents the ways in which white people are understood to earn and spend money. Her perspective is historical and shows the twists and turns of social, economic, and political life in the particular context of Lihir without assuming a linear narrative that becomes more modern as time moves from the past to the present, something popular renderings of fast money schemes as modern day cargo cults tend to do. Macintyre shows how any assumed cultural continuities in relation to *winmoni* derive from local appropriations of external influences. While cargo, develop-ment projects, fast money schemes, or Personal Viability may fold into each other, Macintyre detects influences and convergences that make each iteration of *winmoni* distinct.

In order to draw out some of the distinctions between U-Vistract and cargo cults, I provide some examples from the detailed ethnographic work of Lattas, focusing on the role of the dead, gender, and moral rigorism. These are all ele-ments of the particular cults that Lattas has studied and do not characterize Ponzi schemes generally or U-Vistract specifically. Nevertheless, anthropological studies of cargo cults have helped me understand the working of U-Vistract, and later in the chapter, I consider the most relevant examples to be Burridge's theory of moral equivalence and the history of cargo cult as a term of disparagement once deployed by European colonists and now used by educated Melanesians in very similar ways.

Lattas's ethnographic studies of contemporary East New Britain cargo cults present sophisticated arguments about the mirroring functions of the underworld (2006a, 2006b). Underground, the ancestral dead represent a mirror world where the injustices of the aboveground present can be seen with clarity and ultimately resolved through the cults' ritual practices, including bureaucratic mimicry and the hope of the dead returning with the cargo they have been producing. As we shall see below and in later chapters, U-Vistract certainly spoke to contemporary Papua New Guinean questions of inequality. Its practices of deception also mimicked bureaucratic language, forms, and processes (cf. Macintyre 2013, 143) but without any structural parallel to these mirroring functions of the underground world of dead ancestors.

Some further distinctions between U-Vistract and cargo cults become clearer with a consideration of gender. Jolly (2013) has recently identified the gendered transformations of cargo cults as an underresearched element of the anthropological literature. Lattas (1998, 152ff) describes the Censure cult's belief in a female Jesus who is merged with the traditional ancestor Kewak, a mother figure killed by her brother who thus initiated a patriarchal social order. The procreative properties of women's bodies are combined with the European savior figure to create an image of the "idealized norms of their social order into a feminine figure crucified by the state" (161). The female Jesus then becomes a central figure in the cult's cosmology, inverting and so resolving dichotomies of male/female, black/white, and living/dead. The transformative logic that underlies the cargo cult female Jesus is absent from U-Vistract. Musingku may portray himself in grandiose monarchical and even messianic terms, particularly when writing of his persecution by PNG authorities (Musingku 2009), but he lacks the soteriological role in "mediating alterity" (Lattas 2007) that might otherwise qualify him as a cargo cult Black Jesus figure.

These kinds of views often consider sexual fluids, including menstrual blood, as intrinsic to the production of cargo. This led the Censure cult into ritualized sexual practices and the recruitment of schoolgirls, girls offered by neighboring villages for sexual services in order that they would not miss out on the cargo (Lattas 1998, 187). This resulted in Censure's arrest, as it did for Stephen Tari, the leader of the recent Black Jesus cult ("Uproot Madang Cult of Evil!" *Post-Courier* October 24, 2006).[5]

U-Vistract anticipated a revolution in global financial systems, but this was a Christian reform, not the total reconfiguring of society and cosmos apparent in some cargo cult views of gender. U-Vistract's claimed capacities for generating money may appear ludicrous and without rational means, but they lacked the localized magical and ritual renderings of sexuality as productivity found in cargo cults such as those described by Lattas. The "sexual economy of desire ... where the desire for cargo is figured and realized as sexual desire" (Lattas 1998, 192) has no hint of parallel anywhere in the U-Vistract story, which is shaped by conventional Christian sexual morality. Indeed U-Vistract explicitly avoided transforming desire for cargo into sexual desire by reinscribing strict moral rules for investors that modeled women as chaste and selfless mothers (Cox and Macintyre 2014).

U-Vistract's morality was more routine respectability than the radical reformist rigorism associated with cults. The scheme's warnings against moral laxity do not imply the comprehensive break with the past and inscribing of new rules that have often characterized millenarian movements (Worsley [1957] 1968, 117). Therefore they are not preceded by any antinomian libertinism (Burridge 1969, 167). U-Vistract presumed its investors to be thoroughly Christian and so expected them to have already made a convincing rupture with any pre-Christian traditions or at least to have absorbed Christianity into their ideas of tradition. U-Vistract worked entirely within orthodox Christian, albeit neo-Pentecostal, theology and established relationships with church leaders from a variety of denominations without being seen by them as heterodox or as a cargo cult. This is not to deny the multiple intersections between cargo cults and Christianity (McDowell 1998). Cargo cults frequently draw on Christian imagery, ideas, and practices. Lattas (1998, 271ff) also documents the clandestine infiltration of Christian missions by cargo cult believers.

The moral purchase that U-Vistract held over many of its followers lacked the stringency and asceticism of a cult, at least for U-Vistract investors outside Bougainville. As indicated above, I leave open the possibility that Musingku's relationship to the Tonu community has the controlling features of a cult. U-Vistract was always open to new contributions and wanted to ground itself as a respectable and responsible movement. It therefore needed enough moral rigor to legitimate itself to its existing followers (this included blaming impatient investors and even providing some moral surveillance, as Isaac describes in chapter 6) but not so much that it generated a moral revolution that would exclude new members (Burridge 1969, 147).

Rather than erasing old moral codes, U-Vistract reinvigorated routine Christian moral exhortations, much in the way that Pentecostal and other revival groups do, distinguishing themselves from the older "mainline" denominations. However, as is typical of Pentecostal and Evangelical groups (and of neoliberal self-help programs [Bainton 2011], including microfinance [Cahn 2006, 2008]) these disciplinary exhortations also reconstituted Christians as individuals in moral possession of themselves. If cargo cults were movements of group salvation, U-Vistract was a Ponzi scheme that cultivated proprietorship of the self (Sykes 2007a, 2007b).

"Cargo Cult Mentality": Class and Inequality

The empirical depth and theoretical sophistication of anthropological investigations of indigenous cosmologies and their adaptations in the face of colonial power and economic restructuring has not prevented the development of a popular trope of cargo cult that imagines credulous (or just lazy) natives waiting for goods and money to come by air or sea, delivered by dead ancestors or other magical means. The conclusion that U-Vistract (or any of the other fast money schemes) is a "religious cargo cult"—as a disillusioned U-Vistract "whistleblower" told the press (Kenneth 2005b)—is irresistible and unproblematic for many middle-class Papua New Guineans.[6] Certainly newspaper and other popular reports of fast money schemes give the impression of a headlong rush into the schemes that recalls the ways in which colonial anxieties over Melanesian political and religious were rendered as irrational and threatening in cargo cult narratives (Lindstrom 1993).

Roga, a lecturer at Divine Word University (DWU), follows this path, outlining a stereotypical history of cargo cults, money schemes, and Madang's contemporary Black Jesus—a small-scale cult leader from a village outside Madang who was jailed for abusing young girls while claiming to be a descendant of the famous cargo cult leader Yali—and locating all within an unchanging traditional Melanesian culture that is on the lookout for money in a rather desperate and irrational way. Many people offer similar accounts as folk explanations of the fast money schemes.

> It's something that comes out from deep inside our culture. When they see a white man coming, they think, "Oh yes, here comes some money. How can we get some of that money?" It started after the war with the cargo cults—they wait for the big ship to come, full of money! Now Noah, he's the latest one in Bougainville. And here in Madang we had the Black Jesus—he was promising all his followers, "If you join with me, you can have so much money!" (Roga, *DWU Lecturer*)

The nuance of anthropological cargo cult debates sits somewhat uncomfortably with contemporary usage of the term *cargo cult* by Melanesians, particularly those who, like Roga, see the propensity to consider cargo cult as "something that comes out from deep inside our culture" (cf. Lindstrom 1993, 41ff). Implicit in the cargo cult identification of fast money schemes is the idea that Papua New Guineans are characterized by a cargo cult mentality that makes them peculiarly vulnerable to scams. This can be put in terms of culture, economic transition, financial illiteracy, naïveté, laziness, opportunism, superstition, and plain credulousness, but at the heart of each of these identifications lie essentialisms that anthropologists (most notably Lindstrom 1993) have critiqued, even as Melanesians use the term against their own countryfolk (Lattas 2007, 157).

An opinion piece from the *National* equates cargo cults and pyramid schemes as a developmental issue: "Like sorcery, cargo-cult is a developmental issue which also involves supernatural powers to the extreme of brainwashing people. While the rich and the powerful have access to much material wealth and service, the have nots seek the same. In urban areas, a number of people in recent years resorted to pyramid schemes to get fast money, while in rural areas people believe in gaining material wealth through spiritual means" (Dowa 2005).

Paradoxically, as anthropologists explore questions of inequality through the cargo theme, terms such as *cargo cult mentality* and its variants such as *hand-out mentality* (Gewertz and Errington 1998, 352; Errington and Gewertz 2007, 109) are increasingly used to discredit the aspirations of the poor and on much the same grounds as were used by hostile colonialists (Lindstrom 1993, 15–16). Lindstrom argues that Melanesian elites have inherited the cargo cult legacy and now turn it to the legitimation of their own privilege and the perpetuation of disadvantage for the poor: "cargoism serves negatively within island political debate to label and denigrate anything that may threaten established orders" (Lindstrom 1993, 162; cf. Buck 1989; Lattas 2007).

Politicians frequently describe their constituents as having a cargo cult mentality when asked for money or other forms of petty assistance or acknowledgment (Kaima 2004; also K. Martin 2007 and Okole 2003). The term is also used in discussions of aid dependency (Cox 2009; P. West 2001) or the failure of development programs (Lindstrom 1993). In this sense, the specific term *cargo cult mentality* describes the desire of grassroots people for windfall gains or substantial betterment of their material position and acts as a refusal of obligations that politicians, other patrons, the state, or donors might otherwise be implicated in.

Cargo cult mentality usually entails accusations of laziness and the unwillingness of poor people to work in order to better themselves (P. West 2006, 171–173). In effect, the poor are being criticized for desiring consumption without submitting to their subordinate role in production. West's example has the added nuance of villagers asking an environmental NGO for services in the absence of the state. The NGO worker rebukes them for daring to question the neoliberal model of NGO livelihoods over citizens' entitlements to state services (Cox 2009). As used by Melanesian elites (and their donor partners), cargo cult mentality has no reference to particular traditional beliefs described in the classical anthropologies of cargo cults. Rather, the poor are presumed to have an essentialized backwardness that produces dangerous desires along the lines of Lindstrom's (1993) critique. West's example of cargo cult mentality as a term of disparagement echoes the same sentiments that are often used to explain the spread of fast money schemes in PNG. However, whereas West's story involved direct confrontation between an NGO worker and a village community and focused on laziness, cargo discourse as applied to fast money schemes is more likely to transpose supposed cargo qualities like laziness, greed, and ignorance from the middle class to the rural poor. The editorial from the *National* below provides a typical example of the educated people getting out of the schemes while the simple poor persist in believing they will be paid:

Why do people "invest" in these schemes? At first, when U-Vistract hit the headlines, it appeared that many initial investors had indeed reaped huge returns on small investments. That is precisely the way in which these schemes operate. The first investors will always receive large dividends—but as the scheme continues, and more investors take part, the returns diminish until no returns are paid. That is why these schemes are referred to internationally and in PNG as "pyramid schemes;" the pyramid shape reflects the diminishing returns to those who have entrusted their money to these frauds. Some of the more sophisticated investors back in those days began to realize the truth of the situation. They and other educated potential investors put their money elsewhere.

Today, and for some years past, these cruel and unlawful schemes target the simplest of our people, very often squatters and simple village people. These people believe what they are so enthusiastically and persuasively told. And of course the golden promises have been added to by dark suggestions that the established banks and the Government have some vested interest in blocking the people from the rightful gains such organisations could provide. We still have not succeeded in persuading these thousands of our countrymen and women that such fast money is nothing but a pipe dream, more allied to the cargo cults of old, than to modern schemes designed to improve people's incomes. The old adage "nothing for nothing, and precious little for sixpence" is accurate when describing the whole field of making money. Broadly speaking there is only one sure way of making money, and that is through hard work. That is not, of course, a palatable answer for thousands of our people living at or beneath the poverty line. Anything that can promise some relief from their present situation is bound to be seized upon with enthusiasm. It is not until they learn the hard way, by not only not making profits, but by losing what they have been able to invest, that they come to realise the nature of these schemes. (*National*, November 10, 2005)

As Hau'ofa (1987) argued concisely, Pacific elites share a common culture across the region (and beyond as members of what Sklair [1998] has described as the "transnational capitalist class"). This includes the power to define the lifestyles of the poor, diminishing their claims on common resources and services (Gewertz and Errington 1999). The poor are properly to work humbly and contentedly in subsistence agriculture, staying in their villages and preserving "traditional" ways of life. The poor should certainly not be making homes in the informal settlements around the urban centers of the country, even though the elites prefer city life themselves, nor expecting "hand-outs" from government.[7] Attempts at class mobility or demands to renegotiate the established distribution of resources are regularly met with accusations of having a "cargo cult mentality" (P. West 2006). The charge of cargo cult mentality in this context represents the noncompliant and therefore undesirable side of the "traditional" villager from the perspective of postcolonial elites (cf. Buck 1988). This use of cargo cult mentality as a term of disparagement of lower class desires also parallels the male elite disparagement of Papua New Guinean women's aspirations for modernity through misrepresenting the sexuality of educated women as dangerously uncontrollable desire (Zimmer-Tamakoshi 1993).

Narratives of Inequality

On April 28, 2009, during a visit to Australia, then–Prime Minister of PNG Michael Somare held a press conference with then Australian Prime Minister Kevin Rudd. When challenged by a journalist about corruption and the misuse of Australian aid money, Somare expressed the common view referred to by Allen, Bourke, and Gibson (2005) that there is no real poverty in PNG and that no one really suffers because they can rely on garden produce. This occurred only a week or two into my Madang fieldwork and was intensively dissected at DWU and well beyond. These popular discussions of how a very powerful Papua New Guinean represented the nation framed questions of class and inequality for me as central to understanding the contemporary narratives of nation in postcolonial PNG. Somare's explication of the situation in PNG ended with this summary: "And I don't think anyone in Papua New Guinea starves. If you are talking and you might be talking about the people who come into the city looking for job opportunities and bring their kids along with them and I think that could be the kind of people you are talking about.

"But I just want to give you assurance that Papua New Guinea, no one is starving in Papua New Guinea. We always have something to eat" (Prime Minister of Australia 2009).

This exchange was widely reported in PNG and much commented on—often with great resentment. Many felt it encapsulated how distant political elites were from the day-to-day life of ordinary people.[8] PNG experiences widespread and worsening poverty (Cammack 2008). A 2010 government strategy used World Bank poverty assessments that estimate 53 percent of PNG's population lives below the global poverty line.[9] At the same time, millionaire politicians own substantial real estate assets in Australia, with reports of members of parliament (MPs) living permanently in Australia and commuting to PNG for sittings of Parliament. For some time, anthropologists have noted that villagers are aware of their poverty relative to whites (and elite Papua New Guineans) and find this state of affairs troubling and humiliating. In M. F. Smith's (1994, 230) understatement, "Many Papua New Guineans do appear to notice and react against increasing economic disparities." Indeed, they have been doing at least since Burridge's formulation of cargo cults as an attempt to restore "moral equivalence."

Madang settlement dwellers were particularly irked by Somare's implication that PNG has no serious poverty and therefore no grounds for being troubled by inequality. Some made more specific critical comments about the political and economic power of the Somare regime and corruption. Yet as Thomas, an East Sepik from the Public Tank settlement on the outskirts of Madang (and *Papalain* investor), put it, "he gave us trousers." In other words, Somare's role as the father of the nation makes him unimpeachable, not least for Sepiks, although they themselves roundly criticize him because they feel ownership of him. Thomas continued:

> The Prime Minister says there is no poverty in PNG but he's just greedy for himself. He's not getting down to the provinces, just stays there in Port Moresby looking after himself and his properties. He's just growing himself and letting these Chinese people in.
>
> When government is not assisting, people come up with their own ideas; whether they are good or bad. Like the boys getting into the Asian stores—blame Somare, not us. It's for us Sepiks to criticize him, we don't want others to criticise him. We say, "You criticize him—he was the one who gave you trousers."
>
> Thirty years of independence—there could be so much development. Thirty wasted years. We're here just like in the villages—you walk a distance to fetch water. But there are other villages two days away from a road, past mountains just walking. How can they get basic needs like kerosene, salt. The roads are bad. The diet is poor. If I become an MP, every Saturday will be my day to walk the streets. I'll meet people so they are free to tell me their problems.
>
> In places like Angoram, there's poverty there—no roads, airstrips or government services. Hey, once Papalain is out of the way, then I want to go for political power but if they come and ask me for money, I'll say, "Don't bother me, you already got money! It's voters who corrupt politicians!"

As "disparagement of elites," Thomas's castigation of Somare follows the contours laid out by Keir Martin (2010, 8) who draws on Epstein (1964) to show a long pedigree of grassroots critiques. Martin detects a shift from the "big men" of the past to the "big shots" of the present that reflects growing perceptions of incommensurability between contemporary elites, grassroots, and their memories of past leaders. While Thomas may identify with Somare as a Sepik, he is conscious of the enormous social and financial gap that separates Somare "looking after himself and his properties" in Port Moresby from the daily struggle in Madang squatter settlements or East Sepik villages. Somare seems aware of such criticisms, defending his government as having distributed more money than ever before to the provinces and districts.

Imagining himself as an MP, Thomas visualizes two contradictory roles. One represents the ideal listening politician who is connected to the people. Like Epstein's village entrepreneur ToDungan, Thomas as the listening MP has "little differentiation in the everyday standard of living" (Epstein 1964, 65–66; quoted in K. Martin 2010, 8) from grassroots constituents. However, Thomas can also imagine himself as the type of politician who "go(es) for political power" and so dismisses requests from clients and blames them for corruption. These issues of patronage and clientelism are revisited in chapter 8.

The moral complaint about selfishness and faithlessness of elite politicians serves as a riposte to accusations of a grassroots cargo cult mentality. These are often voiced by politicians seeking to disown the claims of supporters and constituents but have a broader currency and appear in both popular and serious discussions of politics in PNG (e.g., Kaima 2004; Gibbs 2005a). Thomas mimics these characterizations with his quip, "It's voters who corrupt politicians!" Inequality and its justifications are highly visible in contemporary PNG and are the cause of much resentment.

Moral Equivalence

The achievement of the classic anthropological studies of cargo cults has been to explain the underlying moral and political logics of idiosyncratic and often disturbing phenomena that would otherwise be dismissed as curiosities, superstition, sedition, or madness. Anthropologists have found racial humiliation and inequality at the heart of cargo cults, rather than uncontrollable greed and desire (P. Lawrence 1964; Burridge 1995; Errington 1974; Lattas 1998). Whereas racial humiliation during the colonial period was direct and personalized (Stevenson 1984), contemporary humiliations (Gewertz and Errington 1999) are more abstracted, taking an economic turn or turned inwards in an auto-orientalist Christian moral critique (Robbins 2004a).

Burridge (1995) established that cargo cults had an ethical core and were focused on the problem of "moral equivalence" with white people. Moral equivalence in Burridge's sense is the ideal state of harmonious and respectful relationships between persons and achieved through balanced exchange. However, the racial hierarchy of colonialism and the depersonalized and unequal relations of capitalism have made moral equivalence with whites impossible. Burridge particularly saw cargo cults as an attempt to transcend and resolve the failure of indigenous morality to encompass European rejections of Tangu attempts at establishing proper reciprocal relations between black and white. The idea can also be applied to other forms of humiliation and injustice. For instance, Lattas's (2010) study of cargo cults in New Britain argues that elite Melanesians are now seen by many to perpetuate injustices of the colonial period by occupying the same privileged positions and perpetuating the same social relations, institutions and forms of knowledge that whites once had.

The serious questions of moral equivalence raised by Burridge also emerge in relation to fast money schemes. Certainly, in investigating fast money schemes, the interest is less in the money itself than in the implications of the desire for amounts of money large enough to transform the lives of investors. As Burridge has argued (1995, 263), these transformations can also include moral transformations and redemption. As later chapters of this book will reveal, U-Vistract cultivated a moral vision among its middle-class investors that encouraged them to imagine their fortunes as wealth that could be put into the service of the stalled project of national development. Many found this a compelling vision, not least because it promised to resolve the experience of social inequality that Papua New Guineans find particularly troubling.

Colonial and Postcolonial Triangles

Burridge saw cargo cults as emerging from the "triangle" of traditional village life as it interacted with the intimate intrusions of colonial administration and Christian missions. Otto (1992, 264) succinctly summarises the triangle as *kastom* (tradition), *lotu* (church), and *gavman* (government). However, Burridge expressly excluded "traders, planters and recruiters" (representatives of commerce and the market) from the triangle because he saw them as having minimal influence on cargo expectations (Burridge 1995, 141). This omission is curious given the material expectations of cargo cults but perhaps reflects the colonial economy where mission and administration were seen as the source of resources.

Barker (2007b) takes up the ideological role of the triangle among the Maisin in the postcolonial 1980s.[10] Barker argues that the triangle was an important source of identity and authority that could be used in mediating moral debates. Barker thus provides the grounds for understanding why the world of trade and commerce did not appear in Burridge's triangle. The Maisin found themselves peripheral to the cash economy, an exclusion that was a source of shame and self-blame among them.[11] For the Maisin, the commerce was not a moral domain that could uphold "amity": the proper balance of reciprocities.

Barker goes on to note the increasing hold of individualistic ideologies that characterise PNG since independence. These indicate the increasing penetration of global markets into PNG and mark the weakening of government influence across the country. If government and mission were the source of resources in the colonial triangle, now it is the market or the private sector that takes this perceived role, reflecting shifts in PNG's political and moral economy (Barker 2007b, 91). The collectivist values that underpinned the old triangle and its underlying "moral orthodoxy" are being replaced by new choices and identities that foster individualism and disturb the moral ordering of society, particularly as government becomes a site of corruption and distrust.[12] I have argued that this triangle also has a racial dimension as the growing Chinese presence in PNG disturbs aspects of an older moral economy (Cox 2015).

The global scale of contemporary millennial capitalism was a driver of fast money schemes and a form of capitalism distinct from the colonial economy. U-Vistract may be seen as emerging from a new triangle of contemporary post-colonial disillusionment with government, indigenous-led (but internationally connected) Christianity, and the ideology of the global market. Where the old triangle was disengaged from the market as an amoral sphere or, worse, a threat to the moral order, U-Vistract's neo-Pentecostal prosperity teachings valorized the market and so rendered its inequalities morally feasible and remediable through entrepreneurship and Christian patronage.

This book develops the argument that U-Vistract was particularly success-ful in presenting its dreams of global financial wealth within a Christian moral framework. By harnessing these images of global finance, global, and local Christianity and the national vision of egalitarian development, U-Vistract appealed to hundreds of thousands of investors across the nation. While some cargo cults spread regionally, most did not extend far beyond their villages of origin. This was because the highly localized indigenous cosmologies that con-stituted their visions of reality had a limited range of portability that constrained translation into a national or global scale.

Fast money scams offered investors the opportunity to profit from global finance: a world that even village investors had an awareness of, even if they had no better access to the global economy than a Ponzi scam. This was not simply a modern framework superseding a traditional mindset of persistent primordial (even essentially Melanesian, *pace* Lindstrom and Douglas) desires. While U-Vistract envisaged the transformation of individual financial circum-stances and the architecture of global finance, the mechanisms through which this would occur had none of the mythical structures or role of the ancestors that emerge from the traditional cosmologies of many cargo cults (cf. Lattas 2007, 150). U-Vistract's money came from "investments" generated in the inter-national world of finance with its centers in London, New York and Singapore. As Ho (2009), Miyazaki (2006), Zaloom (2006), and others have argued, global finance has its own cosmology and should not be assumed to be "rational," although rationality is indeed part of the mythology of modern economics. Indeed, U-Vistract made itself out to be a rational (although not secular) reform of the global financial system. The scale and portability of global cosmologies of finance are markedly different from the localized cosmologies of Melanesian cargo cults.

Notes

1. Otto (2009, 89) notes that millenarian movements elsewhere in the world are not described as cargo cults.

2. Verdery (1995, 651–652) mentions a cargo parallel for the Romanian pyramid scheme Caritas but notes that it is "decidedly modern" and "lacking the traditional elements of dead ancestors laden with goods triumphantly returning for the world's end."

3. Bosco, Liu, and West (2009, 51ff.) have similar reservations about attributing the rise of a Chinese underground lottery to postcommunist transition because of China's long established monetized economy and evidence that the scheme spread from capitalist Taiwan into China. They argue that the lottery is based on a calculative rationality comparable to capitalist investment practices.

4. Tabani (2013) notes the range of meanings that "cult" has accumulated. Here I mean cultic in the sense of being separated from the world and under the control of group leaders.

5. Opperman (2011, 176) notes that the Hahalis Welfare Society's "baby garden" allowed men and women to engage in casual sex without regard to customary taboos. This was apparently a means of mitigating jealousy.

6. Gesch (2007) and Gibbs (2006) both provide thoughtful examples of this identification. Nachman (1984, 546) sees "cargo cults, chain letters, and other entrepreneurial schemes" as having a "special appeal to islanders eager to obtain immediate results."

7. "The government wants villagers to be 'self-sufficient'; the villagers want government financial aid and management." Pomponio and Lancy (1986, 43).

8. Keir Martin (2007, 296) reports a similar case of resentment after Sir John Kaputin dismissed Matupit requests for assistance in rebuilding, rebuking the villagers for expecting to be "spoon-fed."

9. "Poverty, which is defined as a lack of access to basic services and infrastructure, as well as access to income and income-earning opportunities, was assessed by the World Bank (2007), which estimated that some 53 percent [sic] of the population now live below the international poverty line. This means that people are earning an income of less than US$ 1 per day (using 1993 Purchasing Power Parity). In 1996, some 25 percent of our people lived below the poverty line, but in 2006 this rose to 37 percent. Progress in achieving the Millennium Development Goals (MDGs) has also been challenging. PNG has either not made progress or has lagged behind on seven of the eight MDGs." (Independent State of PNG 2010, 17).

10. Barker (2007b, 76) lists many ethnographic examples of the ideological acceptance of the "triangle" among Melanesians.

11. Hirsch (1990, 1994, 2007) offers a counterexample of Fuguye whose perceptions of economic marginalization place questions of the market at the center of the challenges they face in maintaining their status in their own eyes and, increasingly, in the eyes of neighboring and metropolitan others.

12. Schram (2010) provides alternative examples of moral economies of money that recreate Christian persons as individuals within community.

5 Plausibility, Experimentation, and Deception

Calculations amidst Doubts or the Madness of Crowds?

Narratives of Ponzi schemes are usually stories of mass greed and gullibility: collective madnesses that remove the rationality of the actors involved. As discussed in the previous chapter, in Melanesia these narratives are often framed in terms of "cargo cult." This chapter contests that framing in two ways. First, by explaining how plausible the fast money schemes were in the way they marshalled paperwork and financial babble to present themselves as expert systems.

Second, the latter part of the chapter reveals some of the reasoning of various skeptical and experimental investors, showing them to be people who demonstrate some of the contemporary disciplines of the financial self, such as calculation, even as those calculations extend into assessments of how best to maintain amity with relatives.

There is a strong precedent for exploring degrees of belief in anthropology, as the quotations above indicate (also Engelke and Tomlinson 2006). Stent's recognition of skeptical participants in the Peli Association shows some of the sensitivity possible in detailed treatments of cargo cults. Stent documents degrees of belief, experimentation, rational persuasion, and reevaluation. He attributes this skepticism to the failure of an Australian pyramid scheme in the area, Australian Bonanza,[1] a year or two before the Peli Association arrived (Stent 1977, 196; cf. Nachman 1984). This is an exception to popular portrayals of participants in cargo cults, or Ponzi schemes, as lazy, greedy and gullible, even "Steeped in traditional magic and innocent of modern economies," as a diplomatic cable put it (United States Embassy 2006).

Techniques of Deception

U-Vistract was and is a fraud, albeit a very elaborate one. Placed within Bailey's (1991) typology of lies, U-Vistract is an intentional deception of others for the purpose of profit-making. Such fraud is malicious, not polite or social lying (e.g., Blum 2005), even if Noah Musingku has become self-convinced after years of promoting the scam. For any deception to succeed, it must appear to be very like what its victims imagine to be the real or true way of doing things. Scams operate in the space between how people think the world works and how they think the world *should* work. Clever confidence tricksters can pitch scams to what they know of the victims' visions of "the desirable and the feasible" and not simply to their emotions (contra Nachman 1984). Part of this is a matter of external presentation: dressing smartly, as if one has money or knows business; providing forms that look official or that collect the kind of information that legitimate financial institutions typically collect from customers; or setting up offices with computers. Deploying the language of banking and finance is also crucial to these performances of deceptive mimesis. I now consider some of the techniques used in creating a virtual reality or economy of appearances that was convincing and engaging for U-Vistract's many investors.

Paperwork, Forms, Appearances, and Disciplines

Ponzi schemes may appear as simply irrational exuberance, but there is always some reasoning involved as individuals decide whether or not to join, how much to invest or withdraw, or whether to leave the scheme altogether. For most Papua New Guinean fast money scheme investors, the compelling proof was seeing others being paid large sums of money. This showed that the scheme worked. However, like Madoff's American victims, sometimes they were simply convinced by the sincerity with which they were promised high returns by promoters whom they knew personally. This is the art of deception in any Ponzi scheme: appearing to be able to deliver what investors know is too good to be true.

U-Vistract and other fast money schemes projected an appearance of legitimacy in their mimicry of banking institutions and practices. Setting up offices with computers and filing cabinets gave the impression of open and legal business activities. Investors were asked to complete forms and were given balance statements that showed their investments ever growing. Rather than being innocent of modern economies, their very embeddedness in the modern economy placed middle-class Papua New Guineans in the same relations of trust that allowed Madoff to lure and defraud highly "financially literate" individuals and institutions in the United States.

Signing On

While external appearances can be convincing, particularly within the complex interpretative narrative provided by U-Vistract, paperwork has a particular role in establishing credibility (Riles 2006a). Gewertz and Errington (1991, 235 n1; 1998) note the authority of written and especially printed documents among Chambri, referring specifically to a fascination with get-rich schemes. For Chambri, written documents embody a permanency of knowledge that overcomes problems of forgetting oral testimony. The durability of the written word substantiates competing claims, not least on matters of custom and land tenure. As Fife (1995) argues, literacy is central to developing the "look of rationality," the habitus of being a proper modern subject:

> Literacy is of course one of the keys to the development of a bureaucratized world where humans and nature can be divided and subdivided through the rationalized categorizations of scientistic language (Giddens 1990, 37). It seems there is a direct connection between the older educational goals of missionary schooling for literate salvation in the Bible and what I regard as the new morality of salvation through the look of rationality. By that I mean the development of a moral system in which it is considered good to appear to be following the rules of reasonable explanation, in which the world may be compartmentalized into measurable units, and bad to resist those rules. Furthermore, it is important to note that it is this look of rationality that justifies the division or attempted division of the world into bureaucratic units. (Fife 1995)

Nicely printed forms resembling bank forms and requesting the same kinds of information as banks do (albeit with the addition of Christian mottoes and Bible verses) may be simply a matter of appearance. Yet the act of filling in such forms also entails a performative induction of the investor into the world of the scam. This is not the magical faith in the efficacious power of written characters as agents in themselves that Kulick and Stroud (1990) describe among Sepik villagers who completed lottery tickets and mail order catalogs expecting that this would, if done correctly, deliver them the desired winnings or goods without payment.

Rather, in the trajectory of literacy outlined by Morris (2001), shifting from magical to representational and then mathematical (or bureaucratic) understandings of writing, filling in U-Vistract application forms lies firmly in the bureaucratic context. U-Vistract investors saw themselves entering into a commercial relationship with a financial institution, albeit one later exposed as fraudulent. The "look of rationality" (Fife 1995; McKeown 2006) is of familiar but frustrating bureaucratic processes, not a distant and dimly understood magical power nor the deployment of traditional ideas of the supernatural to manipulate the modern economy. Investors may not have understood how the scam claimed to make its money. However, they completed forms believing that they were dealing with a rational commercial institution, not in some magical hope.

Requests for personal details simply appear to investors as the kind of information routinely required by financial institutions. Being presented with documents often elicits the response of completion rather than serious consideration of content (Brenneis 2006; Riles 2008). Such an aesthetics of completion also entails the abeyance of participants' agency as they acquiesce to the official authority of the scam (cf. Miyazaki 2000).

Completing bureaucratic requirements, such as the mimicry of legal contracts, enacted the appropriate disposition expected of investors entering into relationships with expert systems. This then matched the professional demeanors of the promoters and their staff. The money scheme thus assumed not only the external appearance of a bank but also the institutional demeanor in relation to its clients reflected in formalized processes for dealing with them, including even complaints.

These practices establish a new relationship between the scam and its members, giving it enormous authority. As Kich (2005) notes of Nigerian email scams, successful fraud often inverts authentication: instead of the scam proving itself to would-be investors, investors must now vouchsafe their credentials to the scam. This psychological shift places the scam in a position of relative legitimacy. This authority was based on its status as a business and, of course, its ability to generate money, but, as we have already noted in the case of U-Vistract, there was also a moralistic dimension. U-Vistract's bureaucratic verification demanded letters of reference from pastors or other religious authorities. U-Vistract was a Christian scheme and expected high moral standards from its investors. In Felix's case (see below), this even extended into the suggestion of discipline and surveillance.

This is not simply a matter of re-creating the external appearance of trustworthiness. In the interaction between investors and the abstract system of finance that U-Vistract was mimicking, Musingku and his employees successfully re-created the face-to-face engagements expected of what Giddens would call an "access point." According to Giddens (1990, 85), access points combine trust in abstract systems with face-to-face interactions with those who run them. They are sites where individuals are continually reassured of the trustworthiness of the abstract system, not only by the physical environment but also in the routine demeanor of staff, who reproduce the expert nature of the system. The centrality of trust and reassurance in modern abstract systems provides a context in which to understand how convincing fraudulent mimicry can be.

Such interactions with abstract systems reflect not only the dependence of individuals on expert knowledge in calculating financial risks and benefits but also that the very world of risks and benefits is created by expert systems themselves in ways that encompass modern life Giddens (1990, 84). For example, the profusion of financial products and services means that there is much greater familiarity with the jargon of finance in PNG and elsewhere. Investors show a relative lack of interest in the mechanics of how U-Vistract got its money (cf. Verdery 1995) or what happened to their investments. A few lines about the global economy are sufficient to persuade, perhaps like many investors in much wealthier and notionally more "financially literate" countries. An Australian Securities and Investment Commission (ASIC) legal investigator described the clients of an Australian swindler whose 1990s scam was based on futures trading: "Many people assume the futures market is too complex to ever fully understand. They are satisfied with a quick patter about how it operates and, then to put their trust completely in their broker or advisor" (Brown 1998, 189). Even if the content and implications are not fully understood, jargon creates a new realm of expertise that draws people into imaginings of financial investment and its promised benefits for those who participate in it. As investment practices have become more abstracted (LiPuma and Lee 2004), understanding of financial markets has retracted into the realm of specialist expertise such that laypeople do not feel confident in assessing financial claims themselves and rely on expert advice, even if this is simply quick patter (cf. Giddens 1990, 41). Indeed, Giddens regards this disorientation and acquiescence as a central feature of the experience of modernity: "being caught up in a universe of events we do not fully understand, and which seems in large part beyond our control" (1990, 2–3).

For many U-Vistract investors, Musingku was an expert who had worked out how the world of finance operates. He was also an intimate, available to explain the workings of an expert system to his compatriots, thus providing an access point (Giddens 1990, 83) to the world of finance. Many Bougainvilleans were extremely proud to claim PNG's first international financier as one of their own (Regan 2009).

U-Vistract succeeded not only by promoting Musingku's investment genius and ability to make money but also by adopting the demeanor of an access point within an expert system. This could include a bureaucratic twist, not simply promises of more money to investors. Musingku made subtle performances of this expertise, for example, in telling investors that they could not be paid all at once because the money had to be brought in from overseas and "every country has limits and restrictions as to how much monies may be sent out per day" (Musingku 1999).

U-Vistract could even mimic processes of managerial reform. Musingku (1999) wrote to investors about the new passbooks he was introducing that would allow the scheme to work "more professionally." Investors were told their passbooks would allow them to "go into your branch anytime during business hours and withdraw your monies." Complaints from Madang investors seem to have resulted in a sham restructuring of the Madang branch. The reporting of this restructure echoed the language of management and sounded like a legitimate institution responding to serious complaints by reviewing processes and systems. The scam even warned against investing through the wrong people, implying a legitimacy that the unscrupulous might seek to exploit.

In keeping with the scam's expert demeanor, investors also presented themselves as acting in ways consistent with their ideas of modern rationality. The material elements of the scheme: paperwork and offices and the spectacle of seeing others being paid in cash became the foundation on which new investors could demonstrate their cultivation of proper financial conduct as rational, calculating, disciplined persons.

Ambrose recently retired from his work as a motor mechanic. He is well traveled within PNG and has worked in Rabaul, Lae, Wewak, and Port Moresby. He hails from Bogia village, north of Madang, and had been living in Madang for more than ten years when I interviewed him in 2009. Here he demonstrates his rational credentials, explaining his version of due diligence in relation to U-Vistract:

> I'm not interested in any gambling ways but I as a person always find out how things start and how they work. I don't go in blindly without thinking twice, checking things out and finding out how will I benefit. I have checked it out thoroughly. I know the whole history of U-Vistract so that is why I have confidence. I have confidence because I have confirmed it with the bankers. The Wewak manager knows. He has seen that money is already there. So he tells people to fix up their ID cards.

For Ambrose, checking the credentials of the scheme involved several points of triangulation. It is important for him to know the "whole story of U-Vistract" (even though this seems to be from the perspective of the scheme's promoters). He also positions himself not as a gambler looking for windfall gains but as a shrewd investor investigating how the scheme works and carefully calculating the benefits. He relies on banking authorities, again putting his trust in abstract systems run by experts and requiring particular technologies of verification and recognition. The proper response from investors is to be patient with the process and, in the meantime, to make sure that their own part in the bureaucratic system is in order: they are to fix up their member ID cards.

Plastic or paper ID cards were issued by several fast money schemes in mimicry of formal banking processes and technologies.

Felix, the Sepik hospital worker mentioned in chapter 2, recounts how U-Vistract's Madang agent conjured a vision of technological requirements, reconfirmed issuing plastic cards and copies of the *Papala Chronicles*:

> So she told us we had to buy a broad machine [broadband internet] for Tonu. There's local building and a broad machine and a phone. I heard then I thought, "That's a true thing." My wife and me, they gave us a yellow card from the Royal Bank of Meekamui. That one, my wife has it with the PIN number, card number, everything. They sent our name to Tonu and they print the card in Tonu and bring it back after six months. Maybe about 300 of us got the card. We had to pay K25 stamp duty for the card to fill the form. There was a big meeting down at Tusbab at the same time, about 2005. Susie, she delivered all this news [shows *Papala Chronicles*] so we read it and we believe it. It's appealing! Ah!

Stories of improved technologies of communication featured in the *Papala Chronicles* reconfirmed the narratives provided by the scam's agents and circulated at local meetings. Current events such as elections or natural disasters were woven into the stories of why payments were delayed. This gave the scheme currency and allowed the weekly or monthly "updates" to deliver news of progress that not only kept faith with the scheme but may even have had a genuinely informative element. Delays in payment are not themselves a sufficient trigger for disillusionment as they are nonevents: nothing changes for investors when they continue not to be paid. Rather, the updates give the impression of links to external events that act on the investor's position and so give credence to the scam's claims. Robbins (1998) describes Urapmin practices of interpreting "world news." Radio or newspaper stories of current affairs are woven into apocalyptic narratives of the end times, generating momentum for Urapmin Christians by relocating their practices in a rapidly moving sequence of world events. U-Vistract's updates attempt to achieve something similar, keeping investors' hopes of being paid alive by resituating them in a world of events outside their control and so generating "forward momentum" (Miyazaki 2004).

Consumer Discipline

Participation in U-Vistract required investors to demonstrate their worthiness and used dreams of abundance to cement their dependency on the scheme. Announcements in the Papala Chronicles (2005a) showed Bougainvillean businessmen and other participants receiving ID Cards, a process then replicated in other places, such as Madang. Felix describes his experience:

> We have that card and receipts. They were giving out K25 receipts, K100 receipts, K20, K10. We started with K100 and our total contribution was up to K775. When I got up to that total amount, I found there's nothing coming back. There's no bank statement, nothing. They tell us, "K100,000, that's all you will get that money and you will reinvest again through U-Vistract and you will get K500 a day through your account." Once they gave us this card and told us this: "The card will turn into a banking system. You must use the K500 every day and then another K500 will come in the next day." We were very proud.
>
> The K500, that's for your daily living for your family in the house, *kaikai* (food), *tinpis* (tinned fish), rice. If you want to buy a big thing, car, house, you have to go to the company selling it, get the quotation and we'll get the payment for you. They will process a check through Tonu. They didn't tell us why. K500 was for daily living, pocket money. You could put up to K10,000 request for travel to Wewak or somewhere.

For Felix, the scheme promised money but required imaginary compliance with their regime of domestic discipline so that the money would not be wasted. His everyday desires were relatively humble, but large purchases had to be approved in advance. The K500 per day never eventuated, but Felix and his wife nevertheless felt proud to be associated with the scheme. Rather than resenting the paternalism, Felix was proud to be included in an opportunity to learn the proper discipline of consuming abundance wisely. This willingness to accept external controls on his (anticipated) personal consumption perhaps reflects his low pay as a hospital orderly and the impact of discourses of financial literacy spread through churches and microfinance programs. Later in this book, I show how these financial disciplines overlap with Christian ideas of self-control and the tithing practices expected of Pentecostals and associated with prosperity theology.

Dubious Investors: Skepticism and Reasoning

Many early investors gave up on the scheme very quickly. Nevertheless, there are also many like Ambrose who are still confident of receiving their money in abundance soon. Felix held out hope for ten years after the scheme had been declared bankrupt, only admitting he had been scammed in 2009. Individual U-Vistract investors provide diverse vantage points from which to observe and analyze the social meanings of the fast money phenomenon. Not all of them were true believers or gullible dupes. Some were drawn in reluctantly to appease their kinsfolk and retain a skeptical approach to the scheme. Others had their skepticism worn down by observing the success of their peers and succumbing to fears of falling behind materially. Some were saved from losing their money because the scheme collapsed while they were in the process of saving a large sum worth investing. Others got in early, made money, and kept reinvesting it until the scheme was exposed as a fraud and their money was lost. Still others approached U-Vistract as a gamble, knowing it to be highly risky and so taking their losses with resignation. Some still hold out a defiant hope that their riches will be realized when U-Vistract is eventually vindicated.

The skeptical investors profiled below illustrate the individual texture of involvement with money schemes. Their belief is often "soft" and confused, not fanatical (Bashkow 2000a). There are many contradictions and many lapses of meaning (Tomlinson and Engelke 2006). No one type of investor emerges as typical. No one ethnic or social group can be said to be more susceptible, although there were clearly communities where participation was higher: Bougainvilleans and Pentecostal Christians formed the core "inside track" from which U-Vistract spread across the country, the latter aided by theological teachings on prosperity.

Martin, Geraldine, and Alphonse are three very ambivalent investors. Their stories are followed by Victor's, who had been preparing to join U-Vistract but then thought better of it. In the following chapters the views of more committed believers in U-Vistract are examined in some detail. Here, however, the point is to foreground subsequent analysis of U-Vistract in the recognition that involvement in a fast money scheme did not necessarily imply high levels of belief or commitment.[2] Many were simply content to try a scheme out, without fully accepting the rationale behind the scheme. The motivations and expectations of these investors and almost-investors break up the madness of crowds of the fast money scheme phenomenon into the constituent individuals and their various decision-making processes. While they are presented as individual stories, they also function as types of ambivalent investors who diverge from and rebut key assumptions that underpin popular interpretations of fast money schemes as being the result of laziness, greed, or gullibility. As this chapter reveals, each in their own way demonstrate practices of calculation in relation to money that suggests a widespread dispersion of modern disciplines of personal financial management among PNG's working class. Indeed, each of the investors profiled in this chapter exhibits the cultivation of a "financial self" (Zaloom 2006), an autonomous calculating person capable of making rational choices about the productive use of money.

Geraldine provides an example of peer pressure among Waigani elites. Seeing her husband's peers and superiors making "so much money" made her suspend her initial disbelief, even as a financially literate accountant. Alphonse is another skeptic who defies the stereotype of credulous investors. His involvement was a gamble in what he knew to be a scam, or at least a dubious and risky way of making money. He received an initial payment and then lost it but contrasted his gambler's ability to calculate risks with others who were really taken in by fast money schemes and who lost large amounts of money they could not afford to lose.

Victor had serious plans to invest but withdrew before committing. He learned from his friend's lost investment that U-Vistract had collapsed. Victor is a devout Christian disgusted at the hypocrisy of Christians who gamble their money away in these schemes.

Martin provides an interesting example of a skeptic who nevertheless invested at the behest of relatives. However, the influence of kin did not compel acceptance of the terms of this engagement. Martin invested to detach himself from pressures to invest. An old friend in Honiara told me a similar story of how he joined the Family Charity Fund, acquiescing to an insistent relative. Where popular understandings of fast money schemes assume that such pressures typify the gullible rural poor, who simply accept what they are told by urban educated relatives, Martin provides an example of the pressure working back from the rural kin to the educated townsman.

I include Lindsay as a true skeptic, opposed to fast money schemes from the beginning and attributing their appeal to rural poverty manifesting as a desperate willingness to try anything that might produce some money: Stent's *traiim tasol* (above). Francis had a similar perspective to Alphonse's, investing his money to see whether the scheme was true. A successful journalist, Francis's self-declared *traiim tasol* was not desperation but a self-conscious opportunism that again illustrates degrees of belief and management of risk: Francis was able to use his friendships with the Bougainvillean political elite to recover his money.

All of these investors are working-class urban salary earners with some postsecondary education. They position themselves in relation to the "grass-roots" with some condescension. While the purpose of presenting their stories here is to unsettle assumptions about greed and gullibility, nevertheless they themselves repeat this dominant interpretation of the fast money narrative in ways that reflect their class position and its everyday disparagement of the rural poor as "backward" and credulous. As indicated in the previous chapter, this is a discourse with a long colonial lineage that continues into postcolonial PNG, where accusations of a cargo cult mentality are routinely used to maintain class boundaries and privileges.

Geraldine—Investments Are Not 100 Percent Safe

Geraldine, an accountant, and her husband were United Church members in Port Moresby during the fast money peak in 1999. They were close to some "very, very influential people," including the Clerk of Parliament, who was known to promote Money Rain. He is widely reported to have invested K300,000 of parliamentary funds. As she puts it, "The high class, the very high class MPs, senior public servants were in Money Rain. U-Vistract—more people were in that." For a full year, Geraldine and her husband watched with bemusement and skepticism as members of their social and professional circle joined in fast money schemes. As time wore on, it became more and more difficult to resist the influence of these "high-level" people, particularly when they were receiving very high returns from their investments. The schemes seemed to work.[3]

Like many others, Geraldine tested out Money Rain with a relatively small amount of money. She began with K3,000, which was successful, and then put in a further K10,000 from a pool of long-term savings of K50,000. In a context where their close associates were depositing hundreds of thousands of Kina, Geraldine's contribution was relatively conservative.

Geraldine mentions the fear of being left out as others made large amounts of money. This is similar to Martin's cousin who conjured the shibboleth of separation as an inducement to join the fund. However, the threat posed by the influx of fast money is a threat to relationships and reputation within a particular social class in Port Moresby. These connections rely on workplace ties and political networks, not kinship links. The need for money also goes well beyond the humble expenditures of Martin's country cousins. Socializing at official functions implies a certain competitive lifestyle that Geraldine and her husband risked exclusion from as the fast money schemes delivered huge amounts of money to members of their social circle. Geraldine's experience recalls the atmosphere of exclusivity and high society cultivated by Bernard Madoff among wealthy Americans (Arvedlund 2009; Tennant 2011).

> When you sit together, people ask, "Where have you invested?" Nobody was spending, you want to put it back and get more! So I don't think people benefited by buying things like cars. It was so attractive that when you get it you put it back and get more. It was that attraction that you'd be rich overnight.
>
> This may be a rumour but a reliable very close source told me that Somare put in K500,000 and lost! Maybe they got some in the first place and then they lost. The Speaker was putting in and getting it back. He made my husband weak. You have a boss who's less educated but you can see he's getting so much. My husband he's not very money minded but you get into this frame of mind. Put it in, you'll get it. You get caught up.
>
> The Clerk of Parliament—his close cousin was working as an advisor with my husband. There was a connection, that kind of relationship. During functions, you're all together so it becomes an attraction and something you can do. Luckily our overdraft was paid but we lost so much.
>
> When I first heard about it, I didn't believe for a full year. But I saw someone so close to me, so I should have put less. It took a while, a whole year, to break down our resistance because seeing people get it.... Yes, we knew it was a pyramid. That's why we refused to join. We used to draw the pyramid diagram to show them. I understood but I joined because there was too much influence. I rejected that [the pyramid scheme] completely but he came in and I completely refused for a year. I could sense that it's not real but because of too much influence and all these people, our leader. That makes you feel like you're left out.

Geraldine's story provides an insider's view of patronage networks among the political elite. As clients of powerful politicians and public servants, Geraldine and her husband succumbed to the pressure to invest in Money Rain. Geraldine and her husband were being offered membership of the "inside track" (Verdery 1995). What consequences might ensue if they refused? Behind Geraldine's decision to invest lies coercion from very powerful people whose favor has to be sought and reconfirmed continually. These patronage networks are much more fragile than kinship links, which can become strained but are severed only in extreme circumstances.

This is a very different context from Martin's social relationships where the attempts at manipulation from the bottom of the social scale up are not entirely successful. Martin views his cousin's beliefs in a somewhat patronizing way and is never tempted to adopt them. Geraldine, on the other hand, begins with a skeptical mindset but, under the influence of powerful people, eventually suspends her disbelief and starts to see their returns, receipts, and other documents as real. She and her husband go through a process of re-convincing themselves that Money

Rain might well be genuine and so give themselves permission to join. They are never fully convinced but allow themselves just enough belief to take the chance of making a windfall gain. Later in this book, I return to Geraldine and explore how ideas of risk and investment figure in her processes of suspending disbelief.

Alphonse the Gambler–Investor

Alphonse is a forty-year-old Port Moresby public servant, the son of East Sepik migrants to Rabaul. He met his West Sepik wife while studying at the University of Papua New Guinea, and they have four children. Alphonse is highly educated and completed a master's degree at an Australian university:

> I'm a gambler, that's my entertainment. I bet on the horses. Every payday, I go down to Lamana Hotel and I spend K50 on the horses. I stay until that K50 is finished. Sometimes I go home early but, if I'm lucky, then I stay longer and sometimes I might come home with some extra money in my pocket. Maybe K200 or K300.
>
> So when these fast money schemes came along, U-Vistract, Money Rain, Windfall, I knew what to do, because I'm a gambler. I know you have to put your money in quickly and take it out again because only the first ones will be paid. At first I wasn't sure, so I started with K200. After one month, I had K400. So then I put in another K1,000, into Money Rain. One month later, I went back and they told me I had K2,800. So I took K1,000 out and kept the rest in the account as a rollover. The following month, there was, I think, K3,600, so I did the same thing: took out K1,000 and rolled over the rest. Then the next time I went, the scheme had already closed down, so I lost all that money. I was conned.
>
> But I'm a gambler, so I knew not to put in everything I had. My friends used to judge me because I'm Catholic and I'm a gambler, but they are Assemblies of God, or Pentecostal, CLC [Christian Life Centre]. They used to tell me I shouldn't gamble, but some of them, when U-Vistract came along, they lost a lot of money. Some of them more than K10,000–20,0000. Now I laugh at them, because they were condemning me for gambling and then they did this! One of them sold his house and he lost everything. Me, I lost some money but I also won some money. It's because I know about gambling.

His account may be a product of hindsight but Alphonse claimed that he understood that the fast money schemes would only pay the early investors and that everyone else would lose their money. He took his chances, had some wins and losses, but feels no responsibility for others who also took their chances but without his gambler's nous. Nor did the scheme's closure surprise him, although he was annoyed that he had let himself be conned out of the rest of his putative balance. Alphonse knew he was taking a risk in order to get high returns and did not buy into questions of how the money would be produced. He realized that only early investors would be paid and knew he was taking a risk "rolling over" his money.

Alphonse gambled for personal pleasure. Unlike the social gambling documented by Zimmer (1986) or Alexeyeff (2011), where card games mitigate income inequalities and become a field of reciprocity, his was an individualized sensibility based on voluntary participation and calculation of risks (cf. Binde 2005, 453).

Alphonse tested the scheme with a small amount (K200). When this worked, he put in a further K1,000 and took out a return of K2,000 out of a putative K3,600, making K800 profit for the high risk he took. He wanted to try his luck, but he scarcely entertained the dreams of fabulous wealth that drew his parsimonious friends into losing their money. Where people like Victor were outraged by the hypocrisy of born-again Christians investing in money schemes, Alphonse was simply bemused. His Catholic worldly wisdom and willingness to play gambling games was validated because he did not lose as much as his Pentecostal friends who took large risks and failed to ensure they first recouped their investment, thereby losing substantial assets.[4]

Alphonse's gambler's sensibilities protected him from heavy losses because he understood investment as an activity that placed one at risk of losing one's money. Neither does Alphonse expect that he can control the success or failure of the enterprise, unlike the Prosperity Gospel's leap of faith, which be rewarded by God (or the market) or the deployment of magic to ensure success (Mosko 2012, 2014). Like Zimmer's (1986, 246) Gende and the working class *pilai laki* (playing luck) slot machine gamblers documented by Pickles (2014b), Alphonse set limits to his risk-taking, typically K50 a fortnight for his gambling and higher for the fast money investment. In his fast money investments, as in his gambling, Alphonse was not deterred by the risk of losing his money, but neither was he caught up in displays of risk-taking with other men. He is perhaps typical of the working-class (Cox 2013) *pilai laki* gamblers whom Pickles sees as a counterpoint to the big men these "real gamblers" because they do not enter into displays of wealth but gamble alone and set strict limits to their betting. Alphonse identifies quite explicitly as a gambler. The basis for this is not his willingness to lose money or the hope of finding luck at a slot machine (or eventually working out its recurring patterns) but confidence in his ability to manage his losses and gains when betting on horse races. Alphonse therefore fits Reith's profile of the ideal consumer gambler:

> It is no longer the prerogative of the industry, the state, or the courts to restrict the consumption of games of chance; this is now up to the individual, who becomes responsible for his or her own fate at the tables. It is now the task of the sovereign consumer to temper his or her enjoyment of the thrills of gambling with a prudent awareness of the risks involved, to exercise self-control, to manage losses and, in extreme cases, even to exclude himself or herself from gambling venues altogether—because no one else will. (Reith 2007, 41)

Reith's sovereign consumer gambler is characterized by self-control and the capacity to calculate risks. This bears little resemblance to the competitive gambling among aristocrats she has documented elsewhere (Reith 1999) or, in the contemporary PNG context, Pickles' (2014b) description of masculine contests among the Goroka "big men," gamblers whose willingness to lose large amounts of money (and quickly) qualified them as "real gamblers." Perhaps Victor's desire to save a substantial amount to invest in U-Vistract reflects a similar desire to "make it big." For the world of finance and investment, Zaloom (2006) demonstrated a similar masculine competitiveness among financial traders in Chicago who also make ostentatious bids at high rates as a means of credentialing themselves as (male) individuals who can hold their nerve in the face of the risk of heavy losses.[5]

As is expected in Reith's model of the sovereign consumer gambler, Alphonse exercised his personal discretion and moderated his losses in accordance with his understanding of the risks involved. Indeed he expected to succeed at the investment "game" and make a little money.

If Alphonse used his gambler's wits to manage the high risks of investing in a fast money scheme, the mode of gambling that he was accustomed to is also significant. His bets on Australian horse races, while they involved some male sociality in drinking at the hotel (cf. Presterudstuen 2014), were not a game played with peers or face-to-face adversaries, as is the case with card games. One bets against the bookmaker or the company providing bookmaking services, not against one's fellows (Binde 2005, 452). This type of gambling is more heavily commodified in the sense that it involves an individual consuming a generic gambling product offered by a large corporation. In this sense, the betting agency operates as an impersonal abstract system (Giddens 1990), where the trust that Alphonse has in the fairness of the game is based on a broader trust in the workings of such systems as part of a larger modern urban society. While he might have relationships with some individuals involved in the provision of gambling services through those systems, these relationships do not constitute the grounds of his confidence in the betting system (also Pickles 2014b).

U-Vistract and other associated fast money schemes presented themselves as banks or financial institutions and mimicked the official paperwork, language, and demeanor of such systems, while also being accessible to ordinary people and so forming part of a popular financescape that crossed scales in a manner that was enticing (Appadurai 1996; cf. Bainton 2011; Krige 2011). For many, this mimicry was sufficiently convincing that they allowed themselves permission to invest thousands of Kina. However, Alphonse as a gambler–investor retained a skepticism about such systems, perhaps because he knew from his own experience that the abstract systems of gambling promise winnings but more often deliver losses. His trust was a calculating trust based on his individual discernment, not the surrender of personal agency to abstract systems that represented institutional forms of Providence or markets (Zaloom 2006). Although Alphonse does not use the language of possessive individualism, his gambler's discernment can be seen as a demonstration of his proprietorship of the self.

"I Thought about It"

Several people interviewed planned to invest in U-Vistract or other money schemes but did not end up committing their money. In two separate cases, Victor and Anna were preparing to invest but wanted to save a particular sum of money for this purpose. Typically, prospective investors wanted to contribute a round figure (such as K1,000) as a substantial investment. These would-be investors were influenced by the stories of those around them getting paid and were perhaps a little skeptical to begin with. Their dreams of wealth, travel, housing, and so forth differ little from other more enthusiastic investors and the level of trust they have in those seeking to recruit them is also similar. For Anna, the influence of a Bougainvillean in-law (her sister's husband) was very strong.

Curiously, their very desire for substantial returns saved them from losing their money. Waiting to save a deposit before investing meant that each of them missed the opportunity to join before U-Vistract stopped making payments. Once it became clear that U-Vistract had collapsed, these cautious investors ignored requests to invest more money and withdrew entirely from the influence of the scheme, even as relatives and close friends continued to hope that the scheme would eventually pay them.

In Victor's case a close friend from university, Christian, had invested a substantial amount of money in the scheme, hoping to use the returns to pay for his wedding. With the collapse of the scheme's payments, Victor was called on to help fund a scaled-down wedding for Christian. While Victor did not lose directly from investing himself, he did lose out through his financial commitment to this relationship.

Victor—"Christians Shouldn't Invest in Get Rich Quick Schemes"

But how lucky I was that I didn't invest! It could have been me! I did consider investing but I didn't have the money. I knew it was too good to be true but all the stories of payouts.... It sounded good, so I wanted to invest big money. I didn't want K200, I wanted K1,000. I didn't raise the money in time and, as I thought about it, U-Vistract seemed more like a scam. Even when U-Vistract wasn't paying there was still a lot of hope, so people kept investing. They'd tell them excuses like, "There's such a lot of cash that it will affect our currency and so on." It was my friend not getting his money and the warning by the Bank of Papua New Guinea. I procrastinated long enough that I didn't make an investment.

But it was my belief that it was wrong: Christians shouldn't invest in get rich quick schemes. The fact is that a lot of these schemes are built on deception of some sort. Someone of Christian values should be able to sense that and see something's not right and be cautious. It's not wrong in itself—you can put your money where you like but you should have more insight.

That whole U-Vistract thing has really put Christians to the test and they've failed. It goes against all the fundamentals in the Bible—"A man who does not work shall not eat," "Thou shalt not steal." Gambling is condemned by Jesus. U-Vistract is gambling!

Victor's delay in investing was based on a desire for substantial returns, and so he needed to save K1,000 to make his investment worthwhile. He could not put the money together quickly, and the delay allowed time for his doubts to mature, even in a context of conflicting information about why U-Vistract had stopped payments. The counter story of his friend losing his wedding money provided a lens through which Victor interpreted and accepted Bank of Papua New Guinea warnings. Both he and his friend knew that investing in U-Vistract was highly risky. Therefore, once the scheme stopped paying, they quickly accepted that it had collapsed and would never be able to pay. His hesitation and his friend's loss clarified for him that investment in fast money schemes was basically another form of gambling.

Victor regarded U-Vistract as highly unethical, particularly for born-again Christians of whom he expects high moral standards. Although himself desiring more money, his very desire for a large sum gave him pause to reconsider investing. Consequently, Victor attained a clarity about the scheme that reinforced his doubts and then emerged as harsh moral judgements of Christians who participated. He was scathing of those who spread the scheme through his church and believes them to be hypocrites, yet he himself nearly invested and his good friend was a genuine Christian.

Victor's ferocity had other roots, as we shall discuss in the next chapter, but the charge of hypocrisy stems from his identification of fast money schemes with gambling. Gambling is unquestionably a vice as far as Victor's born-again coreligionists are concerned, so they should not have taken the risk of gambling with U-Vistract.

Anna—"If God Says It, It Is True."

Anna was also tempted to invest but missed the deadline as she did not have the cash at that point in time. A teacher based in a school a short distance by public mobility vehicle (PMV) out of Madang town, Anna would come in to Madang every month or so to receive her pay, do her shopping, and so forth. After being introduced to U-Vistract by her sister, she went home, thought about it and tried to save money for the scheme. However, by the time she returned to town, U-Vistract had collapsed and so her interest withered. Anna was influenced by her sister, who still remains a keen believer despite some ten years of unfulfilled promises. Initially she was also enticed by the excitement of becoming rich and, like Victor, wanted to put in a substantial amount that would achieve this aim.

> My sister would say, "Oh! People are making money left, right and centre and I'm investing too. If you're interested, you can also join." And I took a long time making up my mind. I was interested, I was fascinated by the idea of the amount of money they thought they would make from investing. So I thought it would be nice to make a lot of money and then one time have a big shot of money coming through!
>
> So, it fascinated me. I said, "Ok, I'll think about it and then I'll come back." Well, I never got another chance to come back to town sooner and I kept putting it off until the people who were involved, well, until my interest ran out. And so I didn't get to invest but I thought I would start with K500 but I didn't put that in.

Anna judged the scheme and its participants from a somewhat different position from Victor, whose focus was more on the morality of investing. Anna saw her sister's involvement as demonstrating credulity but nearly succumbed to the fascination of the scheme herself. Her sister was a devout Catholic and Anna herself had a strong Christian faith, but, in the context of money schemes, she saw religion itself as encouraging people to suspend their critical faculties: "People always believe in God, and, if God's name is used, that takes precedence over official Government warnings, official economic, credible economic warnings. If God says it, it is true. And so they disbelieve whoever says otherwise. They do not make that link between false prophecy and fast money schemes, as an example. I think people in PNG are very gullible, they believe everything that might have a spiritual connection.

Martin and the Money Tree Psychology

> The Money Tree is a psychology that people have. They come under stress or need or the economic situation they are in. When such opportunity comes, they very quickly jump and if they have money, they join in. If they don't have money, then they ask others for help.
>
> The economic condition is the main cause. They rely on one cash crop and they don't have much opportunity for other sources of income for helping them out with school fees and daily living. When such opportunity comes, they jump at it. If they don't have money, then they ask their kin.
>
> A few people have cocoa as cash crops. When vanilla came in, they cleared out cocoa. They had a big dream. For two or three years, the vanilla trade was on, but then very soon the marketing and the quality of the beans was not according to the international standard. You see that has an impact on the people. People did not have another income-earning source. They used to rely on cocoa but when vanilla came in they cut down their cocoa tress

and concentrated on planting vanilla. Vanilla stopped and that frustrated the people, so they started clearing vanilla and planting cocoa again. Within this period, people face an economic situation in my village and other areas.

When the Money Tree scheme promoter comes around, they jump on him! They keep on believing him and all he says is wait, wait, wait. They keep on postponing the payments. It continued to fail and some have stepped out. They don't have any hope any more. They realize and stop and don't want to continue.

My cousin is older than me. He's invested in various other money schemes. He has come around to our house and encouraged us to invest but I'm suspicious. My wife's relative came around and put pressure on her. She invested once. Then we started realizing there's no fruit in that.

Only recently my cousin came around urging us to put money in again. But we had bills to pay and we realized and we didn't believe. The first time, it's just a little amount, K100 that we gave. It was not just investing but showing favor to the relative. He comes and then he stays and if he hasn't achieved something and he goes away unhappy—so we invested. It's not just believing and doing it but it's a cultural value, how do you say it? Inside I was not believing but just to appease him and to give him a favor. We were not convinced but it's just our family members— if they go away without accomplishing what they want. It's like returning a favor or something like that.

My wife's cousin came in with care and concern for us. "I have invested and why not you? You'll be without money. Why not put in a small amount?" So what we had, my wife gave just to appease. We were convinced it was not true because they had already waited two years and then they came and asked us. We heard about them investing money and talking about it but they didn't receive anything. So we were not convinced. We said, "OK if you get yours, we'll get ours." But we didn't believe it. I was worried about them saying bad things about us but not black magic. I was more than 50 percent not believing in the scheme. More like 95 percent not believing. They went away happy but then they came back later and we said, "Oh, we'll be all OK." Finally they have given up.

The latest was last month. This cousin came along and asked us to give K60 but by then we have our bills. So we said no and he didn't come around on the appointed time. Because I've questioned him and he knew I was not convinced. He didn't come, so he must be discouraged. He really believes he's [Noah Musingku] not a conman. There's an atmosphere when he comes around. We are brothers. Not really wanting to make him unhappy but if we start asking questions, so he felt I wasn't convinced.[6]

Martin and his wife come from the immediate hinterland of Madang town. His village is perhaps 20 or 30 minutes from town by PMV. He has worked at the same professional job at Divine Word University for years and is much liked there. His salary is modest, but his employer provides good quality permanent housing. Martin intends to build a house in the village and retire living off the land. His relatively privileged position means that he is often called on to assist his rural kin, who come into town frequently and generally call on Martin when in need. Martin himself avoids too many visits to the village and only goes back for special events.

Martin told me his story with some exasperation. He was drawn into investing in U-Vistract not because of an active belief in the scheme but because of continuing pressure from family members. Despite his misgivings, it was more important to keep the peace than risk confrontation over something he cared little for. In the interview, he speaks mostly of U-Vistract but elides other money schemes into the experience. The Papalain scheme has also been very active around Madang (and other provinces).

Keeping with anthropological observations of ambivalent relationships with kin or *wantoks* (Bashkow 2006, 226f; Macintyre 2011; K. Martin 2010; Monsell-Davis 1993, 46; Schram 2015), it is important to Martin that his relatives part from him on good terms, particularly if they had come to solicit money. Therefore, when he contributed K100 to U-Vistract, this was to ensure that his cousin did not leave feeling unhappy or resentful. It was more important to "do a favour" than to question the request. This would shame his cousin and possibly lead to ongoing resentment and gossip, although he dismisses the possibility of any retributive sorcery.

Where many town dwellers invested their rainy day money (savings put aside for contingencies—typically K1,000–K3,000) in U-Vistract, Martin's more modest sum reflects not only his lack of interest in the scheme but also the proportionally smaller contributions of rural people. Subsistence farmers, like Martin's cousin, seem to have limited their exposure to the scheme by investing only small amounts (K10–K100).[7] Martin seems to follow their minimal commitment.

Martin is happy to assist his relatives but would rather respond generously to frank requests for genuine needs than hear long stories concocted to elicit payments. He recognizes that his relatives have little access to money and sees himself as having a duty to help, within his means. Here, asking for money to invest in U-Vistract differs little from routine requests for school fees, bride price, or funeral expenses: the most common stressors of PNG budgets and social relations.[8] Martin does not separate financial investment from the gift economy.[9]

Martin does not mention gambling, but his cousin appears to use participation in U-Vistract in a way not unlike the cardplaying of Zimmer's (1986) Gende. Zimmer argues that cardplaying constitutes a complementary field of reciprocity where questions of shame inherent in the gift economy can be resolved. Collecting money for U-Vistract offered the cousin a way of "demand sharing" without the shame of asking for money. However, Martin prefers to retain his role as patron, seeing himself as generous and responsive to his *wantoks*.

If investment in U-Vistract was a new pretext for sharing money among kin, Martin was more concerned with the implications of refusing a small amount than any factual content in the request. Martin hoped to avoid arguments by pretending to agree. He thought that joining the scheme would obviate the need for the cousin to continue reiterating his fervid beliefs in U-Vistract, including its religious justifications. Martin's lip service to his cousin recalls Nachman's (1984) tale of Balil villagers (New Ireland) who pledged money to a visiting confidence man following his persuasive speech. Far from being credulous, they made their promises with no intention of paying him anything. The pledges were a mark of regard for his oratory and to avoid confrontation.

However, the contradiction of participation without believing in the scheme soon worked its way out. Martin contributed a one-off payment as a strategy for neutralizing the request, but the cousin returned asking for another round of contributions, bringing the latest update on the promised payments. This was exactly the relationship Martin hoped to avoid, but it characterized U-Vistract's ongoing relationships with many unsuccessful investors.

Martin's experience shows a complex relational texture to affinity fraud. Economic and legal understandings of affinity fraud typically assume that shared beliefs and practices within groups allow fraud to be perpetrated using those networks (e.g., Fairfax 2001). This is true of Martin in that he joined U-Vistract only at his cousin's urging. However, he did not actually entertain belief in the scheme and participated only from a self-consciously skeptical position and for motives entirely focused on managing relatives' expectations.

Martin's wife's cousin came "with care and concern" and tried to persuade them to join by conjuring up a situation of incommensurable inequality. What if she were paid millions by U-Vistract but Martin and his wife missed out? Other investors have raised similar concerns. Ambrose (a true believer in U-Vistract whom we shall meet in the next chapter), referring to his close friend Anthony, said, "I don't want to be a millionaire when he's living next door to me." This encouraged Anthony to join the scheme.

These sentiments reflect an underlying ideology of possessive individualism. Martin's relatives do not offer to share their coming wealth but invite him to join them as a possessive individual. They invert the dependency of *grasruts* on elites (often justified as contributions of distant kin to the making of successful professionals or business people [K. Martin 2007]). They imply that Martin risks losing his proprietorship of the self if he does not join U-Vistract. Martin's position as provider is reversed, threatening the amity he and his *tambus* enjoy. His relative privilege as a wage earner and town dweller is stripped away in the face of imagined abundance that may create new social relations if families do not enter into the new world together.[10] This fear of separation in the world to come has been exploited by Christian evangelists, particularly in relation to ideas of the "Rapture" (Robbins 1998).

Yet for Martin, it is his relatives' very position in the subsistence economy that predisposes them to seize on the false hopes offered by fast money schemes. Their lack of ready access to cash makes them economically vulnerable; therefore they look to opportunities for transforming their circumstances. The subsistence economy itself provides precedents: not satisfied with their earnings from cocoa, his relatives sought to increase their cash income by growing vanilla during the recent boom. They ripped out mature cocoa trees, planting vanilla instead. However, the quality of vanilla produced did not deliver the promised returns, and now, within a couple of years, they have pulled out vanilla and replanted cocoa. This exemplifies to Martin an inability to calculate consequences and an impulsive disposition that mobilizes all available resources in the hope of high returns. This he calls the "Money Tree psychology," a phrase he left unexplained but which probably refers to the phrase *money doesn't grow on trees*. Martin's meaning then is that his relatives are habitually looking for a way of accessing money without hard labor.[11]

Martin's subsistence relatives may have a Money Tree psychology, but they cannot pass it on up the social hierarchy to Martin and his wife. Their reluctant participation does not implicate them in the Money Tree psychology because they joined simply to keep the peace, not because they really believed in the scheme. The rural grassroots may extract money from urban kin on the basis of sociality, but this occurs despite differing economic perspectives and aspirations. For Martin, his rural kin have a counterproductive and fickle approach to money that he does not share and sees no value in arguing about. The division between their views and his is explicitly based on class, where the ideas of the agrarian class do not influence the urban working class. Like Keir Martin's (2010) example of New Irelanders who happily give betel nut but do not ask for it, Martin's proprietorship of himself and his stewardship of money maintain relationality to a point but without being encompassed by reciprocity.

Lindsay and Francis—*traiim tasol*

> There are so many of these fast money schemes but I don't believe it. I didn't get involved because I believe you have to sweat work. You have to work hard. People here just sit around. It takes those who have been outside and worked in town to come back and start things but it is very hard because they are jealous of you and they want to pull everyone down to the same level.
>
> But you can't blame these people in the rural areas. Papua New Guinea has an agricultural orientation. They work hard but they are tired. They've worked hard for fifteen years but they can't see any benefits. They are just the same. So when they see an opportunity, they take it. "Mi traiim tasol." Even if they think it is risky, they'll just try it.

Lindsay once worked on large mining projects but has returned home to Karkar Island, near Madang, where he runs a small business. Lindsay describes the participation of rural people in fast money schemes as opportunistic, based on desperation for money, encapsulated in the Tok Pisin phrase *traiim tasol* (just try it). However, he himself was always strongly against the schemes because he believed in hard work. He does not use the term *cargo cult mentality* but neatly expresses a common view of the sloth, jealousy, and opportunism of rural people. However, he also concedes that many have worked hard but without commensurate benefits, making them vulnerable to money schemes. This mix of condescension and sympathy is widely found among PNG's working class.

Francis was a newspaper journalist who joined U-Vistract and put in K3,000. He quickly realized that the scheme was fraudulent and used his connections to senior Bougainvilleans to retrieve the money he had invested. He initially invested opportunistically, rather like Alphonse (above) and echoes the sentiments in Stent that opens this chapter. "Initially I thought there was something in it. I wouldn't really call it a scam. There's thing called "trying your luck": *Traim tasol*. If it works, it works. If it doesn't we're not that shocked.... But the conviction they have is not really *traim tasol*. They say we will get it. It is true! We will get it! There is that conviction."

Francis was not drawn into U-Vistract by desperation but by curiosity and a willingness to test out new things. He distinguishes his *traiim tasol* involvement from those who really believe in the scheme's promises and expect transformation of their financial circumstances. For him, *traiim tasol* implies a short-lived hopeful and somewhat shallow conviction of coming success, not the durable belief embraced by more earnest investors who seriously engaged with the scheme's rationale. Like Alphonse in relation to his born- again detractors, Francis sees "true believers" in the schemes as taking their investments far too seriously and placing themselves at risk of losing large amounts of money.

Such true believers are the subject of the following chapters. However, while it is useful to consider different degrees of belief and engagement as a counterpoint to the popular narrative of greed and gullibility, the skeptics here still have much in common with true believers. As we shall see in the coming chapters, true believers also make calculations and experience doubt, even as they succumb to U-Vistract propaganda. The scheme appears reasonable to them, not because they are inherently gullible, but because it inserted itself convincingly into narratives of global finance, transnational Christianity, and national development. The next chapter provides an extended treatment of the infiltration of fast money schemes into Pentecostal and other Christian churches where ideas of global finance and wealth are filtered through prosperity theology.

Notes

1. Ambrose speaks about his experience with Australian Bonanza in chapter 6.

2. "Certainly membership did not imply full belief in the cult" (Stent 1977, 195).

3. Musaraj (2011) notes the importance of "bags of cash" as evidence for investors in an Albanian pyramid scam.

4. Alexeyeff (2011, 217) provides similar descriptions of Catholic and Protestant attitudes to gambling in the Cook Islands.

5. Miyazaki (2006) writes of similar attitudes among younger Japanese derivatives traders who reject the careful, calculating approach of his principal informant, Tada.

6. Meaning that if Martin and his wife questioned his cousin, this would create tension as the cousin realized that they did not share his enthusiasm for the scheme.

7. Exceptions are those with seasonal windfall income such as the Buka lagoon chiefs who told me they had put in K5,000 of *beche de mer* earnings.

8. Errington and Gewertz (2004, 89–93) document similar demands among employees of Ramu Sugar.

9. Cf. Maclean (1984) where Maring gamblers blur distinctions between spheres of exchange.

10. Compare Stent's (1977, 198) example of pressure to join the Peli Association because the promised money would only come once the whole community was involved.

11. Compare Lindsay's characterization of rural people at the end of this chapter.

6 U-Vistract and the Prosperity Gospel

Aspiration and Discipline

In chapter 2, I noted that U-Vistract presented itself as a Christian organization and argued that Pentecostal Christianity was a key vector for the spread of fast money schemes: an "inside track," to use Verdery's (1995) term. This is not to say that Pentecostal churches were the only Christians involved in spreading fast money schemes. People from all churches were drawn into the scams, but Pentecostals were much more directly involved institutionally. The United Church, which shares some theological traditions with Pentecostalism (McDougall 2013; Tomlinson 2013) and has a completely localized clergy, also provided a welcoming community through which Money Rain and U-Vistract spread in Port Moresby and elsewhere. Not all fast money scheme investors were Pentecostals but neo-Pentecostal ideas and practices based on the "prosperity gospel" provided the grounds for U-Vistract's engagement with Christianity.

This chapter shows how U-Vistract utilized particular aspects of contemporary Christian practice and belief in attracting and retaining investors. Pentecostal prosperity theology was particularly useful in establishing ideologies and practices of wealth that mediated global images of affluence and consumerism, national development aspirations and local moralities of distribution and modern personhood.

I begin with a brief survey of Pentecostalism in PNG focused on the prosperity gospel. I draw attention to the urban character of Pentecostalism in PNG, considering how this form of Christianity creates new types of community and mediates class hierarchies. Prosperity gospel Pentecostalism expands the horizons of what is morally desirable, expanding people's aspirations to embrace global imaginings of lifestyle, personal success and wealth.

The next section focuses on Christian subjectivities in relation to money and vocation. Pentecostals cultivate a Christian version of the "financial self" discussed in the previous chapter. The aspirations nurtured by prosperity theology can only be achieved through the application of appropriate personal disciplines, such as tithing: a fiscal discipline laden with spiritual intimacy for Dorothy.

The chapter closes with a consideration of the interplay of prosperity aspirations and disciplines as seen through the eyes of Victor, the Madang doctor. Victor shares some prosperity beliefs but is suspicious of televangelists and judgmental of Christians who were involved with U-Vistract. His reflections show that Pentecostal Christians do not simply absorb ideas from religious authorities, or in the heat of ecstatic experience, but exercise considerable discernment as they work out their own personal positions in relation to social and moral questions. These discerning Christian selves model a proprietorship of the self that is not simply about acquisition of wealth but that has a role of moral leadership within the nation, a theme developed in the following chapters.

Pentecostalism in Papua New Guinea

As is happening in many countries, Pentecostal Christianity's growth in PNG is fast and substantial, often at the expense of older mainline churches (Gibbs 2006; cf. Gewertz and Errington 1993). Pentecostalism emerged from Wesleyan holiness traditions and catalyzed in the Azusa Street Revival in the early twentieth century (Robbins 2004b). It is characterized by literal interpretation of the Bible and ecstatic behaviour in worship attributed to the Holy Spirit. Since the 1960s, Pentecostalism has grown exponentially, not least in Africa and Latin America (Corten & Marshall-Fratani 2001; Meyer 2004). This latter phase of growth, the "second wave," has also spread lively Pentecostal styles of worship to other Christian denominations, including charismatic Catholics (Gewertz and Errington 1996; Gibbs 2004, 2005b; M. Strathern 1999).

Robbins (2004b) distinguishes older charismatic and Pentecostal movements from neo-Pentecostalism, characterized by emphasis on material prosperity, appeal to middle and upper income groups, and accommodation to global capitalism. This division corresponds roughly to the development of Pentecostalism in PNG. Initially, American or Australian Pentecostal missions were established in rural areas and, like mainline churches, were involved in welfare and service delivery activities. They cultivated personal piety and modern deportment but without expectations of worldly riches. Eves (2003) describes rural Pentecostal attitudes to money as a worldly temptation, not the spiritual reward of the prosperity gospel.

Christian Communities

In the 1970s, a "second wave" of Pentecostalism arrived in urban areas and attracted an educated following, who were welcomed into lay leadership positions (Jorgensen 2005; Gibbs 2005b, 2006). Urban Pentecostals in PNG are often adult converts, who joined when they came to town for work or study. Livelier styles of worship are often cited as a reason for the change, as is spiritual revitalisation. The newness of worship formats points to a broader perception of Pentecostalism as more modern than older Christian denominations: "All members ... saw evangelical sects as new, exciting and progressive—the religion of the educated, contemporary Papua New Guinean" (Gewertz and Errington 1993, 283).

The large Pentecostal congregations in Port Moresby (and in the provincial capitals) create communities of newly forged loyalties based not on customary place or ancestral lineage (cf. Barker 1990a) but on intensified Christian faith and opportunities for interaction with peers of the same social class. This new sense of community is important for professional people whose connections with the village are loosening, who see village expectations as burdensome economic demands, or whose education and life experience puts them in a position where they find social interaction with village kin stifling and prefer to socialize with fellow professionals with whom "they can talk about things at the same level." Christian, Victor's friend from the previous chapter, corroborates this depiction: "So many professionals are attracted to Pentecostal churches, so there are like-minded people. They can talk about things at the same level. It's because Pentecostalism is anticulture, free from traditional obligations. It's an effective and understandable excuse for not seeing relatives and contributing to funerals and so on. There's an identity crisis for town professionals because they can't live in town and meet all the expectations and obligations."

For PNG's working class, ties with the village are already attenuated by distance and economic disparities (Macintyre 2011), so there is a need for new types of urban sociality, particularly communities that can nurture the skills required to negotiate the "ether" (Roeber 1999) of the postcolonial city. These skills are class based and exclude those from "lower levels." Implicitly a national scale is being constructed around middle-class town norms.

Pentecostal churches provide important social networks for urban professionals who form communities with more easily manageable expectations of reciprocity and redistribution. Pentecostalism may have provided a rationale for urban elites to distance themselves from the village *wantok* system (cf. Monsell-Davis 1993; Gewertz and Errington 1999). Nevertheless, financial fraud could flourish just as successfully in new urban social groups as in the village-based networks of "wantokism." Jackson, a senior banking official and elder in a large Port Moresby Pentecostal church observed: "Pentecostal churches are really against the *wantok* system. I don't get around with my real village wantoks. I try to spend more time with my Pentecostal friends. There's a bad side of the wantok system and that makes the Pentecostal church more appealing. Some of the Pentecostal churches are moving to Saturday worship. They are looking for convenient ways to restrict their exposure to wantoks who visit on Saturday, because the wantoks are at church on Sunday."

Urban Pentecostal churches are ethnically inclusive, with members drawn from all over the country (M. Strathern 1999). Ambrose describes his church in Madang:

> I have been at the Christian Outreach Centre for six years. It started in Moresby but it's in Madang town now. There's 200 or 300 people. We have three pastors. Two are from Madang, one is Sepik. They're all mixed from different

provinces residing in Madang. Most would have jobs and live in town. Some are Sepik, some Morobe, Highlands, Rabaul, Kavieng, Madang. Some families have been here for twenty years. There are professionals, people with no jobs.

We have a lot of things to be happy about. We don't go hungry because we have gardens. The highly educated business people make up a quarter of the congregation. This is how the church is developed through these people and their contributions.

Most would have invested in U-Vistract. Some do believe [that they will be paid by the scheme], some don't. It's my money; whatever happens to me it's my responsibility, so there's no argument. People have no job but they have gardens so they are confident taking risks.

Pentecostalism recreates individualistic subjects within new collectivities that "act as a surrogate family" (Meyer 2004, 461) or a "new tribe" (Droogers 2001), or provide support in an urban environment where strangers represent possible danger (Marshall-Fratani 2001). These communities have class-based social norms but their evangelistic mission implies a significant divergence from the logic of exclusion found in middle-class institutions such as Rotary Clubs or golf clubs (Gewertz and Errington 1999). "People with no jobs" are welcome to join the congregation, under the leadership of "highly educated business people." Indeed, outreach programs attempt to resocialize urban *grasruts* youth away from presumed trajectories of criminality. Ambrose's description of his congregation as regionally mixed and economically diverse marks it as an instantiation of the Christian nation: the local manifestation of the transnational Christian community. Christian subjects are relocated within a modern Christian polity that overrides loyalties based on kinship, language, or land and expansively encompasses the nation's ethnic and economic divisions. Even the national ideology of subsistence self-sufficiency is reproduced in his comments about gardens. In the process, class distinctions are naturalized and incorporated into the leadership structure of the church.

Pentecostalism gains much of its discursive power from its fierce demonization of indigenous cosmology and tradition (Piot 2010; Robbins 2004b). Nations and local sites are seen as places where ancient demonic powers are established, particularly in rural areas. Maxwell (1998) notes urban Pentecostal preachers in Zimbabwe who actively disparage rural life itself. The language is of spiritual warfare between true Christianity and pagan practices that have infiltrated the mainline churches, leading them to lose their spiritual vitality (Jorgensen 2005; Meyer 1998; Piot 2010).

For middle-class Papua New Guineans, sorcery or residual paganism is seldom the focus (but see Eves et al. 2014). Rather, the "rupture" is with the accommodations that mainline denominations have made with local socialities: *wantokism*, "worldly living," or toleration of sinful practices of male sociality, such as drinking or gambling. Many Pentecostals reject customary obligations relating to bride-price and funerals or renegotiate the terms to delimit their contributions so that village relationships become financially manageable. Modern proprietorship of the self is foregrounded, not threats of demonic agency.

Ambrose: A Meeting in Madang

He [Noah Musingku] came to Madang and talked to all the members at Apex Hall. It was in 2004, before [Bougainvillean separatist leader Francis] Ona died. He came with his wife. He said, "Your money is rolling over, making money for you. It hasn't gone astray or got lost. So have confidence that you will save your money." He assured all the investors. I was so excited because I knew the money was coming. Whether you invested K5 or K1,000, you're a millionaire!

People asked questions. They said, "We're waiting too long. What is happening now? Is the government going to stop it? How can you avoid it?" Nobody asked for their principal back. Everybody is so excited.

Noah said, "Don't panic because your money is there working for you because I have invested your money overseas and it's making more money. I am a strong believer in God and I believe God will do anything possible for us."

He's a strong Christian. Mainly pastors and Christians have been praying for this thing so that the government would open this thing. I would say that God is behind it. There were 500–600 people there. It was so crowded. We had fellowship and prayer to thank God for the good and bad things.

Here in Madang there are well over 7,000 members. They have an office, everything is computerized. They stopped because there's a communication problem. It will reopen because there's an agreement between U-Vistract and Somare and the Bougainville Autonomous Government.

It started with music and normal fellowship, like a church service. There was a music group from the Foursquare Church. Young people from every denomination were leading the worship. Pastors were there but the musicians lead the fellowship. Most of them were Pentecostals: Foursquare, Christian Life Centre, United Church, and Catholics—the people but not their priests. When you're talking about money, people are always there to listen.

After the singing, Noah started his speech. He introduced himself saying that he's a strong Christian and that in everything he does he must seek God's direction and guidance and that is why there must be a fellowship before he speaks. "I trusted God in everything until now and I still trust him and I will pay you all lump sums." There was cheering and praising God. Some were speaking in tongues during the prayers. Some people were very happy and pleased to see the director himself. They had an opportunity to see with their own eyes such a young man like him. He then gave us a short briefing on what is taking place and we just closed with prayer. He then flew to Port Moresby and Bougainville. Madang was the only place that helped him financially to establish the office and pay for the broadband communications and other office equipment.

> Public servants are members, business people. Everyone from the grass-roots to the high public servants. Politicians. People from Madang villages. At [the local U-Vistract agent's] meetings loads of trucks came in.

Ambrose here recounts Noah Musingku's 2004 visit to Madang and the accompanying worship service that often characterized U-Vistract meetings, usually led by local pastors. In this case the singing group from one of the Pentecostal churches provided the music, as if coming to an ecumenical gathering or a revivalist crusade.

Ambrose's vignette captures the integration of U-Vistract and Christianity. U-Vistract acted as "a Christian ministry," augmenting and revitalizing church life. The use of prayer, music, and other aspects of Christian worship by U-Vistract may seem sacrilegious, but what is notable about Ambrose's recounting of the meeting is how seamless the connections are between the scam and Christianity. Noah brought a Christian message of trust in God. Indeed, the performance of worship was quite unremarkable for Ambrose: there was something normal, even expected, about these rituals. Prayers are common at all kinds of meetings in PNG, whether organized by churches, the government, or NGOs. Rituals such as prayer gave credibility to U-Vistract not simply by invoking the authority of God but by making the scheme familiar by performing everyday Christian routines that accompany most other public gatherings in PNG.

U-Vistract's repeated claim to being a "Christian ministry, not a money scheme" may seem mere fakery in a country where few aspects of life and public discourse are untouched by Christianity (B. Douglas 2000; Barker 2013). However, the scheme involved activities and rhetoric that might be expected of a genuine Christian ministry. Like interdenominational evangelistic crusades, U-Vistract events were peppered with prayer and worship, including music. U-Vistract did not compete with churches for members: it was not a church itself. Rather, it complemented and even revitalized church activities, collaborating with local congregations, just as revival movements typically do.

The Prosperity Gospel

Academic discussion of Christianity and capitalism inevitably returns to Weber's *Protestant Ethic and the Spirit of Capitalism* ([1920] 1976), but for Pentecostal Christianity globally, prosperity gospels are replacing the Protestant ethic of hard work and thrift (Coleman 2000, Hunt 2000, 2002; Maxwell 1998; Robbins 2004b). Where older Pentecostal attitudes to money were more ascetic, prosperity theology promises that God will reward tithing and other practices with even greater material returns. This reflects a "magical" approach to generation of wealth, sanctifies consumerist desires and material aspirations (Robbins 2004b), and even provides a new arena for Christian consumerism to be cultivated. Prosperity or faith gospel thinking emerged from 1960s and 1970s American televangelists and so reflects the material abundance and faith in mass media of that context (Gifford 2001). Prosperity also extends to good health, and faith healing is often a feature of these movements. Poverty and illness are both implicitly understood as failures of faith and therefore as evidence of sinfulness.

Pentecostal churches teaching prosperity theology—or the "healthy, wealthy gospel," as one informant described it—are growing in PNG (Gibbs 2006; Jorgensen 2005). The extent to which this signals the abandonment of older values of hard work and thrift is debatable. It is unclear that the Protestant work ethic was ever really assimilated into Melanesian ideas of money and modernity, particularly as regards its valorization of hard work as ennobling. Schram (2010) notes the Methodist emphasis on charity and generous giving as a sign of true conversion and argues that this forms part of the Auhelawa hierarchy of values, which also incorporate local ideas of business but without a Weberian work ethic. Work is just as likely to be seen as a curse requiring the sweat of the brow (as per Genesis 3:19) but from which there must be some escape to an easier more prosperous life. Rousseau (2015) draws on Gell's (1992) analysis of the "magic standard" of producing value without work to argue that in contemporary Vanuatu, stories of miraculous windfalls are a way of questioning the origins of wealth and the injustices of the colonial and postcolonial economies.

Papua New Guineans are increasingly exposed to American televangelists, such as the EMTV broadcasts of Dr. Creflo A. Dollar.[1] One of my Madang friends receives multiple subscriptions to *Believer's Voice of Victory*, an American magazine published by Kenneth Copeland, one of the founders of the faith gospel (Gifford 2001). The magazine features articles by Copeland and Dr. Creflo Dollar that focus on prosperity and "lifestyle." The subscription is received at Modilon Hospital, and multiple copies are left lying around for others to read. Dr. Creflo Dollar visited Port Moresby in 2001 preaching that "PNG should not be poor" to large crowds and with considerable media coverage (Apami 2001).

Other international evangelists have also conducted mass rallies in PNG: Prime Minster Bill Skate hosted Benny Hinn, a televangelist notorious for his ostentatious wealth (Gibbs 2005a; Gifford 2001; Newland 2010). The Malaysian televangelist, Dr. Jonathon David, also regularly tours PNG. According to U-Vistract, Dr. David endorsed Musingku in a prophecy (*U-Vistract News* 2001).

Describing the prosperity gospel, a United Church pastor succinctly observed, "The common understanding is that, if you're Christian and poor, there's something wrong with you because God wants you to be rich." He thought prosperity teaching was also starting to influence mainline churches. Workers for a microfinance scheme in Madang characterized Pentecostal churches as" full of university graduates and professional people" living "wealthy, decent, upper class" lives. "They seem to know how to make money" was another observation. This was contrasted with the virtues of "poverty, chastity, and obedience" and self-sufficiency through hard work espoused by the Catholic informants. These characterizations are not without substance. Pentecostals do often teach classes on how to handle money, avoid debt, and reduce wasteful expenditure as they nurture new subjectivities among their followers, and this often results in new deportments in hygiene, dress, and appearance that may even extend to a degree of ostentation (Maxwell 1998).

Coleman (2006, 45–47) writes about the Word of Life church in Sweden and its exegesis of biblical passages where an idiosyncratic literalistic meaning is insisted on over a conventional reading of metaphor. Coleman gives the example of Mark 11:23–4 where Jesus teaches that believers have the power to cast a mountain into the sea if they are free from doubt. For Faith (prosperity) Christians, this is a model for "the embodiment of local Prosperity identity" through the demonstration of faith in performance of the spoken (and efficacious) word. Such exhortations encourage an ambitious belief, confident enough to put aside and even denounce conventional understandings of how the world works. True believers expect miracles from a powerful God who can release them from the traditional spiritual and attitudinal constraints that trap people in a "spirit of poverty" (Maxwell 1998). Breaking the boundaries of possibility and dismissing worldly common sense and historical experience refashions the Christian subject into one now characterized by ambition and expansiveness, even entrepreneurialism. Victor (below) provides a further example of this Christian expansiveness.

Prosperity gospel teachings promise imminent transformation of Christians' lives in very material and worldly ways. While many Melanesian cultures link wealth and social amity (e.g., Bashkow 2006, 115ff), this theology goes well beyond traditional moral economies or even modern Christian ideas of thrift, reward for hard work, or a spiritualized idea of reward. Christians should expect to be affluent and should see new cars and other status-oriented signs of wealth as divine blessings.

As with Creflo Dollar's above exhortation to, "Step out now in faith and do business.... Do not fear but do business now in God who is always on your side," prosperity theology is oriented towards ideas of business and profit. It valorizes and sanctifies entrepreneurship, seeing risk-taking as a demonstration of strong faith (Coleman 2000). This disposition is a Christian version of the masculinist risk-taking among North American share traders documented by Zaloom. According to Zaloom (2006, 93), "Risk reaps reward—in money, status, the elaboration of the social space of markets, and the construction of a masculine self." Pentecostal entrepreneurialism promises similar rewards to those share traders hope to receive in status and money and also works on a dual project of constructing a disciplined Christian financial self as well as extending its business-oriented view of the word into every sphere of life.

The expansive aspirations of the prosperity gospel then combine Christianity with contemporary ideologies of finance (Ho 2009; Ortiz 2013), entrepreneurialism, and risk in ways very much consonant with fast money schemes. Prosperity theology thus provided a ready language for Musingku to sanctify his fraudulent activities. The prosperity gospel fosters a sense of entitlement that demands evidence of this-world fulfilment. The need for authentication of the prosperity gospel meant that PNG Pentecostals were already expecting some mechanism that would deliver economic transformation. They were therefore predisposed to accepting U-Vistract. When pastors took U-Vistract money and claimed it as a gift from God (Lutu 2000), this reflected the explanatory power of the prosperity gospel, not a naïveté concerning money itself.

Pastor Paul "I also pray for money to spread the word of God."

Pastor Paul is pastor of a large Port Moresby Pentecostal congregation. Once close to Musingku, Pastor Paul presents himself and other Christians as innocent victims of the schemes. He invested through a Christian friend and thought nothing of the high returns he received until the money stopped being paid. He claims not to have promoted them to anyone else because everyone was already aware of them. For him, the high returns were simply what one would expect from the New York Stock Exchange (see chap. 10). As pyramid schemes were then unknown in PNG, he could not have been expected to have realized the scheme was a fraud any more than the great numbers of others who also invested. The "whole country was taken by storm," "even the government," so how could churches be singled out for blame ahead of anyone else?

> As a pastor, in PNG we're beginning to know value and the importance of money. When you have money you can have what you want—good houses, car, clothes. People look and say, "He's got money." Shoes versus bare feet, a neck tie. Money is everything. In the Highlands, they fight over mineral rights. Unrelated groups come in saying, "At least we can have a share." Everyone has jumped on the bandwagon. Even me: I need money to put bread on the table for my family and to run my ministry, to travel around.
>
> People are desperate for money. In my church we talk about spiritual things but we have to balance it with the basic needs of people. I look around for people in the church who have knowledge. For example, we might have a lecturer in vocational education. I ask them, "Can you train these ladies in sewing, so at least they can get something?" So we try to help everyone so they know how to cook food and bake and they can sell their food in the market. As a pastor I look for opportunities for people to work and get money.
>
> Money schemes have taken the whole nation by storm. Everybody was involved. The main one was U-Vistract and its offspring, Money Rain. A lot

of Christians invested money, even pastors. Me too—I put in K2,000. Every fortnight I was getting K1,000, for four or five months! Then all of a sudden they said, "We're going to stop paying people." It affected every church, every pastor, every Christian.

Some churches split up because of money schemes. Christians had arguments because of it. Some Christians took money as middlemen, so the others took out all their frustrations on them. Everybody in the government was also affected. We can't complain because we willingly gave it. We were not forced into it. So Christians kept very quiet because we're ashamed.

People have given so much money. They've given their heart and want it back. How they get it back is another thing. Some people have died. They might have died because of worry. They lost their hard earned cash and savings collected over many years.

I believe that, in the end times, there will be a lot of crusades, a lot of people wanting to know Christ. I also pray for money to spread the word of God. When I heard Noah, it didn't trigger a reaction in me. If he says these things, I think, "Well, if you have money, give it to us for ministry."

Paul explains that Christians are now ashamed of their involvement in the schemes and refers to the conflict within the Christian Life Center (CLC). The public nature of the conflict may be more a source of shame than the actual financial impropriety. While he claims to have repented of his involvement in the scheme, he is less than forthright in explaining why his name and signature are found on a character reference for Noah Musingku submitted to the courts during the latter's bankruptcy trial: "I believe my name could have been used but I don't think I ever wrote a reference." Paul's reticence is in contrast to a public service of repentance held in Mount Hagen, reported in the *Post-Courier* (Kewa 2003) and reportedly well attended (Mount Hagen Interdenominational Pastors Fellowship, 2003).

Pastor Paul demonstrates how smoothly the U-Vistract system fit into the prosperity theology. Nothing Musingku said "trigger(ed) a reaction in (him)," at least not a negative reaction. As a pastor he still seeks ways for people to earn money and still prays for money for ministry. His comments bear out another investor's cynical observation that Pentecostals "have classes on how to make money and how to be rich." It may well be that some of this entrepreneurial ethos led to church members becoming middlemen for U-Vistract, generating more of the conflict that Pastor Paul mentions.

Pastor Paul knows how hard it is for people to "put bread on the table" in Port Moresby and believes this is what drives people into U-Vistract, rather than greedy desires for luxurious lifestyles. Noah Musingku and his wife are held up as humble exemplars. However, Paul's initial view of money is much more individualistic, focusing on how individuals are perceived by others and how they use material possessions to define themselves and their status. Pastor Paul even mentions the great class divide in PNG, namely between those who wear shoes (*susokman*; Gewertz and Errington 1999; Stevenson 1984) and those in bare feet.

"Money is everything," he says. It constitutes people and determines their value within the modern cash economy. In the Highlands,[2] it drives people into conflict over land and mining royalties (LiPuma 1999, 211–212). In doing so, they vie not only for status but also for access to the essentials of life. Therefore he does not preach against money itself but tries to help people improve their access to cash through training in microentrepreneurship (cf. Maxwell 1998), refashioning the desires of the poor into the disciplines of *bisnis* (Bainton 2010, 2011; Cahn 2006, 2008).

However, it is not individual class mobility that constitutes Pastor Paul's vision of the desirable and the feasible (Errington and Gewertz 2004). Rather, his future is dominated by the End Times and the urgent tasks of evangelism (Robbins 2004b). These cosmic events are played out on the national scale in the manner of the "Third Wave Evangelism" described by Jorgensen (2005). Money is needed for this task, which goes well beyond putting bread on the table and often includes visits from international evangelists. God and prayer no doubt play important roles in generating resources for such campaigns, but, as we shall see in chapter 10, it is the this-worldly, secular mechanism of the New York Stock Exchange that he thinks will generate the means for U-Vistract to finance this work. That is to say that the old Protestant work ethic disciplines of work and saving give way to new practices of investment.

Christian Subjects: Tithing and the Disciplines of Personal Prosperity

The vision of wealth elaborated by the prosperity gospel and mediated by U-Vistract to its investors should not simply be equated with greed or material accumulation (Bielo 2007). Rather, it implies a Christianity that has mastered modernity and that creates a new global community of successful, prosperous, and fulfilled individuals. Debates about the ways in which Christianity generally, or Neo-Pentecostalism distinctively, might prepare or predispose nonmodern subjects for integration into the capitalist economy tend to take an instrumentalist turn. For example, Pentecostals (also Seventh-day Adventists; Jebens 2005) are sometimes thought to make better employees because of the personal discipline and sobriety instilled through the movement. Repudiating vices such as gambling and drink may also allow Christians to accumulate wealth (Robbins 2004b).

A distinctive Pentecostal discipline is the requirement of tithing (giving 10 percent of one's income to the church). This may make Pentecostal churches financially independent (Robbins 2004b), but it also marks a measureable commitment to the new beliefs and a test of faith that such an investment will be rewarded proportionately. Therefore, neo-Pentecostals are not accurately characterized as passive beneficiaries of miraculously produced wealth. In tithing generously, they actively work on their personal disciplines in relation to money. Giving to Christian causes is elevated from mere duty to an act of spiritual intimacy, connecting the believer more closely to God as a person. As Dorothy puts it: "It's spiritual, not like paying a membership fee for a club. Because I'm giving to somebody who isn't seen. I'm giving it to my pastor but I believe I'm giving it to the Lord."

Dorothy, who did not invest in any fast money schemes, has joined a Pentecostal church in Madang, moving from the United Church because "there's a lot of truths in the Bible that I'd heard about in the United Church but they are teachings of spiritual importance that [Pentecostals] put into practice." For Dorothy, tithing is one of these truths and characterizes the revitalized faith she has found in Pentecostalism.

Like Dorothy, Ambrose experiences tithing as an intimate practice as he lives under "God's discipline." This discipline is personalized: God is a benign parental figure protecting his children from temptation and intervening when they have needs. However, Ambrose stresses the link between giving and receiving and reveals a calculus of entitlement that characterizes prosperity theology. Ambrose:

> We have teachings on stewardship. How to look after your money, how to share, how to use money how to give back to God. If my wife gets 1K from the market, she gives 10t to God. 90t to us but 10 percent to God. We give it and that is it, we don't ask. We say, "Thank you, God, for giving us this money."
>
> How we use money in the village: we make sure we have kerosene, soap, salt, sugar, tea. We use money wisely: no drinking, gambling, woman, unnecessary things. Have to save for bride-price, funerals, and compensation. I should be ready. So I save for brideprice. The husband himself has to save up, but the whole family will come together with whatever they have: food, money, clothes. The girl's parents set the price. We help relatives of the deceased buy clothes, food, money to feed to mourners, often transport. The pastor will help with funeral costs and so on. The congregation contributes.
>
> Do not let money control your lives. You'll have to control money so you don't fall into temptation. It is good in itself, so long as we don't let it control us. You give to Him and He gives back. When you come under God's discipline, you give what he desires, then God in return gives back to us. It could be a promotion, more food in your garden, that's what we expect. God talks to people to give you something when you are in desperate need. Maybe you have no bus fare but someone pays the fare for you. God is talking to them to give—that's how we experience it.

Ambrose believes he will be paid and that payment is imminent. Various points of the U-Vistract story are interpreted as signs that the promised payments are finally coming. Indeed, he believes people elsewhere are already being paid—in Bougainville, Australia, and even Israel. U-Vistract encouraged this type of thinking by referring to different phases of establishing the system and explained these in bureaucratic terms, setting in place proper systems for managing the payments and negotiating with overseas banks and financial houses (e.g., Musingku 1999). Technical developments were also a part of this phased roll-out of the U-Vistract system; hence Ambrose refers to the installation of satellite phones and broadband at the U-Vistract headquarters in Tonu.

Despite this heightened sense of expectation, Ambrose's aspirations are actually rather humble. His talk is of stewardship rather than the realiation of extraordinary wealth. God's hand is seen in small things such as being given a bus fare when you have no money. Modest expenses of soap and kerosene are mentioned—not the extravagances of hotels, big houses, cars and travel. Ambrose finds comfort in the idea that he has a U-Vistract account of K105,000 but also believes that his humble stewardship of resources, including tithing and the disciplines of saving for future expenses, place him in the right relationship to God such that he can enjoy a reasonable standard of living. Gardens provide for basic needs and so allow him to take risks in enterprises such as U-Vistract and Papalain. While he may hope for financial transformation, it seems that, at heart, his expectations are more realistic.

My interest here is in the formation of new Christian subjects who are drawn to the world of financial investment. In this regard, there are two features of the prosperity gospel to note, beyond its promise of abundance to all faithful Christians. The first is that tithing represents a personal act of submission to God that is expected to be reciprocated in an undetermined way. The form that the blessing takes may not be precise, but it is expected as a *personal reward to the individual subject*. Delays in the reward may also be reinterpreted as a test of faith, and in a context where all things are possible.

However, nurturing such subjectivities does not automatically create the habitus of prosperity Christianity, which must be worked at continuously, not least through practices such as tithing. Tithing income to the church is a tangible external performance of this subjectivity and it is also a reminder of the need for vigilance and discipline in keeping the new expansive self subordinated to God, not sinful desires. The Christian subject, for all its rupture and ideological individualism, is still relational in practice (LiPuma 1998).

While all things are theologically possible through Christ, sustaining fantastical hopes of transformation is difficult in the context of daily life (cf. the cyclical revivals of Robbins's [2004a] Urapmin). Where Robbins describes a cycle based on the conviction of sinfulness, for Ambrose perhaps poverty is the enduring state from which he seeks redemption (and which is a type of sin in Prosperity Christianity). Ambrose moves through his heightened expectations of becoming a millionaire but then settles into a more familiar narrative of the thrift required to live on minimal income in the village, the importance of gardens for food production, and the reassertion that only a small range of consumer goods (soap and kerosene) are really necessities. The desirable returns home to the humility of the feasible.

Imaginings of prosperity draw on local experience; hence U-Vistract conjured aspirations based on basic needs (food, clothing, school fees) as well as more global practices of consumption. Thrift alone is insufficient to meet day-to-day needs within the urban money economy, not to mention the greater project of evangelism. Some kind of intervention is surely required to remedy the situation: for a while that was U-Vistract. The money scheme claimed to reconnect PNG to the world of global finance, a source of prosperity so vast that God must surely be behind it. This was confirmed in practice by U-Vistract's support to the churches.

Part of the appeal of the prosperity gospel for urban Papua New Guineans is that it mediates modernity from a distant global world that is free from the social, moral, and economic constraints of PNG. This vision is profoundly racialized (Cox 2015). The global world of prosperity is imagined as a white world where white people and their governments know how to produce, manage, and consume money "properly," while black people at home do not. Thus Robbins's (1998, 2004a) observations of "negative nationalism" and its implications for the formation of a transnational Christian identity also apply more broadly to economic matters and national development, a theme I develop in the next chapter.

In the consideration of a distant fantasy world, the quotidian is obscured from view. Ambrose's thrifty village living does not seem to register on the scale of advanced money handling skills that white people are imagined to have and that Noah Musingku has now opened up to Papua New Guineans through U-Vistract. The new disciplines of prosperity may begin in ordinary and familiar practices but accessing abundance requires the spectacle of induction from an authoritative source who is able to mediate the distance and difference of the two worlds. U-Vistract fulfilled that role, resolving the scalar frictions between the local, national, and global.

Critiques of Prosperity

Prosperity Christianity is not uncontested and often attracts reaction. Many Christians are troubled by the involvement of churches with the fast money schemes and see Pentecostal pastors as avaricious and exploitative. This has led to accusations of hypocrisy and not a little disillusionment. Andrew, an NGO worker in Madang (originally from Sandaun Province), and Pauline, a Bougainvillean teacher (now resident in Madang), give some of the flavor of popular suspicion of the behavior and values of independent pastors, particularly in Pentecostal churches. Andrew equates Pentecostal prosperity teachings with fast money schemes and cargo cults. Pauline and her sisters invested some K20,000 in U-Vistract but lost it all.

Andrew:

> Another example of cargo cult is with the new churches. New churches are trying to be established and trying to get people to build pastors' houses from just members' contributions in the name of giving to God. They used to say, "Give 10 percent of what you earn and God will give you more than 100 percent" I do not agree with that. It's a form of making people lazy. New churches—Protestant, Pentecostal, whatever. If they're starting up, they fall under new churches.
>
> One person only benefits: the pastor and his family. It should be shared by all. Church should provide for all through social services. One person gets rich but lazy because he uses theology as a way of getting rich and a way of controlling them. When is God going to give? But it makes people lazy—they don't want to sit and wait. That's cargo cult mentality.

Andrew's comment that the church should provide social services reflects his upbringing in Catholic traditions but is also a communitarian critique of the individualism involved in Pentecostal prosperity teaching, not least in the individual benefits to pastors themselves. His impatience with laziness may appear to embody something of an individualistic Protestant work ethic. However, for Andrew it relates to his communitarian belief in self-sufficient grassroots development. As an NGO worker, Andrew is frustrated that communities do not work harder for their own benefit in the types of programs he promotes and that aim towards "development." Instead, they succumb to the "cargo cult mentality" and wait for logging royalties (P. West 2006, 171) or place their hopes in prosperity gospels or fast money schemes. The hope of windfall income is understood as a threat to the place of responsible and honorable hard work in the minds of the grassroots.

Pauline:

> I see it, yeah. There are a lot of examples. Not necessarily money scams. They use the church to lure people. It's the Bible, they say it's the Bible. Because they are using the Bible, the Word of God, it's more convincing for the public and I think he also used that. Earlier you asked about people investing. There were church workers, especially from the Pentecostal church because they use the concept of spirit to lure people, the way they talk. Very convincing. For example they also use that to further convince people of the concepts of U-Vistract. So he continues to use the church to say that what he's done, he hasn't done anything wrong. He did run a genuine business but the government has pushed him out of business. In the end he's not able to show proof of a lot of things that he says.

Pauline, a devout Catholic herself, criticizes the emotive rhetoric deployed by Pentecostals and regards such practices as also typical of U-Vistract. These types of comments by working class people imply a credulous and uncritical grassroots public, easily deceived by those unscrupulous enough to use religion to defraud them. The emotional nature of Pentecostal worship makes those from more staid Christian traditions suspicious of manipulation by self-interested and poorly credentialed pastors. One senior public servant, described U-Vistract as "a money cult that preys on ordinary people's desire and lust of money" (Ayius 2006). In doing so, he was indexing the cargo cult mentality discourse outlined in chapter 4, with its attendant rendering of the *grasruts* as greedy and gullible. While ordinary people may have lost money succumbing to this "money cult," this person was far from ordinary, having himself made K80,000 over four months from a K20,000 investment in U-Vistract. These ideas of the poor as culpable and the rich as deserving also resonate with prosperity theology, not to mention broader neoliberal ideologies and business-oriented self-help movements such as Personal Viability (Bainton 2010, 2011; cf. Gewertz and Errington 1998).

Taste in Televangelists

Victor's story here is unusual in that he combines a fierce criticism of Christian hypocrisy with a large measure of engagement with—and acceptance of—the prosperity gospel propagated by international televangelists. Victor's judgments reflect more widespread discourses of class in PNG.

Victor:

The Tokorara Christian Fellowship was affiliated with the Baptist Union and it was at the liberal end. There are very conservative Baptists who insist on a dress code, no instruments in worship, and that kind of thing, but Tokarara had all those things. There was some speaking in tongues, so you could say it was charismatic but we didn't make a big deal of that kind of thing. I don't know how it all came about but it did concern me. I was disgusted that the pastors got sucked into this. But it also shook my beliefs. My conscience said it's wrong but I started to think if the pastors are condoning it, maybe it's not such a bad thing after all.

The AOG [Cornerstone Gateway Church] in Gordons put a substantial amount into U-Vistract. They had a building fund, and the church board decided to hasten that process by investing in U-Vistract. Then I also heard of the United Church women's group who fund-raised to go to Samoa (see also chap. 2). They invested the money in U-Vistract because the bishop was a *wantok* who invested their money into U-Vistract. When it didn't come, he accessed money from the United Church coffers to send them. There was quite an uproar in the United Church: when his contract expired, it wasn't renewed. People of such standing! I don't know how you can stand before God.

So I began to look at these superficial things and I wondered how the want for a better life could make people ignore their beliefs. I have to take my hat off to Noah! He's a genius for making all the Christians suck up to him! But my personal feeling to all those Christians who invested—serves you bloody right! Walking around with a holier than thou attitude! Take that!

There are a lot of Christians who look down on other people who don't attend church as being of a lesser race or something, not as equals. Although they don't say it openly, it's a general feeling against them. And there are many pastors who do have this holier than thou attitude (many also who don't). There quite a few in charismatic churches as well as the fundamental[ist] Baptists who have a holier than thou attitude. So if they were fooled, I laugh at them. Because of them investing in U-Vistract, I'm calling Noah Musingku a genius. They try to maintain very high moral standards but it's the subtle ways.

There was one picture in the newspaper that has forever stuck in my mind. It's about a meeting of U-Vistract investors in Port Moresby at Sir John Guise Stadium ("Praying for Reprieve," *National*, September 23, 1999). They've gathered together to fast and pray for the government to release their money. That for me was a triumph! To unashamedly come out in public as a Christian and admit I've gambled my money and I want the government to pay! Something so stupid! Just accept your punishment.

But it was my belief that it was wrong. Christians shouldn't invest in get rich quick schemes. The fact is that a lot of these schemes are built on deception of some sort. Someone of Christian values should be able to sense that and see something's not right and be cautious. It's not wrong in itself—you can put your money where you like but you should have more insight.

There's another get rich scheme that the Baptists told me about. They sarcastically say the televangelists like [Kenneth] Copeland and Oral Roberts and Creflo Dollar get rich quick for the televangelists themselves! I like Creflo Dollar—he's black! There's a guy called Copeland I don't like because of my Christian upbringing. He makes statements like, "God told me as I was walking along ..." Fundamental Baptists believe the Bible is the inerrant and complete Word of God. Any other word of God should be in the Bible, so anyone who says, "God told me," this has to be approached with caution because this guy's bordering on cultlike belief. He's unlikely to be Christian. If something is not consistent with the Bible, you have to question it.

Creflo Dollar never uses that term, he's more biblically based. They're started what's it called? ... this prosperity movement in the Christian church. Because traditionally my background is Lutheran, our impression is that Christians should be like missionaries, not living in mansions or driving nice cars—a poverty mentality. What Creflo and Copeland are saying is that doesn't have to be the case—you don't have to be humble and poor because Solomon, Abraham, and David were all men of God and rich. Riches does not equal evil. You can still have riches and find favor in the eyes of God. That's been their drive and people like to hear that—I do!

[Cox: So why are these guys a get rich quick scheme?]

They sort of ask for money and weave it into their messages. Give and we'll spread the gospel on your behalf. A lot of Christians do that because it's a Christian duty to spread the gospel but they don't do it but it's OK to pay somebody else to do it for you.

[Cox: So what is the appeal for you?]

The appeal is that you can enjoy life more. When you're brought up as a Christian, you're told that you can't drink, can't smoke, can't fuck around, can't go to the disco. You're so inundated with this "can't do that" you're ostracized from social activities that other teenagers were doing. In the 80s it was very popular to go out dancing. Then violence kept people away—there were stabbings and rapes. Then TV came and now people just stay indoors. There's a desire for social liberation so that you want to break out of a modus operandi of going to church on Sunday, go to work or school, and go to bed. Not mixing with people that your parents don't approve of. I don't know, it's probably just parents being strict but it stays with you for a while. You feel afraid to disobey God for bad consequences but then you realize it's not bad to enjoy life—you can drink.

I'm not filthy rich, not in the sense of the accumulation of material possessions or money in the bank. It's rich as in feeling rich, not poor. Being free from debt and being able to afford a few things that I want, as opposed to brewing home brew in a shack in Gav Stoa [the informal squatter settlement adjacent to Divine Word University in Madang] that's poor! I live in a decent house, drive my own car, so it's rich in that sense and not poor. Being able to feed my family, have bills paid, give money to wantoks without it hurting too much. Not living from pay to pay.

The difference between Noah and Creflo is that Creflo preaches riches follow righteousness. You can be prosperous through honest means. You have to have the courage to find the right way to create opportunities for yourself in an honest way. He doesn't make financial guarantees. So you know that if you are dishonest, you may not get there.

Noah is similar, but the thing wrong with Noah is that he promises a set figure: if you put in this much, you'll get so much and it's higher than any of the banks. His main deception is to promise a certain return. All his investors are actually gamblers—it's too good to be true. I used to watch these shows at breakfast time every morning when we had cable TV. The only person who's gone to that extent is Oral Roberts, who built a tower and said, "God said you have to raise this much money or I won't come down."

Benny Hinn is a crook—you can see it on him. He doesn't look all that genuine. He flies in a private jet, always wears white, does this hocus pocus thing, and people fall over. I tolerate speaking in tongues but this is bordering on a cult—a trance is something I associate with voodoo. Having said that, in charismatic churches, people do go into trances.

For me prosperity is about being free from debt and not worried about where your next meal will come from and having a relatively easy life as opposed to being able to splurge.

Victor, whom we met in the previous chapter, is a doctor from Madang. He has worked around the country in various hospitals and also overseas on several occasions. He has a strong personal faith but is ambivalent about institutional Christianity. As a doctor, Victor is often called into the hospital at night and on weekends and so cannot attend worship or other church activities as regularly as other church members. Also as a medical specialist, Victor can lay claim to considerable professional expertise and social standing. Doctors, in their intimate dealings with life and death, have a certain authority that is not merely technical but also extends into a more relational and moral realm.

These factors make it difficult for someone like Victor to submit to the authority of pastors less educated than him. Nor can he tolerate moral disapproval of church members who do not appreciate the rigors of his working schedule. His social and professional position then puts him somewhat outside the norms of the churches he has been a part of, and he resents insinuations that his irregular attendance at church implies that he is a lesser Christian. When he can, he attends church but also accesses Pentecostal teachings through television and American Pentecostal literature from televangelist ministries. Of these, he is distrustful of Kenneth Copeland but likes Rev. Dr. Creflo Dollar "because he's black!" and because Dollar teaches more closely from the Bible, in Victor's estimation.

These televangelists often preach about money, making it difficult to distinguish genuine biblical teaching from those who are simply greedy. Benny Hinn and Oral Roberts are seen as deceivers like Musingku. Creflo Dollar, on the other hand, promises prosperity but with moral requirements and without the specific returns that make Musingku's claims so presumptuous. Musingku, along with Copeland, Hinn, and Roberts, makes claims that imply a unique relationship to God beyond what is found in the Bible and that presume on Providence by promising a "set figure." I suspect also that the set figure represents for Victor a loss of transcendence, representing God's activities as particular sums of money, not more spiritualized principles.

In discussing U-Vistract with Victor, he exhibits a certain schadenfreude in relation to the involvement of Christians in fast money schemes. Although he seriously considered investing himself and his close friend lost a considerable amount of money, he finds something satisfying in what he sees as the exposure of the hypocrisy of many Pentecostal and fundamentalist Christians. In his mind, they have demonstrated that, for all their pious platitudes, they are at heart greedy, selfish people. He is disgusted by their lack of discernment and propensity to follow leadership without question. Their unsuccessful investments in U-Vistract are a public demonstration of how they have no moral right to judge or constrain Victor's attempts to lead a modern life. Victor's schadenfreude follows something of the pattern suggested by Nachman (1986, 57) where "laughing at others requires consideration of relative social standing." The rectitude and moral vanity that Victor detects among Christian investors in U-Vistract is exposed as hypocrisy. Their humiliation in this regard is not the humiliation that

Sahlins ([1992] 2005) leads us to expect of the transition to modernity. Victor's grasp of modernity is grounded in the humiliation of hypocritical others, not the recalcitrant self.

Prosperity as Freedom

Victor makes some interesting comments about his faith and the prosperity gospel. While it is easy to conflate prosperity theology and fast money schemes (as Andrew and Pauline do), for Victor, prosperity has a different texture and is not simply windfall gain. To coopt Sen's (1999) influential reframing of development: prosperity is experienced as freedom for Victor. For him, the worldliness of prosperity teachers stands in liberating contrast to the puritanical constraints of his upbringing and the judgmental "holier than thou" attitudes of the churches he has attended. The prosperity gospel provides a refreshing approach to faith unlike the proscriptive Lutheran Christianity in which he was nurtured. Victor interprets prosperity teaching in a way that embraces his material and class aspirations and relieves him of feelings of guilt at his adoption of more cosmopolitan habits such as a quiet drink (he is a very moderate drinker in my experience). Prosperity Christianity offers a fuller way of being than the duty-oriented life he has been brought up in and regards now as a stifling routine. It offers a modernity that "can open up new horizons for developing the self" (Josephides 2005, 116). Victor likes to hear that he can enjoy the finer things of life, even if he does not have them himself. In fact his long working hours mean that his life is much more characterized by duty than indulgence. Victor's prosperity is not about being able to splurge but is a relatively modest freedom from debt and other pressures, including the intrusive moral judgments of others that might lay claim to his proprietorship of the self. Victor and his coreligionists then exemplify Maclean's (1994, 667–668) distinction between freedom and autonomy, where the latter is "a stance against the world, as opposed to an expansion into the world."

Marshall-Fratani (1996, 2001; Marshall 2009) argues that neo-Pentecostalism is an institutional mediator of global images for local communities in Nigeria and beyond. Global images may circulate through electronic media and migration, but they can also be mediated through transnational organizations and movements. Marshall-Fratani points to the "resources of extraversion" (Bayart and Ellis 2000) that help position Pentecostalism as a credible transnational actor, able to link the local and the global and enter into national public spaces with new interpretations of modernity. Pentecostalism provides a framework through which multiple identities can be prioritized and encompassed. This allows the formation of modern subjects, "not so much [through] the individualism of Pentecostal conversion …, but the ways in which its projection on a global scale of images, discourses and ideas about renewal, change and salvation opens up possibilities for local actors to incorporate this into their everyday lives" (Marshall-Fratani 2001; McDougall 2003).

Victor accepts some social stratification and his relatively advantageous economic position. Yet he still retains some discomfort at the individualism entailed in his vision of prosperity. Certainly, he has wantoks requesting favors (Monsell-Davis 1993), but the aim is to manage their demands or perhaps to commodify them so they become one of many necessary expenses of life. Wantoks do not represent a shared communitarian world that Victor could be drawn back into. Paying bills and giving money to wantoks become equivalents, as both activities require the responsible management of money in a planned and predictable way, not "from pay to pay."

This explains why Victor thinks born-again Christians are such hypocrites for investing in U-Vistract: communitarian conformist claims made on him by church members are exposed as cant when their true desires for individualistic wealth are exposed. Like him, Victor's Christian brethren really want to be financially independent and free from the demands of others. Unlike Victor, they expect this money to just appear by God's grace, whereas he sees prosperity as a reward for righteous behaviour and entrepreneurial risk-taking that requires the virtue of courage. This is not the reckless courage of a gambler but an assertion of the individual's will to achieve his or her goals (perhaps not dissimilar to the "genius" of Noah Musingku!).

In fact, Victor is a more complex individual than this characterization implies. He is certainly not as selfish as is implied above, nor is he much of a risk-taker or entrepreneur. His freedom to do what he likes sits firmly within the bounds of respectable Christian citizenship. Some of his moral courage lies not in seeking to maximize his economic advantage but in wrestling honestly with the ambiguities of sharing and keeping. This stands in contrast to the rigid forms of his fellow Christians that allow only the reassertion of social and religious norms regardless of context. Nor does Victor seek to shrug off all interdependence: he adopted his sister's daughter and made a large contribution to his friend's wedding when the friend lost his money in U-Vistract. The point is, however, that he controls this reciprocity and is not at the mercy of endless shopping lists of requests for assistance: a possessive individual, in command of his fortunes.

Most of Victor's immediate family, including his parents, who are now retired, have cash income and even some substantial assets (his father a large house in Madang town). His wife works and his siblings also have successful white-collar careers in Madang and beyond. His family can be thought of as understanding how money is generated and how far a particular sum is likely to stretch. Not all of the wantoks have this familiarity and some may envy his position but it is his youngest brother that Victor most objects to supporting. The brother lives with their parents but does little by way of supporting himself financially and so is becoming a burden to Victor. The youngest brother has not reached the standards of independence set by this family of high achievers, not only because of his financial dependence on them but also because he is not directing his own life in the manner expected by possessive individuals (Sykes 2007a, 2007b; K. Martin 2007).

In Victor's case, his primary field for moral action is not his family but his career. It is as a skilled doctor who has mastered the personal disciplines of professionalism such that he exercises his Christian citizenship, working for the development of the nation of PNG.

In the next chapter, I develop the argument that the proprietorship of the self-expected of modern Papua New Guinean Christians is to be applied to the project of national development. In Victor's case, this has meant a conscientious career in public medicine. The risk-taking, entrepreneurial, business-oriented aspirations of the prosperity gospel return to a focus on national, state-run public institutions and services led by dutiful, disciplined Christian citizens.

Notes

1. www.creflodollarministries.org.
2. Pastor Paul identified as "East Sepik" but comments on the Highlands as a troubling national moral problem.

7 Negative Nationalism and Christian Citizenship

The Christian subculture created within neo-Pentecostal churches creates a relationship between the self and the world that stretches across several imagined scales. Personal conversion flows on to national revival and then to the redemption of the whole world. O'Neill's (2010) ethnography of Guatemalan Pentecostals demonstrates how born-again Christians there can feel that they are acting ethically as Christian citizens of their own country who contribute to God's salvific plan for the whole world. They experience the global through personal conversion and as Christian citizens working to rejuvenate the spiritual life of their own country. Not only individuals but also nations are "biblical units of salvation" (O'Neill 2010, 7).

As O'Neill argues, these ideas are a feature of the global Pentecostal movement and are spread by celebrity evangelists who travel from country to country preaching revival and seeing signs of God's hand about to irrupt into the history of the local. Their sermons are for the most part interchangeable: the rhetoric of revival flattens out local features such that God is about to pour out his blessings on, say, Guatemala, in much the same way as was prophesied for the Philippines. As noted in the previous chapter, Papua New Guineans host these preachers, watch their TV broadcasts, subscribe to their newsletters, and donate to their ministries. When evangelists like Creflo Dollar visit PNG, their message is tailored to national circumstances but in ways that draw from a reserve of ideas that would be familiar to Pentecostals anywhere.

As a feature of this rhetoric, each nation, like each individual, is assumed to have a distinctive national character: one that is fallen and that poses a barrier to salvation. Like individuals, nations are in need of redemption in order to put their past behind them and adopt a new Christian demeanor. In PNG, middle-class Christians seem to be more troubled by their national failings than their Guatemalan counterparts as described by O'Neill. While both countries are faced with poverty, corruption, and violence, Papua New Guineans have a particular imaginary that draws on a colonial racial legacy. Robbins (1998, 104) has called this "negative nationalism": an auto-orientalist critique of the racial failings of Melanesians who see themselves as not civilized enough to be able to run a functioning nation. Negative nationalism is characterized by disparagement of the state, its representatives and even a racial critique of its own citizens' moral capacities. Negative nationalism in PNG frequently imagines Papua New Guineans as inferior to white people (Bashkow 2006; Brison 1996; Clark 1997, 73–75; Cox 2015; Leavitt 1995, 2005). Echoing colonial racial narratives, "black" Papua New Guineans are seen as lacking "white" moral qualities and so are to blame for their own underdevelopment. This critique is particularly focused on the supposed lack of self-control that characterizes black people (Robbins 2004a, 177), particularly in relation to jealousy and disharmony (Bashkow 2006, 130ff).

As noted in earlier chapters, the perceived failings of national character can also include skills and demeanors imagined as intrinsic to the mastery of modernity, such as handling and saving money (LiPuma 1999, 208). This racial critique even extends to conceptualizations of the process of "development" as "becoming European" (Clark 1997, 79; Cox 2015; M. Strathern 1992, 250). Keir Martin (2010, 14) provides examples of Tolai who regard their own *kastom* as a retardant of development.[1] Such sentiments imply some of the characteristics of Anderson's (1983) "imagined community" but constitute an inherently inferior or subordinate nation: national identity but hardly nationalism, if it is to be understood as the "cultivation of civic consciousness and patriotic loyalty" (Thomas 1997, 214).

Pentecostals, Money Schemes, and the State

In PNG, the negative nationalism described above is applied to the state as a moral critique of the national character. Personal qualities such as greed underlie pervasive corruption, which is rarely understood in systemic terms. Personal morality and piety have become central to political debates (Barker 2013; Hauck, Mandie-Filer, and Bolger 2005). Standish laments that in PNG "most of the anti-corruption campaigning remains at the level of moralising rhetoric (2007, 150)."

The above quotation illustrates how U-Vistract addressed problems of poverty and inequality in PNG through discourses of citizen and nation. U-Vistract envisaged a Christian citizenship based on access to the cash economy, although the consumption practices referenced in this passage are hardly conspicuous or prestigious demonstrations of abundance. Rather, they evoke a vision of egalitarian grassroots development where the basic needs of all are met in the modern nation.

However, educated urban Pentecostals were also exposed to repeated warnings against fast money schemes (Bank of Papua New Guinea 2005). Typically, neo-Pentecostalism accepts worldly governments as established by God, albeit temporarily until the Kingdom of Heaven arrives in the end-times. How could devout Christians who supposedly submit to state authorities ignore these warnings?

Perhaps the answer lies in widespread perceptions of the state as inherently corrupt and therefore lacking legitimacy. Among Christians there are a variety of theological responses to questions of the state and corruption. Pentecostals in

Africa and beyond have actively opposed corruption but usually on the grounds of personal moral integrity rather than on any developed theologies of the state (Meyer 2004). Studying corruption and 419 fraud in Nigeria, Felicia Smith (2007) demonstrates how Pentecostalism narrows the sphere of public morality to individual behaviour (cf. Maxwell 1998). Another Africanist anthropologist, Gifford (2004, 167–168), draws the implication that the Pentecostal emphasis on personal morality and evangelism distracts from questions of service deliver— "only the Word of God can change society for the better and not governments." This critique of the state is grounded in Christian discourses of the sinfulness or moral rectitude of individuals who work within the state. In this line of thinking, reform of the corrupt state is imagined as a project of redeeming the sinful individuals who constitute (or "personate" the state [Golub 2014]).

Pentecostal engagements with the state contest the state's legitimacy as a producer and manager of public values (Marshall-Fratani 2001). This contest is imagined as a global spiritual battle against the forces of Satan, allowing local concerns and cosmologies to be drawn into an intensified experience of conflict. Such "spiritual warfare" can revitalize local non-Christian religious traditions and elevate traditional spirits into minions of Satan (Meyer 1999; Piot 2010; Robbins 2004b). Jorgensen (2005) explains how "Third Wave" Christian evangelism divides the world into nations and regions that then become a focus of its spiritual warfare and revivalist activities. The nation becomes a battleground where Christianity and locally embedded demons fight over the nation and its people.

Working from a similar paradigm, *U-Vistract News* (2001) explained PNG's lowly economic position not only as the work of the Devil but also as a result of not having God as "our centre of focus in order for social, economic and spiritual prosperity." This communal failure to be faithful to God was also applied to individual investors, who were told that they would not receive their payouts unless they repented and led godly lives. I argue that this intense Christian moral surveillance gave U-Vistract investors permission to ignore the many official warnings against the fast money schemes that came from secular authorities whose motives were easy to cast as corrupt, greedy, or jealous.

Negative Nationalism as Dependency

The "negative nationalism" Robbins describes focuses on lack of self-control, predominantly in terms of conservative Christian reinterpretations of willfulness. This reflects the primacy of religion in the Urapmin world and the potential of Christianity to redeem Urapmin from their subaltern moral and economic status (Robbins 2004a, 171ff). For those more embedded in capitalist market cultures within PNG, negative nationalism reflects different types of national moral failings in the light of imagined virtues that equip citizens for success in the modern economy. Martin's Tolai informant described the success of "big shots" in terms of money power (2007, 293), characterized by proprietorship of the self and the ability to rely on oneself for resources. Yet big shots are also disparaged as self-centered, not conforming to expectations of sharing. These modern day class-based dilemmas are a problem of moral equivalence that Burridge (1995) identified as the underlying social desire of cargo cults and originally applied to the racial inequalities of colonial rule. However, in contemporary negative nationalist discourse, colonial racism is turned in on the nation itself and read as an inherent moral failing.

Moral concerns about the failure of the national character often focus on "dependency." In something of a popular Washington Consensus manifesto, "Jay Pee Gee," in a letter to the *National* ("Handout Mentality Aids Dependency," February 5, 2007) traces the theme of dependency from national dependency on aid donors to the patronage of politicians and "elites." He decries expectations that government should have a role in social well-being and dismisses any government capacity to resolve social and economic issues:

> Most of our politicians hand out money, willingly or unwillingly, to win votes and the admiration of the people.... Consequently the voters feel they have a right to expect cash and other gifts.
> This adds to the tendency by politicians to commit corruption to sustain themselves.
> Many Papua New Guineans do not even bother to seek employment because they feel that they are entitled to depend on their well-off *wantoks* for survival ...
> The handout mentality must be stopped because it only makes people become dependent.

Like Balthasar and Rebecca later in this chapter, Jay Pee Gee understands government primarily in terms of direct patronage, but he regards these dependency-based relationships as generative of corruption.

Papua New Guinea's thick social ties are implicated in dependency through the discourse of *wantok*. As Schram (2015, 15–16) points out "wantok is more than simply a practice, new or old, but it is also a discourse people use to analyze their own practices." For PNG's working class, this discourse is laden with concerns about the economic threat that wantoks pose to household budgets. These sentiments are routinely echoed in "working class" discourse by wealthy Papua New Guineans (Gewertz and Errington 1999, 58), by village "big shots" (K. Martin 2007, 297), or by NGOs (West 2006, 171–173) and are even formalized in the popular Personal Viability self-help course (Bainton and Cox 2009; Bainton 2010, 2011) and by Papua New Guinean academics (Okole 2003, 58–60).[2] This can even undermine the efforts of people to become proprietors of themselves. Jay Pee Gee in the letter quoted earlier exhorts "elites" to "educate and discipline" their importuning wantoks, lest they have their ability to "improve themselves" constrained. The failure to exercise the necessary personal discipline is the root cause of corruption.

Wantoks are not the only social grounds of dependency. Royalties from resource developments based on claims to land ownership may also foster the moral peril unproductive national subjects who expect windfall payments without hard work. Port Moresby Governor Powes Parkop (2009) even accused the PNG state of "promoting the culture of fast money scheme (sic)" through incorporated land groups and other bodies established to receive mining benefits (Filer 2007), the logic being that such mechanisms discourage people from working the land themselves and create expectations of wealth without work. The critique of the nation thus provides a site for projecting a moral critique of possessive individualism and so advances the possessive individual (Sykes 2007b) as a citizen within a personified nation that fails to act as a possessive individual.

These ideas therefore constitute a "neoliberal negative nationalism" focused on the failings of Papua New Guineans to integrate into the imagined norms of the global economy. In the next chapter, I discuss how U-Vistract drew on these anxieties about dependency in constructing a global scale.

Winning the State and Redeeming the Nation

Alongside disciplining or demonizing the unregenerate nation and its institutions is a parallel project of colonizing the state and accessing its resources (Coleman 2000). As Robbins has argued for the Urapmin, even very remote communities in PNG have a high level of awareness of themselves as citizens of the PNG state and may even feel trapped in this identity: "inescapably Papua New Guinean" (Robbins 2004a, 171). In this context, Christianity offers redemption from the original sin of membership of a dysfunctional black nation and creates an alternative identity that connects the Urapmin with a white transnational community "that they imagine is far more successful both morally and materially than their national one" (Robbins 2004a, 174).

The state of PNG is often portrayed as a distant entity, irrelevant to the lives of most of the country's inhabitants. Even after a decade-long mining boom, the poor reach of essential services, undermined by decades of corruption, limited human resources, and so forth, certainly leaves much of the country with little day-to-day interaction with visible reminders of the state (Howes et al. 2014). Subsistence living and local forms of organization persist independently of political independence, even in cases where remote people are able to imagine the workings of the state and other features of modern and urban life (Robbins 2004a, 314).

The absence of the state is not simply naturalized and accepted by Papua New Guineans. Rather, it is a source of much disaffection and disillusionment. A well-functioning state is a national aspiration: many rural communities in Melanesia also work hard to try and enact the state through local courts and committees

(Demian 2003; Opperman 2015; McDougall 2016). Sykes (2001) argues that Lelet exercise a moral relationship to the state based on local ideas of reciprocity that she terms "critical citizenship" and that are characterized by rejection of state-imposed hierarchies and market relations. Lipset and Halvaksz (2009, 133) argue that negative nationalism provides a counternarrative that points to inconsistencies and shortcomings within the national polity. Constitutional ideals of egalitarian national development are seen to have been betrayed by corrupt and immoral politicians, even in remote corners of the country (Robbins 2004; Clark 1997). This critique of the state often extends into a critique of the nation, as Robbins has argued (Robbins 1998; 2004a). This critique often finds its way into mass media such as daily newspapers (Foster 2002a). Below is a typical example: "Papua New Guineans are used to promises. In fact they will tell you that they have been fed with promises after promises from politicians for the last 30 or so years that today their stomachs are really full. Too full that many people around the country today have lost their trust and confidence in the Government system, that they want to have nothing to do with the Government" (*Post-Courier* August 10, 2011).

Whatever the state of the state; whatever the divisions between ethnic groups within PNG; and however primary local identifications may be, there is also a widespread and vigorous articulation of the nation, often characterized by vigorous discussion of corruption and expressions of disillusionment. This is so widespread as to be a key part of the national "cultural intimacy" (Hertzfeld 2005). Jacobsen's (1995) argument about the role of the state as the creator and maintainer of national traditions is then reversed for PNG as dissatisfaction with the failing state gives rise to negative national traditions.

As Christians, many Papua New Guineans have strong feelings of vocation in their professional expertise and work (Weber 1999). In the PNG context, this vocation is not oriented towards personal fulfilment so much as a commitment to national development. As noted in the previous chapter, even Victor's "prosperity as freedom" is exercised in the delivery of public medical care. However, for many others without a strong belief in the legitimacy of the state, this commitment is often displaced onto church activities and institutions. In Pentecostal and other evangelical traditions, which emphasize the priesthood of all believers, professionals typically rise into lay leadership. Each member brings their secular vocation into the community and places their skills and a proportion of their income at the church's disposal.

Like the discipline of tithing discussed in the previous chapter, the Pentecostal vocation represents a spiritual submission that will be rewarded with further success. However, the Pentecostal life of prosperity is also coopted into the project of evangelization and expansion that are paramount cultural values of the movement (Robbins 2004b). A related Pentecostal trend develops traditional ideas of vocation by seeking to "shape the nation in their own image, to accomplish their project of a Christian nation" (Roca 2007, 322). Because of their assumed moral superiority, Christian professionals have a unique mission to guide the nation (D. J. Smith 2007). Bill Skate, seeking legitimacy after losing the prime ministership in 2000 (Gibbs 2005),[3] echoed these sentiments at a Christian meeting reported by the *Post-Courier* on September 25, 2001: "Opposition Leader Bill Skate yesterday urged all Christians "to rise up and become politicians, prime ministers and departmental heads, as the ones now in office were liars and a bunch of hypocrites.... He said "wicked people" were running the nation and called on Christians to show that there was hope at the end of the day. He urged all Christians to put Jesus Christ as the head of the nation and as the "bridge" to growth and prosperity."

As noted in the previous chapter, Pentecostals have succeeded in attracting successful people, in turn establishing informal networks within government bureaucracies and other centers of power: "this thing was heavy in Air Niugini" as Jackson noted. Having born-again Christians in positions of influence begins to realign state institutions towards church goals, especially evangelism (Coleman 2000). From here come arguments that the state should pay tithes to the churches (and not that churches should pay taxes to the state).

While Christian capture of the state might seem to be an inappropriate sectarian ambition, Pentecostals believe they have peoples' best interests at heart. The project of placing Christians in key positions is not simply nepotism but a necessary step towards rectifying the corruption, poverty, and misfortune that beset the nation. Once the nation undergoes the conversion expected of individual believers, placing "Jesus Christ as the head of the nation," God's blessing will be restored and everyone will flourish again. The personal discipline that Christians work on in their projects of proper governance of the self are applied to the nation as a whole. As O'Neill writes of Guatemalan Pentecostals, "The active Christian citizen shoulders an accountability for himself or herself but also the larger responsibility for the production of the nation" (O'Neill 2010, 83).

"Our senior pastor was the heavyweight behind Noah Musingku"

As the following story makes apparent, Musingku and his cronies successfully used U-Vistract's Christian reputation to override concerns about fraud within Pentecostal churches. Jackson's story below is of a dutiful Christian bureaucrat ostracized for defending church and national financial systems against a Christian network that would appropriate money for church purposes, regardless of any improprieties. Jackson works for BPNG and was also an elder of the Christian Life Centre (CLC), one of Port Moresby's largest Pentecostal churches. The CLC had several influential members, including high-level public servants and businessmen. Other Pentecostal congregations in Port Moresby had similar constituents, as did mainline congregations associated with U-Vistract and

Money Rain. Jackson's tells a story of betrayal: he had placed his professional skills at the disposal of the congregation and risen into a leadership role, but his vocation as a financial manager was not respected by the pastors and he was effectively excommunicated:

> During 1998–99, the money schemes were more at an underground level. I got all these messages from my nephew, so I raised it at the bank to draw BPNG's attention. They were just sitting on it. They weren't doing anything then. I knew who the people were. Our senior pastor was the heavyweight behind Noah Musingku. He and another pastor were using the pulpit to promote U-Vistract.
>
> There was an elders' meeting in early December on a Wednesday evening. We went to the church and were talking through issues and we came to the investments of the church. So the senior pastor raised the issue of investing in Noah Musingku's U-Vistract. I said, "Can I make a comment because I've been hearing things from my nephew and others?" I told them I was very concerned about the operation Musingku is running. I explained that this is not allowed under government regulations. I raised the alarm. Some were trying to side with me saying, "This is a serious issue." So they asked me to explain. So I said, "Collecting deposits from church members constitutes banking business. It is my professional responsibility to safeguard this, so I have to discourage illegal deposit-taking without a licence."
>
> They were clear about where I was coming from, so they said, "Let's have another meeting to discuss this further." But there was no follow-up. When I went to church on the Sunday, I could see there was a tense atmosphere. The Sunday preaching was totally different. There was no Bible just promoting money schemes and speaking against those who want to stop them. Some members asked me and I told them the scheme was illegal but this thing traveled quickly that I was against U-Vistract. Some who had deposited their money changed their minds and wanted their money back so they were reluctant to support me openly because they were afraid of losing their money. So I had to push this very hard to try to get the church out of it.
>
> The next week two elders came to talk. We had lunch near my office. I wasted my money buying them lunch! They said, "Thank you for telling us about Musingku. We met without you and we discussed what you said. We came to the conclusion that we will stand with Musingku and support him in this activity." I said, "OK. I'm very disappointed in this decision and also disappointed that there is no transparency. All of you have an interest in U-Vistract! I must tell you that what you've done is a mistake. You've given the church's money to a pyramid scheme and a lot of people will lose their money and families will break up. Their blood is on your hands!"
>
> The following Sunday they preached against what I had said: "There are two brothers in here who are against what the church believes is a biblically sound operation by our brother Noah Musingku." They said this thing is good and made an altar call. "Let's pray for those of us who are not in tune with the church. Who wants to be prayed over?" Then the senior pastor called my

friend over and he came forward with anger on his face. The senior pastor came around to my side and told me to come and stand with the others. So they started praying for them one by one. It took a long time. I was the last.

They came to me. I was looking at him with my eyes wide open and my fists clenched. I said, "What are you going to pray about?" My eyes were wide open staring at him. He was laying hands on people. In my mind, I was thinking, "You're not going to lay hands on me." He realized that I wasn't cooperating and he thought I was going to hit him. I caught him off guard and he lost the idea of praying.

I went home and told the family that we have to move out of this church because it's not preaching the Word of God, it's just preaching about money. So I wrote a letter to them and resigned from the church. They sent my nephew to talk to us and he took us to have lunch with the senior pastor at the Holiday Inn—he wasted all his money. He asked me, "Why are you leaving the church?" I didn't want to offend him, so as the head of my family I said, "There's nothing I can give you—you know why. I can't tell you any more."

At that moment all the best churches all seemed to be linked up with Musingku: CRC, CLC, Assemblies of God (AOG), United Church. Then a young man came to see me and told me he was thinking of starting a new church. I told him I was furious about people losing money after putting all their savings into these fast money schemes. I went along to his church, and my two friends were there from the CLC, the ones who had opposed U-Vistract straight out. The new church is still going, it's the World Outreach Christian Centre.

The CLC elders lost their jobs. One was high up in Papua New Guinea Banking Corporation, one was the director of a statutory body. One worked for Air Niugini. This thing was heavy in Air Nuigini. The church hit the dust. The board was fed up with the pastors, so they called the Founding Pastor from Holland. He set up a new interim board and brought in an Australian AOG pastor to oversee it. He preached to the CLC after the conference, saying, "There's a curse upon the CLC church because their involvement in pyramid schemes. This is killing the church. The curse won't come off until people truly repent." He really came heavy and hard.

So the senior pastor came to me and the pastor of the World Outreach Christian Centre and apologized to us because of the money schemes. He told us, "When you left the church I felt something was wrong. I have been repenting since 2000." The following week they had a meeting at the church and everyone came to the front to repent, including one of the other pastors. He said, "I want to repent for my involvement in fast money schemes and for encouraging Noah. I won't do any more money schemes but Noah is still my personal friend." The pastors are spared— they should be kicked out. Maybe God says, "I'll treat you differently later."

Jackson comes across as a sober and responsible Christian, without the emotive enthusiasm and religious jargon that can characterize some Pentecostals. His integrity in relation to government regulatory systems in which he works is laudable but is perhaps theologically more at home in churches with longer term accommodations with the state.

Against the influence of the pastors and other elders, Jackson tried to fight the scheme. He was outraged that his warnings were ignored and that people acted behind his back to invest church funds in the scheme. Indeed, the pastors reendorsed U-Vistract as "biblically sound" and Musingku as a "brother," knowing that Jackson had declared the scheme illegal. The final straw came when he was denounced in church. His resentment at this mistreatment has not been resolved by the public repentance of the pastors, nor their apologies, which came long after the exposure of U-Vistract as a scam and the loss of church money. Their apologies were not proportionate to the damage done to the church, nor to the disrespect shown to him. In Jackson's opinion, CLC pastors were responsible for spreading U-Vistract and escaped lightly. Like Victor, he still believes them to be hypocrites. His hope is divine judgment in the future.

The Transfer of Wealth

Proponents of the prosperity gospel have few qualms about how wealth is produced within the global capitalist economy. Risk-taking for entrepreneurial purposes is reinterpreted as "following God's guidance" or taking a "leap of faith" and therefore understood as a heroic performance of trust demonstrating the strength of one's relationship with God. Because the prosperity paradigm is based on abundance, there is no ideology of scarcity that would make the accumulation of wealth morally or spiritually suspect as an improper impoverishment of others (cf. Comaroff and Comaroff 1999; Taussig 1980; Verdery 1995). In fact the reverse is true: wealth is seen and even expected as a sign of divine blessing.

Some Pentecostal churches teach the "transfer of wealth." This holds that God wants to transfer wealth from the faithless to the faithful in order to build his kingdom through the church. This idea is based on an (idiosyncratic) exposition of Haggai 2:6–9 (RSV):

> For thus says the LORD of hosts: Once again, in a little while, I will shake the heavens and the earth and the sea and the dry land; and I will shake all nations, so that the treasures of all nations shall come in, and I will fill this house with splendour, says the LORD of hosts. The silver is mine, and the gold is mine, says the LORD of hosts. The latter splendour of this house shall be greater than the former, says the LORD of hosts; and in this place I will give prosperity, says the LORD of hosts.

The implication is not only that faithful (Pentecostal) Christians have more claim to the world's wealth than others, but also that the church is the only significant social institution—government agencies are corrupt and will be replaced by God in due course. This way of thinking explains why Jackson was treated so poorly by the CLC and why his warnings were ignored.

Some further implications may perhaps be seen in the investigation of a high-level Ministry of Finance official, also an Assemblies of God pastor, who is alleged to have made illegal payments from public funds (*National* 2006). These monies are suspected to have been used for church activities, such as buying land for the new Jubilee University, run by the Assemblies of God. Here the state has been reduced to a resource to support evangelism and church expansionism.

As loyalty to the state is encompassed by loyalty to fellow born-again Christians, ideas of good governance become blurred. Daniel Jordan Smith (2007, 217) gives a Nigerian example of a devout Pentecostal doing business with a politician, allowing him to launder stolen money. Because the politician in question was a fellow Pentecostal, the businessman was untroubled by moral questions around the origins of the money. Smith attributes this to the separation of private morality from secular business and economic life. This example also illustrates an earlier point: prosperity theology allows people to claim money as a divine blessing, regardless of its origins. After all, "the gold is mine and the silver is mine"—all wealth has its ultimate origins in God. The importance of the individual's intimate and trusting relationship with God also foregrounds and prioritizes relationships with other Christians. Indeed, prosperity gospel preachers such as Benny Hinn (n.d.) quote Proverbs 13:22, "the wealth of the sinner is laid up for the just," to imply that faithful Christians need only ask God to receive worldly wealth.

Material prosperity is expected to accompany a spiritually vital relationship with God. This will in turn bless others, particularly through making funds available for evangelism. God has an unfolding plan to gather the world's resources into the church for this purpose, transferring money from the unfaithful to the faithful. Therefore outcomes that produce money successfully are accepted as evidence themselves of divine abundance, except for forbidden areas of previously established immorality such as gambling, stealing, or prostitution.

Balthasar and Rebecca: U-Vistract Insiders

If the prosperity gospel creates a rationale for the concentration of wealth in the hands of true Christians and especially charismatic pastors, then this raises the question about how such wealth is to be redistributed. Indeed this is a familiar question within PNG's political system where politicians oversee increasingly significant proportions of the national budget through various direct grant systems badged as "constituency development funds."

Across PNG, people are troubled by inequality and frequently express this discontent as moral critique of politicians—the "disparagement of elites" described by Keir Martin (2013). Alternatively, elites also bemoan the dependency of the lower classes as a moral failing. This failure is a failure to become the right kind of moral person: economically self-sufficient, having mastered the disciplines of the financial self and thus prudent in consumption. However, I suspect that the ubiquity of these discourses is itself troubling to working-class Papua New Guineans who may deprecate other people's politicians while remaining fiercely loyal to their own patrons. Nor do the majority of people I know strike me as ruthlessly dismissive of the claims of importunate kin. Many take great pride in having negotiated workable relationships with people "back in the village" where they send money to their parents or pay for their younger siblings or cousins to attend school.

The long interview that I did with Balthasar and Rebecca encapsulates much of the substance of these dilemmas. It provides a rare insight into how U-Vistract inserted itself between the two narratives of blame outlined above and presented itself as a positive solution to seemingly intractable problems of inequality and poverty.

Balthasar and his wife Rebecca live and work in Madang town and have family from different parts of the province. They are both well educated and identify as working class in the contemporary PNG idiom. Balthasar works in a clerical job with Madang Province. Rebecca is a teacher. They were initially drawn into U-Vistract because they saw other people receiving payments and have been members for some ten years. They continue to believe that the scheme will pay all of its investors and supporters. Since 2007, they have been involved in organizing U-Vistract meetings in Madang. Their role within U-Vistract has become more central since the departure of Susie Hapoto, the Bougainvillean woman who acted as the scheme's agent in Madang.

Their views closely follow ideas propagated by U-Vistract in its literature, to which they explicitly refer. They make their case with some passion and come across as sincere and convincing, despite their work promoting and sustaining the country's biggest scam. Interviewing them, I warmed to their genuine concern for the nation and for redressing the disadvantage of their rural kin. Indeed, I was surprised by how my own concerns for the future of PNG intersected with theirs.

> Balthasar: I don't know if it is a money scheme. I've only read from the *Papala Chronicles*. In my opinion from the director, they say PNG is a rich country but in actual fact there are a lot of poor people around. So he wanted to make something to help people live an equal life. The founder is a God-fearing man and reads the Bible every day, so that's why we believe the man above is guiding and directing him, giving him wisdom.
>
> Really in PNG, it's very hard for the people. The government system is very hard for the people. They have microbanks but there is no good road

system, schools, health centers. People get about in grass skirts. That's the whole view of the people because they don't benefit from the government system and the banks they set up.

[Cox: But you're urban people with good jobs?]
Rebecca:

Yes, but we all come from villages and we have to think about our village people. So the government can't provide for people. Kids are walking for five hours to go to school, there are no roads. So we invest thinking we can do something better when U-Vistract pays us.

Balthasar:

At that time, the government didn't stop this. If I put K4,000 and roll it for five months, I'll get K20,000—that's a lot of money! I could pay school fees, etc. It's a good system for us. The government, the banks here, they cannot do it.

U-Vistract is presented as an alternative to the government system and its banks, and therefore as a means by which rural poverty and disadvantage can be addressed. U-Vistract has the capacity and will to act where the government and the banks have only a legacy of failure and self-interest. Unlike its opponents, U-Vistract also "has a heart for the people" and is scandalized by rural underdevelopment and signs of backwardness (such as people wearing grass skirts).

With actual payments to investors now but a distant memory, these types of claims come across as very thin. However, the explanations of why U-Vistract has not paid out also incorporate the narrative of failed development outlined above and produce an elaborate conspiracy that is credible because of the high levels of disenchantment with government in PNG. Disillusionment fosters rumor and conspiracy theories (Verdery 1995, 638). The government system has realized that U-Vistract poses a threat and so has acted to stop the scheme from making payments.

Good and Bad Patronage

The promised effectiveness of the U-Vistract system is attributed to its moral foundation in generous Christian leadership. Rebecca contrasts the workings of government in PNG and Australia in highly personalized terms: "There's a lot of money there [in Australia]. Old people, single mothers, they get paid by the government—not like here. Why don't we become like Australians? We see it on TV and in the newspapers. The leaders in Australia are really blessed to share things with the people. We saw the system worked, otherwise it would be happening and a lot of people would change their lifestyle because they've got money."

Australia, as the former colonial power, is still regarded as a model country by Papua New Guineans. Australians are known to enjoy much higher standards of living than Papua New Guineans and are often perceived not to have to work for these benefits (Bashkow 2006; Biersack 1996; P. Lawrence 1964), hence Rebecca's interest in how welfare supports old people and single mothers in Australia.

In Rebecca's understanding, doing things properly is not so much a matter of impersonal rational bureaucracy as personal patronage: "the leaders in Australia are really blessed to share things with the people." Here Rebecca envisages Australian politicians giving generously to individual constituents, rather than the workings of bureaucratically managed welfare programs funded by taxation. Her model is the expectation of direct contributions from politicians to their constituents, a common practice based on ideas of the state as "big man" redistributing wealth in a spirit of reciprocity (Clark 1997, 81; Dinnen 1998, 248; Foster 2002b, 242–243). This redistributive role is often glossed by politicians and their constituents as "represent(ing) the people directly" (e.g., Jacobsen 1995, 237–238).

Such expectations of reciprocity often bring disappointment to Papua New Guineans hopeful of support. If the state is personalized as a big man, then trust can be betrayed (Foster 1999b, 225). This is perhaps most evident in the millions of Kina assigned to each MP, ostensibly for development projects in his or her electorate but in practice having no checks on how the money is spent (Standish 2007). Martin notes Berman's (1998) African work on patronage and the state where economic restructuring has placed pressure on elite patrons who can no longer redistribute favours and wealth as freely as in the past. This strains the "relations of trust underpinning patronage networks" (Berman 1998, 337; quoted in Martin [2010, 19]). I agree that something similar is happening in PNG. U-Vistract's promises of wealth can then be seen not so much in terms of personal prosperity as the provision of new resources for patrons to service their trust-based networks.

Rebecca and other U-Vistract investors embrace the role of Christian patron, a theme developed in the next chapter. Indeed, Rebecca conceptualizes the state itself as a system of patronage. She is not troubled that her altruism might lower expectations of the government to provide services, bearing out Schoeffel's analysis (1997, 8): "People lost faith in the state as health and education services, public works and the administration of justice deteriorated and placed their hopes increasingly upon political patronage and wantokism. Because government is weak and incompetent, people have no faith in it, and their cynicism and recourse to alternative means of self-help keeps government weak and incompetent."

In Rebecca's imagination, Australian politicians are generous and indeed are "blessed" to be so, meaning not that they come from a wealthier country with more efficient government systems but that they have the right moral attitudes towards their constituents and, by implication, a genuine personal relationship with God. These idealized Australian politicians are implicitly likened to Noah Musingku, who, Balthasar says, "is a God-fearing man and reads the Bible every day." Musingku's righteous persona as a humble and withdrawn other worldly prophet demonstrates that he is a different kind of leader, a "servant leader" embodying the biblical type of the suffering servant (Isaiah 53). Musingku's own writings (e.g., Musingku 2009) deliberately play on these images and use biblical language to create an aura of mystery about his person and establish him as a moral exemplar (Tomlinson 2011). Unlike the "pregnant with twins" beer bellies of politicians (Gewertz and Errington 2010, 114) that signify their greed and self-indulgence, Noah's virtuous, even holy, persona creates a strong foundation of Christian trustworthiness.

As argued above, failures of the current economic and political system are frequently analyzed in moral terms. The lack of personal integrity and greed of politicians and public servants allows corruption to flourish, diverting money from its proper purpose. Not only is the current system failing to deliver much-needed services to the people, but it is failing because of the moral weakness of its leaders. U-Vistract established its credibility as an alternative banking system by playing to these views and presenting itself as a Christian agent of moral reform. By speaking to the ethical dimensions of systemic failure at the national scale, U-Vistract addressed what many Papua New Guineans would see as a fundamental prerequisite of genuine political reform: the need for Christian moral regeneration.

This framework is not simply Christian parochialism or naïve inability to conceive of depersonalized institutions. There is an underlying logic that relates to the centrality of trust in abstract systems such as governments or financial investment. As Foster (2002b, 243) argues, embedding the PNG state in Melanesian conventions of reciprocity has actually eroded people's trust in government. By reembedding the nation and its money in a Christian ethic, U-Vistract addressed these questions of trust through a moral narrative, albeit for the purpose of defrauding those who placed their trust in it.

Initially Balthasar and Rebecca (and many others) had been convinced that U-Vistract really worked because they had seen the payments made to individuals. Published five or six years after the last big payments were made, propaganda such as the articles below was a clever attempt to maintain investors' faith in the scheme by shifting attention from unfulfilled promises of high returns on personal investments to the national scale-making project of grassroots development, a project that all Papua New Guineans have a moral investment in. Like many Papua New Guineans, Balthasar, and Rebecca see the country going to ruin with individuals having to bear the costs of development in the face of government corruption and inaction. They believe U-Vistract to provide the only viable alternative, apparently taking the stories in *Papala Chronicles* as factual.

According to the *Papala Chronicles*, U-Vistract will deliver the facilities and roads longed for by Balthasar and Rebecca and will do so by dispensing money to local landowners through fictitious governors and their budgets. While politicians fail to listen and keep public money for themselves, U-Vistract promises to restore community confidence by implementing policies for the "long term well-being and happiness of citizens" (Sapan 2005h). Articles such as these provide spurious evidence that U-Vistract is more effective at delivering "development" than the "government system." U-Vistract mimics, or perhaps reappropriates, the jargon of development agencies by using terms such as "greater sense of ownership" and "effective governance," buzzwords that themselves respond to concerns about dependency (e.g., Leal 2007). Indeed, these are the very discourses that politicians themselves use when disbursing money in their own constituencies and reflect a convergence of development and patronage politics (Cox 2009).

In the next chapter, I show how U-Vistract cultivated an ideal of its members as Christian patrons of national development. Mirroring the benign patronage of Musingku as King David Pei II of the Royal Kingdom of Papala, successful investors in the scheme would have the resources and the moral integrity, the "heart for the people" that would allow them to rectify corruption and to initiate development projects that would address the needs of the worthy *grasruts*.

Notes

1. Hirsch (2007), on the other hand, makes a case that Fuguye attempt to redeem themselves as modern precisely by showing their proprietorship of culture.

2. Writing of reforms to provincial government in relation to compensation claims and development more generally, Okole (2003, 60) concludes with a statement that Jay Pee Gee would second: "Hopefully dependency would then be replaced by self-emancipation from one's own mental siege and this would be followed through by self-reliance."

3. "The two years under Bill Skate were widely viewed as the most corrupt, and the worst administered, in PNG's brief but increasingly sad history as a nation" (Callick 2000).

8 Christian Patrons and Cosmopolitan Sentiments

In the previous chapter, I set out some of the features of the dissatisfaction that Papua New Guineans feel in relation to their own country. Underdevelopment and moral failure are closely linked. Patronage politics is widely declaimed as corrupt (Kurer 2007), yet Christians hope not so much for the reform of the political system as for the replacement of the sinful individuals whose lack of moral fiber is seen as the root cause of the nation's troubles. This chapter maps out the ways that Christian citizenship was molded into a particular fantasy of being able to act as Christian patrons.

Middle-class Papua New Guineans do not feel that they are benefiting from the system in the way that they might once have expected. They are also conscious that there are many grassroots who live in far worse conditions and do not have access to basic services. However, they despair of being able to change the situation, as they believe powerful politicians have the money to buy voters' loyalty and that rural people are so desperate and ignorant that they will simply acquiesce. Beyond exhorting people to vote for Christian candidates of staunch moral character, there seems to be little they can do.

Within this political void, U-Vistract offered a new hope for middle-class agency. With the large sums of money they were to receive from the scheme, investors could imagine themselves as so well resourced that they would be able to redress the failures of development themselves. Whereas selfish politicians are seen to have failed to act and to have kept public money for themselves, U-Vistract investors would initiate a new politics of distribution, reaching down directly to the village level. This kind of rationale is the same as that used by Melanesian politicians to justify the allocation of increasing resources to constituency development funds under their personal purview. Absent is the Weberian ideal state ruled by dispassionate public servants taking expert advice (Mitchell 2002). Thus the vision of U-Vistract investors as dispensers of development is still clientelistic, albeit with a more explicitly Christian rubric shaping these aspirations. I therefore use the term *Christian patrons* to describe the model that investors in the scheme were encouraged to follow, even though the term does not appear in the U-Vistract propaganda nor is it used by any of my informants.

Moral Vision

The construction of a successful economy of appearances (Tsing 2000b) is more than simply creating the outward appearance of legitimacy—it is about entering into the subject's internal narrative of the desirable and the feasible. As Isaac (below) puts it, "They knew our brain, where we're heading, what kind of … system we are in." Isaac's interview concerns the moral vision of the scheme as a Christian ministry and the inculcation of participants' desires such that they conformed to the virtual world of the scheme.

A whistle-blower from within Musingku's Tonu community denounced U-Vistract as a "religious cargo cult" and described the moral code that governed U-Vistract employees. This code proscribed liquor, smoking, betel nut, "unhealthy, unhygienic or non-nutritious food," extramarital sex, and "worldly" entertainment, including music (*Post-Courier*, October 10, 2005, referring to the code above). These examples illustrate attempts to establish moral control over investors and staff along patterns familiar to those involved in Pentecostal or fundamentalist Christian movements. Presumably the "moral torment" generated over questions of willfulness (Robbins 2004a), reinforced by the threat of losing money, was effective in minimizing attempts by investors to criticize the scam.[1]

As Isaac explains, U-Vistract called up not only a world of money but of ethical application of that money. In so doing, the scheme found ways of presenting this vision to its members that engaged not only their desires for more money but also their moral agency as Christians. For investors such as Isaac, this was thoroughly compelling, and his world became dominated by the virtual world of U-Vistract's vision. Describing his feelings when he realized he had been tricked and his money was lost, he says, "During that time I felt that I lost everything. Even I thought that I lost my life also but my life didn't go."

Isaac is a policeman based in Madang. Originally from Mount Hagen, he comes from a business family. Even after losing a considerable amount in U-Vistract, has managed to amass substantial property assets in Madang. Displaying stereotypical Highlands entrepreneurship, he claims to have made his money from sewing waste rice bags into the plastic bilums now available at almost every market in the country for K1 or K2. Isaac invested in U-Vistract some years back. He was introduced by a "Buka fellow," a Bougainvillean colleague, at a time when:

> The police force, I think, we, even some of our big men in the police force like, ah, provincial police commanders, even the commissioner of police— they all invested. Even now my brother is also a deputy commissioner in the Highlands region—he invested very heavily.
>
> I don't know why but some of our guys, policemen teachers, everybody, in the workshop, everybody. They did that because they saw that somebody was, you know, successful—the previous and first people who started. They were successful, so we want to think that we will be like that too. So we invested.

Isaac here describes the now familiar rush into fast money schemes. He invested heavily himself, putting K24,000 into U-Vistract, mostly his own savings. While in the scheme, Isaac exhibited a remarkable discipline in saving most of his fortnightly pay and depositing it into U-Vistract, thinking he would maximize his returns. He also borrowed K10,000 from his brother in Hagen to put into the scheme but when the scheme collapsed, Isaac was subsequently humiliated by the family as they refused to contribute to his bride-price. He clearly still resents having missed out on a wife with better education and higher status, although makes no complaint about his current wife, who is, after all, a tertiary educated woman who helps him in his business activities.

Isaac's standing within U-Vistract in Madang was such that he, along with other "big investors," was asked to make additional contributions to allow the scheme to continue operating even though it had been stopped by the government and had run out of money. His extra money paid rent on U-Vistract offices and housing. Some of these additional collections were supposed to fund a lawyer who would fight U-Vistract's case and persuade the government to release the money. Similar contributions were also collected for additional expenses such as the broadband connection in Tonu that was supposedly going to allow Musingku to bring the money into PNG electronically. Madang's additional contributors are said to have sent in K10,000 for these costs alone.

Moral Visions of the Nation

Isaac is also an elder in one of Madang's Seventh-day Adventist (SDA) churches and describes some of the processes involved in joining the scheme. Below he outlines the kinds of Christian moral "guidelines" and visions that U-Vistract engendered in its members. Isaac now understands that U-Vistract was simply a Ponzi scheme and understands how Ponzi schemes work: Some of them who invested money before us, they were a bit successful. But when we saw that they were making money, so all of us put in the money. And we really didn't realize that when we were putting in the money, these people would remove our money out. We didn't realize it. That's what actually happened. So we were putting in the money and the people who joined first, they were getting our money. They were benefiting.

Isaac has come to regard U-Vistract's use of Christian practices and ideas as deliberate trickery and rather cunning manipulation of his values. He is one of relatively few investors who expressed their anger at the scheme directly and violently. After realizing that he was never going to retrieve his money, he "dispersed" a U-Vistract meeting, firing his gun, chasing away the promoters, and smashing their equipment. Perhaps his status as a policeman gave him a certain license to act in this way. Certainly, he did not need to fear being arrested by police for creating a disturbance. His physical attack on the scheme's meeting may have been the trigger for the chief U-Vistract agent in Madang to escape to Bougainville, as she left soon afterwards and has not returned.

Isaac:

I signed something like, "I want to be part of U-Vistract, in the system to promote and then make money"—something like that. I signed that one. "I want to be in the system or whatever, U-Vistract." You know, principles and guidelines. That's what I said and I signed something. So at that time, the guidelines were, you know, nothing is restricted or something like that. So I, I took it and then I signed it. And I was a member of U-Vistract.

Yes, you were asked to bring some sort of witness or something like that. A pastor or missionary or boss, our superior or something they wanted us to provide. But me, as a policeman, I went there as a policeman so I went in. Nobody authorized this, I went in. So other people, they were authorized by the pastors.

We were issued with pamphlets, some books, information. We were issued with all these things. Yes, I still have it. I don't know if I can produce it because I smashed everything. I was mad. They issued us with pamphlets, *U-Vistract News* all that, additional stories. I don't know. Now I got booked a lot of people, so I don't think I will locate them.

To a religious side and all these: they were introducing to us, ah, it's from a Christian man. It's sort of a religious type of scheme and then it's coming here to help people, the poor people, and then bring the poor people up to a standard where people can live in a same level, something like that. So, at the first place when they introduced, they didn't want the money put in first, they want the poor people and must be recommended by the pastor and all this so that everybody can have the money. Reset the balance in the society (and all these things) where we live.

And the money we get, we have to pay tithes, offering, and then pay the pastor's house, mission schools, and all these things. That's what they told us. We can't get the money and, you know, make problem with the family or, like putting the money into beer and organizing, all this. They said "no." Those are some of the rules where U-Vistract has set aside. If you get the first payment and then come back and get, ah … if you get the first payment and go and misuse this money, ah, with beer and women and all these things, you will never come and join us, you just get your money and go. That's what they said. Because it's sort of a Christian type of scheme where people, ah. That's what they said. So all the things that the principles, they said: the guidelines and all these things, they are from a Christian principles where we thought this was true. They were doing it with prayer, asking in God's name, open the door of the office with worship and all this, you know, we don't know!

[Were you going to church at that time?]

Yeah! I was going to church. I am from the Adventist, I go to church on Saturday.

[They let you in as an Adventist? They weren't prejudiced against you?]

They were, they let me in. I even, I told them "I am an Adventist." They were people around me and they know me, I go to church, even I preach around the streets and all this—they know me.

[Not all of your colleagues would have been good Christians—how did they join U-Vistract? They might have been tempted to spend their money on beer or other things that were not allowed.]

Yeah, yeah. Even they told us, "If you come and go and get the money and then drink beer and all this, there are some people who will monitor you. They will monitor you and if they catch you drinking beer or if they see you in a dark-glass car with another girl apart from your wife and all this, they have to come and report and put you out of the list. They won't be a member of U-Vistract because those were outside the guidelines that we have signed. So if you break it, you are going out." That's what they said.

[So they were pretending to be quite strict?]

Ah! That's exactly, exactly. We were thinking that's it's like belief: it's true and real. Because they said, even they told us, "If your money goes, reach K200-300,000, then you have to go back and start a school or *haus sik* or hospital or even build a church, build a church in the village and all these things will funded. That's what they told us.

So, nothing obstructed us, there was no stone, you know, that could obstruct us from investing or something like that. So we invested because all of us, we got, you know, ah, they knew our brain already, the man who introduced that thing. He knew our brain, where we are heading to, what kind of, you know, the system we are in, he knew already. So he pulled it out from our brain and then he was pulling it out so we would think that it's true. (Laughs). So we acted on it.

Now I come to a realization. Now, I'm realizing that people tricked me (laughs) and then they observe my brain already and my money and everything, they tricked me (laughs)!

[Did you talk to your pastor or other people at church about U-Vistract?]

Pastor? That I wouldn't tell lie but, ah, we would talk. I am also a church elder in the church. So one time, several times, the pastor told us that, ah, "Some of us are investing in U-Vistract." He told us. "So you people are not finding the thing properly and new people are investing in it. That's something against Christian belief, some people are putting it out. So if we find out that all of you are doing this, we will penalize you from church." That's what they told us. I invested, even he told me. He told me and then I heard some members are arguing with the pastor. They were saying, "If he's saying this, what are we going to do now? Are we going to take our money back or what is it?" And then they were conflict of interest inside the church. A lot of churchgoers, especially the SDA church, some of them invested. Even church elders and all these people invested. So when our pastor, a very strong pastor, got up and (we got a lot of pastors, some were, first, directors and assistant directors and then pastors in the church and all this). So from the top down, he directed people, "Some of you pastors are involved with investing money. If you are doing it with a member, I'll penalize the church." These are some of the things that happened during that time too. And then at the same time the government went and stopped it.

Penalizing the church is close the church: the members also. Close the church: no, no church, no going to church, whatever they have until they fix this one. Fix this matter up and then, you know, people who are joining this U-Vistract thing, they have to go out—no communion. They are not following the right church rules so they will not have communion. Something like that they wanted to put in place. So that's what they said. So that's something that happened in the church I attend.

I was frightened too. I was thinking that I must not have to put myself in public. So before my church intervene and find something and penalize me from the church and that's where I walk and all these things, so I was hiding it from my church too. Because I was thinking that I was going to get money. (Laughs). Ah, really! We were doing something that was hypocritic [*sic*].

Conjuring a moral vision was an important tool for creating and sustaining belief in U-Vistract. This began with admonition, setting boundaries, and establishing a negative antitype of how not to use money. Investors were warned not to use their newfound wealth to indulge in alcohol, gambling, and prostitution, all emblematic of waste and irresponsibility, of selfish indulgence and sinful gratification at the expense of others (Macintyre 2008). As is common among Pentecostals, members were subject to surveillance to ensure their moral compliance. Breaches of these standards would be monitored by U-Vistract and offenders expelled. Investors underlined their commitment to this framework by signing a quasi-legal code of conduct.

U-Vistract's moral claims over investors were further established with warnings against the love of money, drawing on Christian spirituality and quotations from the Bible. The scheme deliberately cultivated a relationship of pastoral oversight of investors. Musingku (Jagui 2005a,) warns of an early investor who died because he spent his money improperly and of another "millionaire (who) went through many wives, changing them like they were toys or playthings." Here the scheme is working to reinterpret the conspicuous indulgence of early investors. In the article, a pastor speaks of the need to "seek God's guidance on how to control and use their money, or else they could find themselves in really big trouble." An influx of money could even induce "money drunkenness (which) is also similar to being drunk with power or on alcohol which drives people to do things they won't normally do."

Good investors were not to follow this path of trouble. They were to discipline themselves so that they would be fit to engage in what we might gloss as "development": understood here as a morally purposeful commitment to resourcing communitarian objectives, something the failing state of PNG had failed to deliver for the nation. As we saw in the previous chapter, for Balthasar and Rebecca, the vision of good investment and development was about building roads and clinics for their rural kin.

Some needed little persuasion of the need for moral oversight. Ambrose tells the story of investing in an Australian pyramid scheme in the 1960s when he was working in Rabaul. The story prefigures U-Vistract and includes the scheme being shut down by the government. As a young man, he did not have the wisdom to use his money properly: "Almost every day for a month, I received money from Australian Bonanza.[2] I bought a car but I didn't even know how to drive it! (Laughs). But I was reckless, a drunkard. I was not wise enough. I spent all the money—beer, women. Somehow Somare stopped Australian Bonanza. He was Chief Minister then." This tale of wasted opportunities forms part of Ambrose's "moral career" narrative (Goffmann 1962), where selected events of his life are related "tracing certain pasts to certain futures for distinct categories of persons" (Chu 2010, 62). As a foolish young man, Ambrose had yet to learn the disciplines of managing money and acknowledging God in his life. Now, as we saw in chapter 6, he has had an evangelical conversion that has reoriented him towards a deserving and grateful life of Christian prosperity. In the present this gives him the security of knowing that God will look after his basic needs and in the future he will be blessed by the returns on his U-Vistract investments. Unlike the Chinese peasants studied by Chu, however, Ambrose's moral career is less indexed to questions of his social status before the state and more focused on the governance of the self as a worthy Christian citizen. As we saw in the last chapter, Christian citizenship in PNG has little faith in the state and regards Christians as transformative agents for the redemption of the nation and the provision of social goods.

Isaac also had a similar vision, explicitly couched by U-Vistract promoters as a reproach: he is warned not to waste his money. At the same time he was encouraged to dream of riches but riches that first go to the glory of God or to the benefit of the community in the form of building a church or a school in the village. This is a modern vision of development where Christian citizens take up the role of the state and deliver "projects." Compare Musingku's (1999) exhortation to investors: "For others, Christians, etc., we expect you to come up with noble and honourable projects for which God must receive glory and honour. We will *not* allow you to withdraw your monies if you have a project that is ungodly." U-Vistract propaganda regularly appealed to this vision of grassroots development, a vision that refers back to the egalitarian ideals of local development enshrined in the PNG Constitution, which also imagines the nation as a Christian polity. In this spirit, Isaac mentioned, "resetting the balance" towards "poor people," who should be the beneficiaries of the scheme. The *Papala Chronicles* also carried stories modeling how ordinary investors would use their money in these ways. In an early memo to investors, Musingku (1999) spelled this out in detail for Bougainvilleans: "For Bougainvilleans, priority will be given to the purchase of items used in the reconstruction of our island(s) such as tractors, chainsaws, boats, building materials, trucks, etc., to be used directly on Bougainville. We will *not* allow you to spend your monies unnecessarily on investments outside during this time of restoration of services." These are dreams of a nation of villages, rather than conspicuous consumption of global images of wealth and "lifestyle." Nor is this the kind of utopian city envisaged on Lihir (Bainton 2009, 2010). The scale-making that U-Vistract and its investors engaged in linked the village and the nation by mirroring and addressing the development of distinct rural and urban social and economic classes. Rather than encouraging a dream of mass consumption (and urbanization) perhaps more in keeping with its connections to global finance, U-Vistract engendered an egalitarian hope of meeting modest needs in the development of a rural nation led by the grassroots (Errington and Gewertz 2005; Golub 2014). Here Trouillot's (2001, 129) observation that the "global production of desire does not satisfy the cultural needs of specific populations" is borne out in the form of PNG's national ideals of egalitarian development. Whatever personal greed investors may have brought into the scheme with them is concealed by (and so transformed into) a vision of prosperity for all and a critique of injustice. The materially desirable becomes morally feasible and the morally desirable becomes materially feasible.

While U-Vistract reshaped these visions of the desirable and the feasible, it did so by manipulating and reenergizing existing aspirations. "They knew what was inside my brain, where we are heading," says Isaac of U-Vistract's successful appeal to his Christian values and disciplines.[3] Rather than focusing on personal gain, Isaac was encouraged to imagine his coming wealth as a moral project. He obliged by diligently saving his fortnightly pay and depositing it in the scheme. U-Vistract offered the prospect of righting of the imbalances between townsfolk and their rural kin according to the elusive promises of national development. In doing so, it established its moral authority over investors and evaded scrutiny of its implausible claims to be capable of delivering on these promises.

The vision of becoming suddenly wealthy but obliged to channel the first fruits into rural development is intriguing. On the one hand, there is simple utility to consider: the scam bought time by setting investors like Isaac a target of K200,000–300,000 that would take months to amass. Watching their notional gains multiplying each month and spending time calculating future benefits, investors were less likely to withdraw funds for present use. This was particularly so for disciplined investors like Isaac, who was committed to saving his wages for the future returns promised by the scheme. Meanwhile, these deferred expectations allowed the scheme time to redistribute the remaining money and new contributions either to U-Vistract insiders or to investors who did demand their money, showing that the scheme could still pay.

For Greed or Good?

There is a more subtle moral transformation at work here as well. While the popular press might decry the greed of investors, the attention of those involved in the scheme is engaged by new possibilities for their own altruism. By investing in U-Vistract, they will become stronger moral actors because of the much greater capacity to do good they imagine that they will have when paid. Money is then an enabler of the self (Barber 1995). Like the remittances from Chinese emigrants that are invested in temples (Chu 2010), U-Vistract investors were encouraged to imagine their coming returns as an enduring form of social capital. Contributing K200,000 to a community facility such as a school or church represents a substantial achievement that would be highly regarded by the recipients for years to come, establishing the reputation of the donor as a highly respected moral leader and patron. Not only so, but returns from U-Vistract would be so abundant that the successful investor would be able to bestow his patronage so freely as to banish the specters of jealousy and sorcery that often haunt successful businessmen in PNG (Zimmer-Tamakoshi 1997; Sykes 2007b).

Far from feeling greedy, their motivations are channeled by the scheme away from personal gain to collective benefit such that investors feel already like moral entrepreneurs and even leaders of their community. Herein lay the dilemma for Isaac: when his pastor condemned the fast money schemes, Isaac had to choose between U-Vistract and the church. Both were credible Christian vehicles for executing his righteous vision. This was a choice not between greed and good but between two types of good.

Which good would be more efficacious in furthering Isaac's own moral agency? He could either submit to the pastor's authority or become an autonomous leader himself. Taking action independently would come at the heavy cost of being ostracized by the church and losing his leadership status as an elder. Nevertheless, Isaac had too much money invested to simply abandon the money scheme. So he chose to stay involved with U-Vistract but did so secretly, as exposure before the money came through would thwart his aims and leave him isolated and discredited. Had he received the promised returns, his involvement would have been vindicated by the results and so have justified disregarding the pastor's warning. Isaac's experience thus embodied dilemmas of willfulness and leadership similar to those of Urapmin big men (Robbins 2004a, 194ff).

In Guyer's (2007) terms, U-Vistract was a merger of "evangelicalism" and "monetarism." However, Isaac's experience raises questions for her argument that these parallel movements "empty out the near future." Guyer's near or foreseeable future is a temporal space of human agency, rationality, and planning in contrast to the utopian horizons of finance and Christianity that require faith in transcendent markets or divine will. Although based on deception, Isaac's near future involved purposeful planning[4] for communal benefit—the school or church or *haus sik* in the village—and this required attention to personal disciplines such as saving and avoiding sinful vices.

Cosmopolitan Sentimentality and the Reconciliation of Class

For Pentecostals and many other Christians, Christian citizenship demands not only evangelism but also charitable application. O'Neill (2010, 143ff.) outlines how urban Guatemalan Pentecostals constructed their relationships with rural indigenes in terms of charity. Such charity involves acts of ranking whereby deserving recipients are classified and distinguished in class terms from their donors.

U-Vistract's use of the rural poor, widows, and children as worthy beneficiaries evokes Black's research into cosmopolitanism, "a mode of belonging that implies a heightened sense of responsibility for an expanded view of community" (Black 2009, 169). Sentimentality, "emotionally suffused sympathy for others," is, for Black, the key to understanding how cosmopolitanism produces affective ethical engagements that are not grounded in more familiar forms of social identity based on nationalism or ethnicity.[5] For Sykes (2005), the expression of sentiment is a defining element of the possessive individual.

Black studied the high-profile American microfinance website, Kiva.org, where metropolitan donors from the United States and other developed countries exercise their social responsibilities by lending money to microentrepreneurs in Africa, South Asia, or Latin America (Schuster 2015). Kiva, alongside many other aid agencies, made strong use of personal testimonies from its clients and used its website to link them with the program's donors. The sentimentality of these narratives fostered a transnational sense of social connection that aimed to link donors and recipients in relationships of mutual respect. Black argues that the cosmopolitan identity of the donors was based on affective responses to the sentimental narratives of the testimonies. This sentimental attachment allowed donors to sustain their ethical involvement with an imagined community of recipients that is global in scale yet small enough to allow the intimacy of emotional engagement, even across great physical distances.[6]

Black (2009, 270) notes the use of "familiar sentimental tropes, such as the woman in distress, the self-sacrificial mother, and the virtuous poor" in the Kiva narratives. U-Vistract websites and other propaganda used very similar approaches, presenting testimonies of successful investors as the deserving poor whose lives have been transformed.

The *Papala Chronicles* gave particular attention to payment of school fees by U-Vistract. Several stories described benefits to schools, parents, widows, and children. One typical example focuses on a nine-year-old boy, pictured riding his bicycle (Jagui 2005b). The child's potential as a future "educated elite" (Fife 1995,

129) is alluded to, indicating the rhetorical place of children as innocent agents of the future (Bornstein 2001, 601; O'Neill 2010, 155).

In the case of Priscilla, a young U-Vistract client starting a business (as reported in the *Papala Chronicles*), U-Vistract "guarantee(d) the financial capacity" to help widows and orphans: the paradigmatic biblical deserving poor. Yet Priscilla is a rural *grasruts* herself, providing for her own needs and those of her community through her U-Vistract investments (Sapan 2005g).

For Gewertz and Errington (1999), the middle classes in PNG find the poor threatening. They see middle-class discourse as defensive of private property rights against claims of rural kin on the one hand and undersocialized criminal urban grassroots on the other. U-Vistract propaganda reformulated these class distinctions by portraying the poor, like Priscilla, not merely as morally deserving but as hearteningly capable of achieving their own development without making undue demands on middle-class resources. Through entrepreneurial engagements with U-Vistract, the fantasy of independent grassroots development upheld by microfinance programs and other interventions (Gewertz and Errington 1998; Bainton 2011) could be realized, validating the model and its class-based sensibilities. While class distinctions were mollified, they were not erased. Middle-class Papua New Guineans could still feel "ontologically superior" (Gewertz and Errington 1999) to the grassroots while still retaining a less defensive noblesse oblige, more sentimental and intimate than found within, say, the Wewak Rotary Club (Errington and Gewertz 1997).

Satisfaction Guaranteed for Possessive Individuals

In addition to affective narratives of the deserving poor, U-Vistract propaganda also featured cosmopolitan entrepreneurs whose careers have flourished in the scheme's bosom. This was a way of grooming the scheme's members to be able to tell narratives of their own "moral career," relating their life experiences to broader social transformations and establishing themselves the right kind of middle-class subjects (Chu 2010). The testimonial from Peter Lising, a governor of the International Bank of Meekamui below was used by U-Vistract to show how its investors might be able to live out these aspirations by joining the scheme:

> Satisfaction Guaranteed!
> I guess its satisfaction and fulfillment of life that matters most! I'm a seasoned banker, having worked with now Bank South Pacific for 23 years, rising from teller to branch manager. The satisfaction I derive today from pioneering a new global monetary and banking system based on Godly principles, just cannot be compared with anything else. I joined the U-Vistract system in 1998 as an investor. Then in 2002 I was appointed to manage one of its Reserve Banks. Today as Governor of the Central Bank overseeing the operations of IBOM, I just cannot believe my eyes. I derive my greatest joy when I see our

people increasingly becoming multi-millionaires/billionaires who would otherwise remain poor in the old/other system. I myself am a living testimony and I too have become a multi-millionaire through the system.

(IBOM 2006b)

Just as Kiva encouraged its donors to post their profiles and become visible to themselves and their clients (Black 2009), so narratives like the one above from Peter Lising allowed U-Vistract investors to imagine themselves following a path of prosperity that implied not simply material riches but also professional success and personal fulfilment (Carrier 1997a, 1997b). Base greed for money is replaced by imaginings of individualistic progress and well-being within a communitarian (albeit paternalistic) national community linked to a global Christian cosmopolitan outlook (Cox 2011; Robinson 2007; Werbner 2007).

American neo-Pentecostal prosperity-oriented magazines available in PNG[7] use similar testimonies. Hemry (2009) tells the story of how "the Lord taught Mike how to build a business." After a life of alcoholism and marriage difficulties, Mike is healed of a stomach ulcer and finds the Lord. Giving his life to God, a series of postprayer coincidences guide Mike from business to business and eventually to a very profitable oil-drilling company. Mike and his wife enjoyed the benefits of their prosperity by starting a Christian school and supporting Christian conferences. Their consumption was not self-centered but communitarian, just like Isaac's U-Vistract-inspired vision of building a school or a *haus sik*.

U-Vistract investors were clearly to be proprietors of themselves in the manner expected in theories of "possessive individualism" (Sykes 2005, 2007a). Christian patrons felt that they were conducting a rigorous scrutiny of themselves just as U-Vistract scrutinized their moral character. Like Were's (2007) Bahai, they "search inwards to establish the constancy of their proprietorship over the self, even carefully fashioning a self to possess spirituality (251)." This in turn qualified them to be proprietors also of the common good, as predicted by Macpherson (1962, 204–211, referenced in K. Martin 2007, 297, n6) and Sahlins (2005). Their position of benign leadership on behalf of others obviated any association with selfishness based on private accumulation for personal consumption or risk and therefore the vice of gambling.

This case appears to provide another example of Sykes's (2007b) insight that possessive individualism advances by its own critique. Here Christianity, specifically business-oriented neo-Pentecostalism, provided the grounds for the moral critique of possessive individualism both in the surveillance of the self and as a vision of an ideal society. For U-Vistract, the proprietorship is of a vision of prosperity applied to grassroots development and overseen by enlightened Christian patrons. These grounds of the moral critique imply obligations to society but they are delineated as within the control of middle-class patrons (Foale 2001; West 2001).

Keir Martin (2007) argues that in contemporary PNG there are debates about the proper social context for the possessive individual. He gives the examples of "Big Shots" who attempt to contain the extensive reciprocal claims of *kastom* within ritual exchanges in the village. However, U-Vistract's Christian patron is an incipient ideal of the self, awaiting fulfilment in imaginary riches to come. It is constructed jointly by investors and U-Vistract but has not yet taken a social form enacted by investors and their kin, except where all are members of the scheme and share in the anticipation. The act of investing does not accrue debts to kin[8] because it is a fantasy of future prosperity. It does not yet actualize wealth that would need to be distributed according to the relational calculus of kin (K. Martin 2007). This is because such claims are typically retrospective (e.g., Errington and Gewertz 2005), and since no payouts have actually been made, there is nothing to redistribute. Nevertheless, as we saw in chapter 5, where investors like Martin were drawn into the scheme because of persistent pressure from relatives, the forward momentum of promised wealth has the potential to unite and divide kin.

For U-Vistract investors contemplating engagements with village kin there is no imagined negotiation of the field of *kastom*. Rather, their relationships with the *grasruts* are cast in the idiom of national development being implemented at the local level under the beneficence of middle-class Christian patrons. In Karp's (2002, 87) terms, they become "agents of development" and their rural kin the "raw material on which development is worked." They therefore assume proprietorship of "development," rather than *kastom* (Hirsch 2007), *bilip* (faith; Were 2007), kin (Sykes 2007b), personal property (Wendel 2007), *bisnis* (K. Martin 2007), or land ownership (Filer 2006). In so doing, the accumulation of capital that U-Vistract investors imagine themselves about to possess is imbued with moral legitimacy as a reinvigoration of a national moral and economic project.

The Gender of the Model Investor

In conjuring a model Christian investor, U-Vistract moved away from moral questions about the origins of money, placing the moral weight on the personal ethical qualities of investors, their worthiness before God by virtue of their proprietorship of the self. Appropriate demeanors of patience and faith, with accompanying practices of prayer for the scheme's success, modeled the positive elements of the ideal investor–citizen, while negative admonitions against the ever-present temptations of drink, gambling, and womanizing served to draw boundaries and were used to explain the scheme's failure to pay or to expel transgressors from membership.

Noah Musingku himself emerges as a model Christian man. Many investors describe him as "God-fearing," quiet, thoughtful, somewhat eccentric in his habits but not prone to violence, drunkenness, or womanizing. With the exception of his lavish wedding, he is not given to extravagance or self-aggrandizement. The latter claim might seem strange for someone who has anointed himself king, but

Musingku presents himself (e.g., Musingku 2009) as a humble servant of God, obediently fulfilling a divine plan despite the hardships and persecutions this means for him personally. This evocation of the biblical suffering servant stands Musingku in sharp contrast to the political leaders of the nation who are widely condemned as corrupt and morally weak, not least in relation to the temptations of women, drink, and gambling. Such things are forbidden in some detail (and Musingku's own sexual propriety emphasised) in a "Code of Work Ethics" published in the *Papala Chronicles* as an example to other investors (Memoinenu 2005).

The vices that U-Vistract sought to guard against were predominantly male. Papua New Guinean men are often regarded as bad managers of money, prone to wasteful and careless expenditure (Sykes 2007b, 259). Alcohol in particular has a direct impact on women in the form of domestic violence (Memsup and Macintyre 2000; Zimmer-Tamakoshi 1993; Macintyre 2008). The vices listed, emblems of men's irresponsible expenditure, represent direct threats to household budgets across the country. Macintyre (2003, 126) argues that, despite an influx of money during the construction of the Lihir gold mine, there was no benefit to women because male workers shared little of their wages within the household and their labor was withdrawn from the village sphere, creating more work for women.

Memsup and Macintyre (2000, 26) note that where Lihirian men spent upwards of 50 percent of their wages in beer, women would give a similar proportion of their (much lower) income to church or women's groups. Men's indulgence is counterpointed with women's Christian sacrifice. This duality is also reflected in U-Vistract's literature and practices, raising interesting questions of the gender of the ideal investor. U-Vistract's admonitions against male vices may serve as a signal that conventional masculinity can be contained by the scheme, marking U-Vistract as a place where women particularly can be confident of the genuine transformative power of Christianity and feel that the gains they make on their investments will not be dissipated in male consumption.

Bainton (2010) provides similar examples of moral virtue in the Personal Viability self-help scheme. Schram (2010, 456) also notes Auhelawa disapproval of "eating money" in "heedless, selfish consumption." There are many other examples from PNG of those whose windfall gains are quickly lost in beer or gambling.

Fast money schemes could also play upon male vices to make investing seem responsible. Michael explains how his Chimbu uncle was manipulated:

> These people go around and campaign. They use arguments and language that are very convincing, so people really believed in them. My uncle told me, "K50! If I take it to a beer club, I'll buy twelve bottles and that's the end of it. But if I deposit it in Papalain, it's better than going to a store." That's what they told him. It's not good for my uncle to contribute this Kina but he was convinced through this campaign so he thought it's good to contribute to the scheme. These people are cunning. They can change around to confuse the minds of the people and that's the language they use.

Michael sees his uncle as being deceived by the promise of mastering the financial disciplines of saving and investment (cf. Bainton 2011) set against modern male sociality as represented by drinking beer. A similar negative contrast of gambling and financial investment was seen by one woman as "an act of desperation by people who don't understand how money works." (Macintyre 2011, 115). U-Vistract presented itself as able to curtail these male vices and redirect men into productive and fulfilling pursuits.

These vices are also located within a particular class of men as they characterise undesirable behaviour common to politicians and other "big shots," (K. Martin 2007, 2010) or at least heads of households; men with responsibilities (cf. Gewertz and Errington 2010, 114). Significant are the male vices not listed: while identifiably male, there is no trace of the bravado of listless *raskol* youth, whose vices go beyond drinking, gambling, and womanizing to include the even more socially destabilizing vices of intimidation, violence, robbery, guns, and drugs (Macintyre 2008). U-Vistract is appealing to a type of man who has some respect and the possibility of gaining more respect. He might attempt to pursue this goal through enhanced male sociality in drinking alcohol but U-Vistract warns against this.[9]

The Lihir experience of men failing to redistribute their earnings to the household is replicated in many comparable situations around the country (Koczberski 2007). Nevertheless, some husbands do hand over their pay packets or a portion thereof to their wives in order to moderate these discretionary male expenses and establish their credentials as responsible Christian heads of their households. Indeed, Ambrose, a resiliently faithful U-Vistract investor, makes the following observations, noting that his evangelical conversion reoriented his relationship to his wife and their management of household monies:

> In 1997, when I heard about Money Rain, I put in K2,000 and then a few weeks later I heard about U-Vistract and I put in K1,500. I already had some savings but I kept half. I didn't put everything in. At that time I was working as a Telikom officer, earning about K200 or 250 a fortnight. I budget myself well on those fortnightly wages. I looked after my family, my children, myself.
>
> I became a Christian about 1988. It was in Wewak. I was a Catholic but I joined a different denomination, the Evangelical Brotherhood Church. It's like the Lutheran Church with Swiss origins. When I became a Christian I knew how to look after my wife. I give money to my wife and she gives money back to me.
>
> Women in PNG ask to see pay packets. Men are always the boss. He is the head of the family, he controls everything and makes all the decisions, but the wife just follows. But now people are changing due to colonization. The husband has to change. So I changed my attitude at church. I trusted her to take full responsibility because she's my wife and I love her. She had Standard Six education. In Madang I'm Evangelical Brotherhood Church but I go to the Christian Outreach Centre.

Here risks of male dissipation are curtailed by handing responsibility to the woman as the dependable household manager, a change in relations that flows from Christian conversion. "The husband has to change" is Ambrose's realization, underlining both men's consumptive irresponsibility and the sober role expected of good Christian women. Marilyn Strathern (1975, 321) notes precedents among Hagen migrants in Port Moresby as pragmatic action to avoid male dissipation but without the explicitly Christian rationale Ambrose gives, nor the expectation of transformation.

However, as Ambrose himself adds, this transformation is not simply a pragmatic way of managing money more effectively. It is based on a new affective disposition where a man is expected to love his wife in a more equal conjugal relationship, an understanding of marriage that owes much to the circulation of global images, not least including Christianity (Rosi and Zimmer-Tamakoshi 1993). While not entirely free of hierarchical relationships, this Christian companionate marriage is characterized by mutual love, not male dominance. Indeed, men like Ambrose understand this love as deeply fulfilling for themselves and their wives. Wardlow (2006a, 63) argues that Christian "love based unions" are "an essential aspect of modern personhood." In the context of PNG Anglicans, Tim Anderson (2012, 11) has identified a very similar "move away from the macho connotations of being a 'real man'" to a Christian masculinity characterized by listening and spending time with other people, particularly family (cf. Wardlow 2006b, 128). However, such ideals stand in considerable contrast to marriage practices prevalent across PNG, where violence against women is severe and unexceptional (Macintyre 1998; Jolly 2012), where educated men may profess ideologies of romance in courtship but expect submission in marriage (Rosi and Zimmer-Tamakoshi 1993), and where educated women increasingly reject the enforced inequalities of marriage, preferring individual freedoms and professional fulfilment (Macintyre 2011; Spark 2011, 2014).

U-Vistract offers not only the fulfilment of desire but also the promise of transforming desires from venial male sins to respectable Christian virtues. For women this offers the prospect of men who, like Ambrose, acknowledge that, "the husband has to change" (cf. Robbins [2004b, 133] on the role of Pentecostal Christianity in condemning traditional male activities while upholding the domestic sphere). This is not to argue that U-Vistract has any genuinely emancipatory value for women. If the ideal investor is not prone to the national male vices, he is still implicitly a male figure, albeit a regenerate one.

Women as the Deserving Poor

Women occupy conservative social roles in U-Vistract propaganda. Although some, such as the Madang agent, were able to take on local leadership roles in promoting the scam, the various pseudo-dignitaries (governors and so forth) presented in the *Papala Chronicles* are all male. Gorethy Kenneth, a journalist with the *Post-Courier*, recently ventured to Musingku's headquarters in Tonu and writes of being surprised at arriving to find that she was inappropriately dressed. Wearing "three-quarter pants" was inappropriate for meeting the king, and she was furnished with a long skirt "that looked like a curtain" by protocol officers (Kenneth 2010a). Women wearing trousers or shorts is surprisingly controversial in contemporary PNG and is widely regarded as precociously modern if not rather indecent or even salacious (cf. Zimmer-Tamakoshi [1993] on miniskirts). One educated young woman recently told me of how her boyfriend had instructed her that she would not be wearing three-quarter length pants again now that they were seeing each other. Maintaining this protocol is an indication of U-Vistract's conservative view of women as sexually abstemious and obedient mothers.

Women rarely feature in U-Vistract propaganda leaflets. When they do, it is as recipients of largesse or as microentrepreneurs. These roles for women are typical of the ways the male elite of PNG marginalize women's interests by consistently promoting a "myth of chaste and selfless village women contrasting with sexually promiscuous Westernized women living in selfish abundance in town" (Zimmer-Tamakoshi 1993, 62). Within this gendered national framework, also shared by a large number of urban and rural women, good women exhibit the disciplines of good housekeeping, including thrift (M. Strathern 1999, 93). As national consumers, women should not waste money on frivolous personal expenditure such as Western fashions but should take pride in channeling their available resources into the family (Zimmer-Tamakoshi 1993, 84).

In the article "Women Helpers at Equal Par with Spouces[sic]" in the *Papala Chronicles*, the author boasts of the scheme's gender equality within an idealized Christian companionate marriage (also affirmed by Ambrose above). However, it locates the potential expenditure of women who receive U-Vistract payments squarely within the domestic realm where women are now able to "decide with authority what they want to buy for their families." The article implies that the women are worthy recipients of this largesse, having suffered through the Bougainville crisis, and so again represent the deserving rural poor for a presumed urban cosmopolitan audience (Sapan 2005a).

Cosmopolitan Sentiments

Both narratives of deserving poor and successful believers were designed to appeal to the cosmopolitanism of middle-class Papua New Guineans. Like Borenstein's (1999) account the Russian pyramid scheme MMM using melodrama to place its investors within a narrative of national hardship followed by prosperity, U-Vistract's use of sentimentality reembeds investors in a new community that will ultimately redeem the nation. This community is based on Christian moral principles, not on greed or selfishness, nor, like Schram's (2010) Auhelawa (Milne Bay Province), on traditional social values.

Schram (2010) makes a convincing case that Auhelawa tensions between ideas of business and charity reflect a "moral metalanguage" that entails a distinct hierarchy of values. Money for Auhelawa emerges not as a threat to the moral order but as an opportunity to remake the community as a Christian society in accordance with these values. The new Christian model is based on voluntarism, not the "obligations of normal sociality" (465). Like the cosmopolitanism outlined above, Schram's Auhelawa enjoy a new set of social relations, "based on an ethic of mutuality and emotional intimacy, rather than respect and reciprocity" (464). A similar mutuality and intimacy can certainly be found in Pentecostal churches and more broadly among other Christians (e.g., Macintyre 2011, 105). These dispositions stand in stark contrast to the disturbing lack of empathy towards women documented by Zorn (2012) and Hukula (2012).

As Fassin (2011) reminds us, even the "pure gift" relationships of donor and worthy recipient imply hierarchical difference. The images of women, then, speak not only to Papua New Guinean national stereotypes of chaste village women but international discourses of (deserving) aid recipients where "women" become a category of "faceless, helpless uneducated victim(s) of discrimination and receiver(s) of assistance programs" (Riles 2001, 127). For the women's rights activists that Riles worked with, women were an essential category that grounded their networking activities. Through similar discourses, U-Vistract investors were placed inside the network development actors. However, by evoking affective ties between donor and recipient in the manner described by Black, they were also able to enact a cosmopolitan moral sensibility.

This sentimental cosmopolitanism was highly attractive to working-class Papua New Guineans sensitive to accusations of selfishness leveled by *wantoks* and perhaps discomfited by their own practices of class distinction and exclusion, including the rehearsal of individualistic ethics that relieve the middle classes from any moral obligation to the poor (Gewertz and Errington 1999). In propaganda such as the *Papala Chronicles*, U-Vistract engendered a voluntaristic communalism similar to what Schram describes, and that proved compelling to investors like Isaac. The remaining chapters explore how this voluntaristic cosmopolitanism engaged with ideas of national development, global investment, and Christian citizenship.

U-Vistract's scale-making work of turning Christian citizens into Christian patrons involved three related steps. These three steps constitute a "moral career" for investors like Isaac or Ambrose, creating an evolving story where their involvement in the money scheme becomes a narrative of personal moral growth that culminates in aspirations of fulfilling the promises of national development. First, financial investment was rendered as a Christian moral field requiring high ethical standards of those wanting to participate. Second, the teleological end of investment was shifted from self-centered personal gain to a rejuvenation of national development. Third, the scheme cultivated the right moral sentiments in relation to the deserving poor, moving obligations to rural kin from being an ever-present encumbrance to a more purposeful act of charity exercised along class ranking (O'Neill 2010, 159). In cultivating these cosmopolitan sentiments, middle-class investors could resituate themselves in relation to two troubling aspects of their class status. On the one hand, their charitable intentions provided a riposte to the grassroots' disparagement of elites as selfish. On the other hand, their doubts about having mastered modernity were allayed by their ability to replicate the kinds of dispositions modeled in international Pentecostal literature and reconfirmed in their own urban Christian communities.

Notes

1. Compare Morauta (1974), who mentions a Madang cult where failure to produce money was attributed to unconfessed sin and resentment.

2. Stent (1977, 196) mentions Australian Bonanza: "a chain letter racket run from Sydney and almost everybody in the Maprik Sub-District had been involved in it."

3. Stasch (2008) notes a similar case among Korowai where claims to know what people think are also statements of moral authority.

4. Verdery (1995, 642–643) mentions "near future" planning: "With Caritas, people could plan an economic future different from the past. They could buy consumer goods not otherwise affordable, could obtain tractors and plows for working newly acquired land or trucks for transporting goods to make extra money, or could at least contemplate doing these things."

5. Gewertz and Errington (1996, 487) argue a similar case for the charismatic Catholic fellowship group Antioch, which was characterized by "a subjectivity that elicited responses of empathetic identification."

6. Dolan, however, critiques such connections in the free trade sector. She argues that the promised egalitarian relationships between producers and consumers are hardly realized and that patron-client relationships more accurately characterize the industry (2008, 280).

7. *Believer's Voice of Victory* is routinely distributed by Pentecostal staff at Modilon Hospital in Madang (cf. Cox and Philips 2015 and especially Street 2014, on the influence of Christianity on clinical practice at this hospital).

8. Isaac provides an exception here as he borrowed a substantial amount from his brother and lost it to the scheme.

9. Powerful men may have access to guns and even paramilitary groups (Macintyre 2008), but the point here is that, unlike street criminals, powerful patrons do not wield weapons personally in acts of violence.

9 "Some of Us Are Fed Up of Banks!"

From the virtual moral world of Christian patrons explored in the previous chapter, I now turn to how these ideas are read into financial institutions and practices of investment. Banks are distinctive as a highly symbolic type of institution that not only stores and makes money available but is also deeply implicated in the project of development and of nation-building (Foster 2002a, 36–60). It is hard to disagree with U-Vistract investors who claim that banks are an integral part of the "government system." As we see below, banks (along with their informal competitors such as payday lenders) are also part of the experiential "financescape" (Appadurai 1996) of Papua New Guinea's "working class" and are seen as institutions that embody national moral failings. The chapter moves through concerns about debt and disillusionment with banks (and their competitors) to explore ideas of risk, security, and investment.

Banks and Debt

> That's why we got into these money schemes! (but not ours!) It's because we are living poor. Banks' loans are excessive—they're only for the top people—we can't afford them. So we do this—*traim tasol bai em kamap*. We take some risks. (Thomas, Madang U-Vistract investor and Papalain money scheme promoter)

> Some of us are fed up of banks! So we don't want to listen to them. Here in PNG, banks are ripping us, so such schemes as U-Vistract are giving us an opportunity. (Balthasar, Madang U-Vistract organizing committee)

Several fast money investors reflected on their experiences and ideas of banks. Much frustration was expressed with banks, particularly in relation to high fees and stringent loan conditions. PNG's commercial banks find lending a high-risk business characterized by limited appreciation of assets and problems with enforcing defaults on loans. Loans are therefore often issued under very short-term repayment periods and stringent conditions. A housing loan might typically have a ten-year term, meaning onerous repayments through the course of the loan. The vulnerability of household budgets to extraordinary expenses, such as funeral costs, means that even disciplined borrowers may find themselves in circumstances that strain their ability to meet repayments.

The ways in which people envisage the social hierarchy are evident in talk about banks and finance. Banks are not there to provide for the needs of ordinary people. Thomas, a Sepik living in a squatter settlement on the periphery of

Madang town, has a clear sense of the class basis of banking: "they're only for the top people." With no assets or regular income, it is unclear what relationship Thomas could have with any of the commercial banks.

Victor also invokes class in describing the power of banks. "I feel they're running my life," he told me. However, Victor's class position is different from Thomas's. He is a doctor, earning a relatively high salary, while Thomas only has occasional employment as a laborer. Nevertheless, Victor distinguishes his standing from "rich people." Victor has spent some time working in Australia and owns and reads popular financial self-help books bought there. This seems to influence his idea that rich people can manage money in an advantageous way.

> Rich people know how to manage debt to their advantage. For us it's more the loan shark–debtor relationship. If I'm in debt, it rides on my conscience that I'm still in debt to this person. I've been to the bank. I feel they're running my life. It's a big chunk out of my pay. You look at your pay slip and 30 percent had been cut from the bank. I took a loan for about K2,000 from PNGBC [Papua New Guinea Banking Corporation] and I had to pay K3,600—never again! If I take a loan it has to be for a house or some form of investment.

Many Papua New Guineans fear being in debt. In earlier chapters, Anna expressed her reluctance to enter into a loan, and Victor defined prosperity in part as "being free from debt." Below, Pauline, a senior teacher living in Moresby during the peak of U-Vistract activity, describes how anxiety about her mortgage led her to invest a substantial sum in U-Vistract.

> I think people were triggered by the pressures they were experiencing and here was something coming up that could relieve them of that pressure. For me personally, I had a major loan. I had purchased a home and I was, I think I had taken care of just a quarter of the payment. I think that may have been a factor that drove me into this. I was thinking that if I can make money from that to repay my loan in a short time. I recall now, I think it's more that that drove me to invest because they're saying you can make a lot of money in a short time.
>
> [Cox: Did you put a lot of money in?]
>
> I put in a lot, once you consider our level of savings in PNG, I put in quite an amount.
>
> [Cox: A couple of thousand Kina?]
>
> Me and my sisters, we put in, it's unbelievable, it's a hell of a lot more than that! We put in K5,000 each, more than 10,000 when you add us all together. There were four of us. We were working and we had some savings. I can't speak for my sisters but I think it was the loan that was driving me.

Rather than incrementally paying off her housing loan, Pauline allowed her anxiety about the size of the loan to push her into investing with U-Vistract. Her hope that by investing she could pay off the loan in a short time reflects the kind of near-future planning that Guyer (2007) believes is disappearing into evangelical and macroeconomic time. Pauline and her sisters may have been the dupes of a Ponzi scheme, but her account of her involvement shows her thinking of herself as a proactive manager of household finances. As Ewald's (1991, 207) comments on insurance and risk elucidate, "to provide for the future does not just mean not living from day to day and arming oneself against ill fortune but also mathematizing one's commitments." Pauline and others used U-Vistract as a locus of risk calculation and therefore as a tool for "disciplining the future": extending their financial discipline into the future and removing potential risks such as housing debt. Sadly for Pauline, this financial risk management failed to identify the risk of U-Vistract's pyramid collapsing without paying her any of the promised interest.

Payday Lenders

Not all working-class Papua New Guineans have the means to manage their way out of cycles of debts. Coercive relationships with banks are mirrored in the world of informal lenders or loan sharks. These are the moneylenders described by Goddard (2005, 121–148; also Gewertz and Errington 2010, 110 n19), not the informal and rather benign loans among friends and relatives documented by Marilyn Strathern (1975, 332). Loan sharks are regularly lamented in popular discussion and media,[1] particularly in relation to the heavy debts incurred by tens of thousands of public servants:

> 60,000 live on loan cash
>
> MORE than 60,000 public servants are living on "borrowed money," Chief Secretary Isaac Lupari said yesterday. Mr Lupari said these public servants are paying K7.5 million in loan repayments to various finance companies every fortnight from the Government payroll. They owe these companies K56 million. The staggering figure has prompted Mr Lupari to direct that by November this year, Government department pay offices will no longer process loan repayments through the government payroll system. Mr Lupari said public servants could still borrow money "as it is their right but they won't have their borrowings repaid through the government payroll."
>
> He told parliamentarians at the orientation program of the eighth Parliament that 80 per cent of the 76,000 public servants survived on borrowed money. Some were in fact "seriously in debt." He said many of them had borrowed money from three to five different finance companies which charged interest rates ranging from 25 to 50 per cent. Mr Lupari said as a result of high loan repayments, "the net pay some of them take home each fortnight on average is K50 or none." Mr Lupari said one officer, he knew, had been taking home K15.51 home for the last five fortnights.
>
> Another senior departmental head said later that one of his officers was taking home K4 a fortnight with the rest going into loan repayments. The Chief

Secretary said with this level of income, public servants will resort to "other means to survive." "In fact they are forced into doing illegal activities to support their families. "Or sometimes families are abandoned by their fathers because they can't afford to take care of them," Mr Lupari said. He said 90 per cent of these public servants' time was spent outside of the work place, many chasing new loans or looking for food to provide for the families. If they are at work, their minds are not focused on their job, he said. (*Post-Courier*, September 20, 2007)

Payday lenders charge as much as 30 or 40 percent interest, starting at 10 percent and adding a further 10 percent for each per fortnight that the loan continues to be outstanding. Repayment of such loans is difficult and can trap borrowers in cycles of recurring debts. For both commercial banks and payday lenders, high interest rates reflect high risks of default, particularly with larger sums of money that cannot simply be collected from fortnight to fortnight.[2] A letter to the *Post-Courier* equated fast money schemes and loan sharks:

Legitimate payouts must not be cancelled

It's about time someone in authority came out and assisted the police, courts and Bank of Papua New Guinea take a stance against loan sharks and fast money scams. Both types are fraud activities preying on the unsuspecting employees both in the public and private sector and the churches. Fast money schemes get money from the public by false promises of large returns and con the bulk of the people by making large initial payouts to demonstrate their scheme then they fail to pay back any money they receive from their so-called investors. Many of the money scheme operators have made their money from the gullible and foolish public and they have taken your money and fled. Some have left the country and are living off your earnings in Australia and the Philippines.

... A loan shark usually charges interest rates that could be up to 500 per cent a year or more. You public servants who are decrying Mr Lupari's move about these lenders should listen and take a close look at the realities. If you borrowed K100 every lose week and repay K120 in the next fortnight and you do this every lose week, you are in fact borrowing K2600 a year and paying interest of K1040 on top of the original amount of 40 per cent interest rate on your loan.

... Both operators, loan sharks and fast money scammers all survive from human misery and create more misery ...

James Jafas, University of Papua New Guinea (*Post-Courier*, September 12, 2007)[3]

Usurious interest rates also generate a context in which parameters of what might be considered reasonable become distorted. Goddard (2005, 131) notes a lender who was offered a repayment of K1,000 as a promise to secure a K500 loan. Such proportions are akin to the 100 percent returns promoted by U-Vistract and other fast money schemes. As Balthasar and Rebecca indicate later in this chapter, U-Vistract cleverly manipulated these ideas of what interest rates might be considered reasonable.

Loan sharks form part of a disillusioning financescape of high living costs, low incomes, and limited access to credit among the working class of PNG. These struggles are further compounded by pressure from kin for redistribution of money (Monsell-Davis 1993). Fast money schemes then fit into the informal world of finance alongside usurious payday loans; loans and donations to and from relatives; rotating credit associations (*sande*) among women (Sexton 1986) and men (Stevenson 1984, 27; M. Strathern 1975, 329f); informal workplace contributions to funerary and other expenses (Errington and Gewertz 2004, 91–92);[4] and more structured microfinance programs such as savings and loans societies (Kavanamur and Turare 1999). Formal microfinance schemes such as the AusAID-funded Bougainville Haus Moni program were particularly affected by competition from fast money schemes (Newsom 2002). Depositors withdrew tens of thousands of Kina from their microfinance accounts to invest in U-Vistract and other schemes (Shaw and Clarke 2004).

Interest and the Critique of Banks

The flip side of debt is credit. On the one hand investors were typically fearful of being debt, especially to loan sharks. On the other hand, many felt that the banking system was not paying a fair rate of interest and certainly not enough to make a savings account a viable means of getting ahead.

> Balthasar:
>
> [I was first attracted to U-Vistract] because the bank couldn't give us that kind of interest. So I'd have to leave it in the bank for ten years to get that type of money but my wife said it was just one month! We were planning to buy a small car. We were planning only for the next month so we could take out the money for the car but we didn't know the government would stop it. So we said, OK, let it roll over. Until now, we're still waiting.
>
> [Cox: Were you aware of the Bank of PNG warning against U-Vistract and other money schemes?]
>
> We were not aware of the Bank putting any warnings. Only after they stopped the Principal and then when they stopped the Reserve Bank of Papala, then they put warnings. Some of us are fed up of banks! So we don't want to listen to them. Here in PNG, banks are ripping us, so such schemes as U-Vistract are giving us an opportunity.
>
> Rebecca:
>
> One time we got a K1,000 loan at PNGBC.[5] It was for a fridge and TV. We had to pay interest of K800 over six months, so they're ripping us. So if we get K10,000, then we would have to pay K15,000 interest to the bank. For us,

it's a lot of money, so we say, "Forget about the bank!" and we invest in such schemes to sustain our living.

Balthasar:

We don't know why BPNG [the Bank of Papua New Guinea] took action against U-Vistract. I think they don't want us to be rich, so we can work. If they allow U-Vistract to continue, the commercial banks will eventually lose customers putting deposits in, so the banks will eventually close.

U-Vistract was doing the opposite thing: one thousand and one thousand, but in the bank if we get K1,000 out, then we have to pay K800—it's the opposite thing!

The car is for personal use, but still I've got plans behind for five months as it grows.

Because the bank can't provide that kind of interest, so that clearly shows us that the bank is using my money to make money somewhere else. They're taking my money and keeping it for themselves! That's what the banks are doing now! But because U-Vistract is honest—if they take my K1,000, they give me back my 100 percent interest.

Balthasar and Rebecca explain their involvement with U-Vistract and move from their unsatisfying experience with a commercial bank to elaborate the alternative offered by U-Vistract. They had borrowed money for household electrical goods, something they regard as a modest aspiration, but were charged 80 percent of the principal as interest over six months. This high rate of interest, alongside experiences of being paid very little interest on their own savings account, exposes the true predatory nature of the conventional banking system as far as they are concerned. One might think they could have used the relatively short loan period to save for the television and refrigerator and so avoided these charges, but they do not seem to have considered this, nor, apparently, did the bank discuss this with them. Their domestic consumption of such white goods vindicates Lattas's (2007, 153–154) rebuttal of Lindstrom's (1993) treatment of lists of consumer goods as mere projections of Western desire. Balthasar and Rebecca clearly provide an example of "actual Melanesian desires" (Lattas 2007, 153) that articulate with global models of domestic consumption.

High interest rates are explained within a narrative of disenchanted nation-building: as part of the "government system," banks are exploiting PNG and, like government, have neglected their responsibilities to its people, particularly in rural areas. As Balthasar puts it, U-Vistract is the opposite of the banking system: rather than charging exorbitant interest, U-Vistract pays it to its clients. In so doing (or promising or appearing to pay), the scheme acts as an ideal bank would: not "ripping off" its customers but promoting their best interests and giving them their full entitlement. The aim of banks in PNG should not be to make a profit for their shareholders but to finance national development.

The promise of returns of 100 percent interest sets a new standard for investor expectations. Investors like Charlie (below) told me it was "illogical" to leave his money in the bank when U-Vistract was paying out so much more. However, for Balthasar, the 100 percent return exposes the secrecy, dishonesty, and corruption of the banking system. If the bank pays investors 5 percent interest, it must be withholding the other 95 percent and, worse, doing so without telling investors what it is doing. As the *Papala Chronicles* put it, "Whatever investment the people make, we pay the straight forward percentage interest, which is very different from conventional banks which deduct a lot of money from the interest and give very little to the investors ... from the interest paid by the borrower, the bank gets about 80 percent and give only the twenty percent back to the investor or owner of the money" (Jagui 2005c).

Questions of basic numeracy aside (although this may indeed be a significant deficiency of the PNG education system),[6] this logic relies on a re-rendering of the idea of "100 percent" to stretch expectations of what returns might be plausible. Here Balthasar elides rates of return with the question of how much of their investment depositors are entitled to claim. Nevertheless, this sleight of hand convinces him that U-Vistract is honest. Of course people are entitled to 100 percent of their own money, but the distinction between this 100 percent and the idea of 100 percent return on an investment is obscured and then validated by stories of payments. In this way, investors came to see schemes like U-Vistract as paying them "their full due."

Far from being just a rate of interest that was too good to be true, 100 percent now represented payment of their full entitlement, a fraction of which was offered back to them by commercial bank deposits, as if a commercial rate of 5 percent represented how much of their rightful return the bank would give them.[7] U-Vistract rates of payment are then subtly made the norm by which other banks and investments should be judged, creating a logical circle whereby U-Vistract appears reasonable and the commercial banks selfish and underhand. For Balthasar and U-Vistract, official banks are inherently deceitful as they are founded on exploiting their customers.[8] The *Papala Chronicles* explains this as a "straight forward return," unlike the complicated and deceitful machinations of banks in the government system.

In the article "Straight Forward Percentage: No Deduction like Conventional Banks," (Jagui 2005c) U-Vistract takes on the banks and delegitimizes them as "shams." The scheme daringly redeploys the very same language that is routinely used by financial authorities to explain how Ponzi schemes work: according to the scam "most banks do not have any money of their own and only make money from monies put in by their customers" (Jagui 2005c). Here this language is reversed and applied to the banking system as the real scam. By implication, U-Vistract is the true bank and even makes an evolutionary claim to its own superiority (or perhaps competitiveness): "the conventional banking and monetary systems will eventually die out" as people realize its merits and transfer their deposits across.

The idea that "banks do not have any money of their own" shows an underlying immediacy in conceptualizing the relationships between withdrawals and deposits. This is also reflected in the views of other disillusioned U-Vistract investors who explain that the scheme failed because (then–Prime Minister) Bill Skate withdrew millions to fund his reelection campaign, leaving nothing for other investors. Money held by the banks belongs to particular individuals.[9]

If U-Vistract were allowed to succeed, people would not only leave the conventional banking system, they would also become rich and stop working. To keep people under control, the government had to stop the scheme. The (false) claim that BPNG only put out warnings after it had shut down U-Vistract also implies some underhand activity. These are the actions of a perverse, capricious government run by corrupt politicians, bureaucrats, and bankers who are out of touch with ordinary people.[10]

Ambrose, who invested in both U-Vistract and Papalain (and believes the two are connected) reflected on BPNG's opposition to the Papalain scheme:

> The manager of Central Bank has seen the money himself and knows it belongs to Papalain. Several bank agencies have confirmed this.
>
> [Cox: Then why does BPNG put out warnings against Papalain?]
>
> Because of jealousy, the position in the job (he looks after government money). So this is a competition on his side. So he has to try his best to chuck it out or stop it because people in PNG are trying to find ways to find ways to help themselves get money.
>
> In Australia there are lotteries, horseracing, welfare, but here there's no benefit. The government is closing the door. So we're trying to rely on our own efforts and be self-reliant.
>
> To my surprise he himself [the governor of BPNG] was involved himself in Papalain, trying to cover up, just following the instructions of the government. Many public servants and politicians are involved but they want to keep it secret.
>
> The government won't allow it because everyone will resign and nobody will work. When I get my money, I'm not going to be on the payroll—I'll quit! When everyone's a millionaire, the unemployed and students will come up and take over from the vacant people.

Here, as for U-Vistract, Papalain has failed to pay because of the many bureaucratic and procedural delays. The mention of taxation implies a certain procedural legitimacy and gives the impression that the official processes are adhered to. Several fast money schemes circulated fake documentation that implicated high-level BPNG officials such as the governor. This propaganda is repeated by Ambrose. It is also likely that some lower-level workers with BPNG made personal investments in schemes like U-Vistract.[11]

The Bank of Papua New Guinea has been particularly obstructive because of professional jealousy, the fear of people giving up their jobs when they receive their millions, and the pernicious influence of double-faced officials who are secretly involved with the scheme.[12] Jealousy may seem a petty accusation, but, as Bashkow (2006, 136ff; cf. Wardlow 2006, 30–31) has argued, jealousy underpins a moral economy of value in Melanesia based on egalitarian principles of sharing. Bashkow notes that Orokaiva attribute social and economic failings to the inability to maintain social harmony because of jealousy. The success of "whitemen" in "development" therefore implies a superior moral standing and ability to maintain cooperative social relations (Bashkow 2006, 115). This is a more recent version of the problem of "moral equivalence" that Burridge believed lay at the heart of cargo cults and that contemporary Papua New Guineans find deeply troubling (Cox 2015; Robbins 2004a).

Like Rebecca's imagining of blessed leaders in Australia, for Ambrose, Australia is also a place where people have opportunities for access to money that are supported by the government. This reflects the idealised cooperative relationships among "whitemen." By contrast, the PNG government has "closed the door," leaving people to fend for themselves. More intriguing is Ambrose's equation of gambling on horse races or lotteries with welfare. While not from Gende (Zimmer 1986), Ambrose appears to see gambling as a means of redistributing resources. More common is the view that gambling is wasteful consumption (Cox 2014a; Hayano 1989). These three sources produce money without visible cause and allow consumption without apparent production but they also allow a general benefit to the people that the PNG government system is withholding because of its greed and corruption.

Ambrose expects that, as fast money millionaires leave paid employment, new generations of students and unemployed youth will take their places. His imagined position of wealth and privilege, then, is not unjust but will actually create opportunities for those currently excluded from active economic participation.

Transparency and Spectacle

Rebecca talks about the establishment of the "Royal Reserve Bank of Papala" by Musingku. This was an audacious attempt to set up a (pseudo-) bank in downtown Port Moresby in 2002, flying in the face of previous court actions against the scam ("BPNG Raids Illegal 'Bank,'" *National* 20 August 2002).

Although she and Balthasar regard commercial banks as deceptive, something about U-Vistract presenting publicly as a bank (and in a former bank's offices) was convincing to her. This was not simply mimicry of the external appearance and physical location of a real bank. The open and public scale of the Royal Reserve Bank of Papala was a performance of transparency (and so legitimacy) that convinced Rebecca because it is the very opposite of the secretive and underhand practices she would expect of a scam: "We really believed when they were setting up the Reserve Bank of Papala. If it's something not real, they wouldn't come out publicly like that in such a big place in a big city. The Director was on the top floor of the Bank of Hawaii building and on the second floor they were setting up ATMs, they were trying to put in those machines so that makes us confident that he's really trying to set up something to help people."

The apparent transparency and openness of setting up a bank office in town indicate the reality of the scheme to Rebecca. Like Tsing's (2000b) expectation that spectacle is intrinsic to finance capital, for Rebecca, the Reserve Bank of Papala is a spectacle of virtue irrupting into downtown Port Moresby. It is a short step from transparency to other virtues. The public spectacle of the new bank premises also implies a good motivation, "to help people." This "heart for the people" is something that distinguishes U-Vistract, not only from commercial banks but also from other institutional pillars of the nation, including its political leaders. This contrast was borne out in the theatre of the Royal Reserve Bank of Papala, which was raided by police, BPNG officials and lawyers (with journalists also in tow), not two days after opening.

While the Royal Reserve Bank of Papala may have provided a spectacle in downtown Port Moresby, during the early period of the fast money rush, all the U-Vistract offices around the country generated local spectacles as people walked out carrying bags of money. Rebecca describes how her attention was drawn to U-Vistract by the sight of queues of people:

> I was lining up. I went in myself to see what was really happening. They said, "This is U-Vistract paying last month's money." They explained that if you invested K4,000, you would get K8,000 after one month. I didn't know them but I saw them getting cash out, so I had to go in to see with my own eyes to see if it was true. I asked one of them and they said, "Last month we got K10,000, so now we're getting K20,000." I saw their bags. There were some working-class business people. Small people in the village were putting K50 and they would get K100 or K100 and they would get K200 back.

Whatever doubts Rebecca (and other investors) had about the scheme were quickly extinguished by the compelling evidence of others receiving their payments. Musaraj (2011, 90) argues that the materiality of bags of cash in Albanian pyramid schemes made "the abstract concrete, all the while embracing the neoliberal promise of capital reproducing itself exponentially." This interpretation also applies in the PNG case. However, there is a relational dynamic also at work for Rebecca. That strangers, working class and grassroots alike, were being paid only increased her confidence in the scheme as they provided a performance of national prosperity under the new U-Vistract system.

Banks, Risks and Security

Disillusionment characterizes popular discussion of banks. Banks may exist only for the benefit of the "top people" and do not provide loans (or interest on deposits) commensurate with people's aspirations for development. However, this disillusionment is not complete. Banks are still regarded as safe places to store money. They may not generate new money but are reliable institutions where one is not at risk of losing one's money (account fees notwithstanding). Charlie and Isaac describe different aspects of these more stolid perceptions of banks.

> Charlie:
>
> At first it was only Bougainvilleans, then there was clearance for a bigger group to join [U-Vistract]. So it came to our workplace and I was encouraging other staff to join. Because I'm already in, I was promoting it. The ones who got in first were paid, so I thought, "let me wait and see if others get their money." I was afraid of putting my money in an unknown place, so I thought I would wait and see. So when we saw others getting 100 percent, it's a big difference to Bank South Pacific (BSP). I wouldn't be stupid keeping my money in BSP. It's logical to go into U-Vistract.

Charlie is the well-respected director of an NGO based in Madang. He is highly educated and well traveled within PNG and abroad. We met in Melbourne when he was conducting a speaking tour to promote some of the NGO's programs but this conversation took place in Madang. Originally from East New Britain, he was introduced to U-Vistract through a Bougainvillean *tambu* (in-law).

Charlie's initial caution, waiting to see whether the scheme really worked, is typical of many investors. The evidence of others getting their money is compelling, whatever doubts one may have about how the money might have been generated. Charlie's fear of putting his money in an "unknown place" reflects a belief that money is safe in the bank. He imagines money as tangible banknotes located in a physically safe bank vault (Foster 2002a, 42; cf. Peebles 2008, 245). In contrast to U-Vistract's conjuring of the immaterial global financial system, BSP may be safer but the returns are not rewarding. Once U-Vistract demonstrated its capacity to pay, Charlie's confidence in the safety of his present savings in the bank shifted to concerns about future returns. It no longer made sense to keep his money in the bank if he knew he could get far higher returns through U-Vistract, and he knew these high returns were possible because he had seen others being paid. While a bank deposit might be safe, the opportunity cost of missing out on the high returns of alternative investments was too high.

Once prospective investors minimize their consciousness of risks and foreground high returns, the scene is set for a fast money scheme to succeed. This is a key step in any high-risk transaction but it stops short of being an unthinking failure to consider risk altogether. For some, high returns may indeed justify taking a great risk with their money. Indeed, this was the experience of those early investors who received their payments. If the desired end was to become very wealthy, then fast money schemes provided the only available means proportionate to the goal. Investing one's money "sensibly" in the bank would not achieve the outcome of being rich. Therefore, the high risk and uncertainty of fast money schemes was preferable for many, even if this involved taking leave of the security of keeping money in the bank.

Security and Responsibility

Isaac:

We were collecting money. Even I went and collected K10,000 from the bank. They questioned me, "Why do you want to get this K10,000?" My brother sent me K10,000 through my account and then I went and asked the bank to give me the 10,000 to invest and then the bank knew I was trying to invest this money into something else—to U-Vistract. So they told me they would not release this money unless you provide a document saying that you're going to do business with K10,000 or you've got a problem sort of, whatever, whatever. Until we receive this, even though it's your money, we will not release it. That's what he said.

So I went back to the bank and I said, "Look, this is my money. If you don't give me the money, I'll fight you. So I went to the bank straight. I went to the manager and I argued with him. The manager gave me the money. The manager knew me that I am a policeman around here. I was arguing, I was talking too much, I was disturbing him, so he gave me the money. I was thinking that I was going to invest this money and get more money, not realising that the bank was trying to help me (laughs)!

Now I apologise to the bank manager, "Sorry!" When we go to the hotel or something like that, I say, "Sorry. Look you saved my life but I struggled and I got the K10,000. That is down, right in the grave. I did not get any benefit. You saved my life and then I would like to stay like this. Every time he sees me, he laughs and says, "Oh, you nearly fight me and now that K10,000 is down in the grave!" Sometimes we joke but that's exactly what happened.

Isaac had the unusual experience of the bank actively trying to stop him from withdrawing his money. While commercial banks were no doubt concerned about the loss of deposits to fast money schemes, there was no effective mechanism by which they could prevent their clients from accessing their money. In this case, the bank manager seems to have felt some duty of care to Isaac, as a well-known police officer. Perhaps the bank manager feared that Isaac's involvement (together with other police) would further exacerbate the spread of U-Vistract in Madang and make it much more difficult to rein in the illegal scheme. Ignoring the warning, Isaac ended up losing a substantial amount and now admits his mistake. He apologized to the bank manager he once threatened and it is now a running joke between the two of them. He has now learned his lesson and saves his money, investing in property. Once again, the bank emerges as a secure place to store money but not as an "investment" that will increase money. The image of the bank manager trying to "save his life" but Isaac struggling and sending his money to the grave is an interesting image of safety and responsibility but not of reproduction or growth of money.

This story offers another highly personalized interpretation of how abstract systems work. The bank manager was trying to do the right thing in stopping Isaac from withdrawing his money, and Isaac sees himself as foolish not to honor the personal connection they had. From a different perspective, there is no reason why banks should prevent customers from withdrawing their savings, nor do banks have any legal or moral authority to determine what customers should do with their money. However, this example shows business connections that are embedded in personal trust, not detached and disinterested ideals of commodity relationships.

U-Vistract also exploited ideas of money and security. Playing the part of a responsible bank, it extended security warnings to investors, even when they had not been paid. Anticipating large payouts, investors would need to be careful as their substantial payments could put them at risk of robbery. This was a clever ruse, designed to make U-Vistract appear authoritative and official (the appropriate demeanor expected of an expert system such as a bank) while at the same time subtly encouraging investors to visualize the experience of receiving their fortunes. Ambrose, for instance, believed it was necessary for Musingku to hire Fijian mercenaries because the amount of money to be paid would create new security risks.

A warning published in the *Papala Chronicles* "Take Care with Cash" discouraged investors from withdrawing cash from their accounts (Sapan 2005f):

> People investing in new products of the Royal International Bank of Meekamui have been warned to take care when handling cash from their investments, to avoid holdups and similar incidents which could result in them losing money.
>
> They were told that such incidents could be mounted by people from their own communities who may be disappointed that they do not have enough money to take advantage of these investment opportunities.
>
> In sounding the warning, Siwai District Manager in the Meekamui Government, Hon. Thomas Wawoitu, urged investors to deposit monies they make from their investments with the RIBM, into their bank accounts and only carry enough cash for their daily needs.
>
> One is at risk of losing one's money not by depositing it in a fast money scheme but by taking it out of the safety of the scam!

An article by the Bougainvillean journalist Gorethy Kenneth ("I Have Lost Trust in Banks," *Post-Courier*, September 2, 2010) on Bougainvillean businessmen who carry large sums of cash around, indicates that loss of faith in fast money schemes could flow on to loss of trust in banks: "Paul said he didn't trust the two banks operating in Buka—Bank South Pacific and the Nationwide Micro Bank because he lost almost K50,000 to U-Vistract, and as if that was not enough, he lost another hefty amount at a local finance company now operating in Buka. 'Because of this I carry around with me every time when I travel to and from Buka sometimes K50,000, at one stage K200,000.'" (Kenneth 2010b)

Paul and the other men profiled in this article indicate that the *Papala Chronicles* fantasy of walking around with large amounts of cash is actually a common practice for Bougainvilleans who run businesses. Yet *Papala Chronicles* encouraged investors not to walk around with cash but to have confidence in the system by depositing their investment returns into their (U-Vistract) bank accounts. The scheme thereby reaffirmed its own legitimacy as an expert system.

This appearance of legitimacy was rather like the 419 story Keir Smith (2007, 1–4) describes from Nigeria, where an international executive comes to Nigeria, is met at the airport and ferried to a smartly appointed office where he hands over his banking details. By the time he realizes the fraud, the office has disappeared along with the former business partners, and his money. There are differences between this Nigerian story and U-Vistract: the 419 scam was targeted at a wealthy foreigner and was fleeting to the point where the scammers have a ghostly ability to disappear. U-Vistract, however, has not gone away, even if it had a public rise and fall. It has a known physical headquarters in Tonu. Its offices around the country closed because of government action (or else their failure to pay the rent) but not because they were set up as short-term illusions, intended to be dismantled at the completion of the scam. U-Vistract had pretensions to (banklike) permanence and even transparency that reinforced its appearance of genuineness.

Banks and Development

Foster (2002a, 36–60) elaborates on the importance of banks as a modernizing and nation-building project of the Australian colonial administration. However those who have adopted the disciplines of saving promoted by the colonial-era Commonwealth Bank (and more recently through microfinance institutions)[13] have not been rewarded with prosperity. Financial institutions, even microfinance schemes specifically targeted at the needs of the poor, fall short of aspirations for development.

The commercial banks (and BPNG) also feature in popular critiques of PNG's economic system as they are taken up by U-Vistract and its investors. Banks are often thought to represent elite and foreign interests and are therefore in an exploitative relationship to ordinary depositors. Many feel that banks hold back development by not approving loans for small-scale "development" (for example to expand agricultural production for income generation) or charging exorbitant rates of interest for housing loans or loans for consumables. People feel strongly that banks should free up the supply of money, although this is rarely matched to an awareness of the liabilities and risks of default that banks would then be accepting. When the financial system is seen as inimical to the interests of the majority of the people, there is no reason to fear its collapse, certainly not when a notionally viable alternative is ready to take over the functions of the banking system.

Balthasar and Rebecca refuse distinctions between government and private sector (Mitchell 1999, 83–84). Banks are not accepted as independent commercial institutions regulated by government and mandated to make profits for their shareholders. Rather, banks are an integral part of the government system that falls short of its responsibility to deliver equitable development for the nation.

This is not least the case for the National Development Bank of PNG (NDB). In recognition of the difficulties of rural people in obtaining credit on commercial terms, NDB was originally founded "to provide accessible development credit to citizens to engage in income generation to improve the quality of lives of our people especially the people in the rural areas where 80 percent of our people live" (NDB website, http://www.ndb.com.pg/aboutndb.htm). However, many rural people express frustration at the lack of service from NDB and feel that their applications for business activities are not taken seriously. Balthasar captures neatly the disillusionment with the NDB and its failure to support development by grassroots entrepreneurs: "The government is not flexible about giving funds out for people to develop their land. For example, the National Development Bank—its criteria are too strict. It's too difficult for simple villagers. 90 percent of people own their land in PNG. I myself own about 20ha but I don't have the money to develop even if I own the land. I have a forest but the government is putting difficulties so I can't develop it."

As individuals insert themselves into these national scale-making projects, they regularly meet with disappointment. Perceptions of inequality and unfairness amplify this discontent to a point where the narrative of living within one's means becomes discredited. Other explanations are required to resolve the dissonance between the practice of patient thrift they are told will bring them prosperity and their knowledge of elites enjoying far more than their fair share of the nation's wealth.

Cephas runs a guesthouse on Karkar Island north of Madang town. He applied for a loan to rebuild and expand some of his guest rooms. Despite having clear title to the land and good cash flow (not to mention help from expatriate visitors in completing the application), his request was rejected. Cephas remains bewildered about who could qualify for such a loan and is disappointed at NDB's failure to reward his virtuous hard work and entrepreneurial initiative.

For Cephas, his proposal was so solid in its content and meticulous in presentation (not to mention the underlying motivation which he brought to the project) that he cannot believe it has been assessed on its merits. He has seen other less viable projects approved that simply amounted to cash payments to relatives of the NDB manager. I cannot discern whether there is any substance in his implication of wrongdoing. It may be, for instance, that his request for money was set at a level the bank judged to be too high relative to his current income and likely increase in patronage, but these considerations do not form part of Cephas's thinking on the matter. He is convinced that his application has not received a fair hearing because of personal issues: some grudge or jealousy on the part of NDB officials, or just plain laziness and incompetence. These imagined vices are perhaps an inversion of his own hardworking entrepreneurial virtues that ought to, by rights, be rewarded by the system.[14]

Cephas's view of why NDB fails to provide development capital to rural people is similar to the view of the NDB managing director's criticism of his staff, as reported in a newspaper article "Bank Managers Warned against Lying" (*Post-Courier*, February 25, 2010). Both interpret NDB's poor performance in terms of personal failures by officers who are lazy, greedy or at the mercy of *wantoks*. As we shall see below with Balthasar's wife Rebecca, this moralistic analysis is typical of how many Papua New Guineans view the shortcomings of the state and its failure to deliver development. Indeed, personal failures of individuals also symbolize national failings and characterise the dysfunction of the system. This Papua New Guinean dysfunction is often contrasted with ideals of governance and economic activity imagined in more developed countries and forms a central part of popular imaginings of the national "scale."

> [NDB Managing Director Richard Maru] said a culture had emerged whereby managers that were not doing their jobs were lying to customers and telling them their loan applications were being processed when they were not doing anything about them....
>
> "How can you be a servant leader when you are a 'con-leader'? This nonsense must finish, we must have integrity in what we do," he said....
>
> He said there had been instances where bank managers were seen hanging around clients including defaulters and even drinking with them ...
>
> "This kind of attitude must stop. As bank managers you are supposed to wring their necks, not go drinking with them," he said. (Evara 2010)

The above reproach from NDB's managing director reveals systemic unprofessional behavior. His critique appeals to the Christian vocation of NDB managers, particularly through the image of the servant leader, a reference to the model of the suffering Christ. The managing director encourages staff to ensure that NDB exhibits the cosmopolitan demeanor of "caring," something U-Vistract conjured successfully, as we saw in the previous chapter. However, the righteous servant leader is not to interpret this "caring" attitude as a reversion to familiarity. The governance of the self-expected of a good Christian bank manager entails "neck-wringing": the enforcement of financial discipline, not the male sociality of drinking. The failure of bank managers to live up to their vocations also requires NDB itself to adopt more proactive surveillance.

The managing director goes so far as to characterize staff as "lying" and being a "con-leader," drawing a connection between the bank and confidence tricksters. Here fraud provides an explanatory referent. Fast money schemes, based on deception and unfulfilled promises, have become a metaphor that characterizes the licit and illicit financial systems of PNG and perhaps even the nation itself.

"Too Much Nepotism in the Bank"

One letter to the editor ("Too Much Nepotism in the Bank," *Post-Courier*, August 6, 2007) by "JRopex111" complained about preferential treatment of wantoks by bank staff:

> As a customer of the Bank South Pacific (BSP) I've noticed over the past years and up to now that most of the BSP tellers practise nepostism in almost all the BSP branches in Papua New Guinea....
>
> It is mainly happening in all its branches where the tellers tend to give their first priorities in serving to customers especially those who are related to them. The rest of the customers meanwhile are queued at the counter for banking purposes, it's an embarrassment to see the tellers playing wantok system by serving them first. (JRopex111, 2007)

As part of the "government system," banks are institutions that reflect the failings of national character. The unprofessional and paradigmatically Melanesian behaviour of bank staff serving their own wantoks before other customers is no innocent practice but "leads to corruption." BSP, the "largest bank in the country" faces the same perils as other institutions. Moreover, as a Melanesian bank, it does not work the way banks normally work (or are supposed to work in developed countries such as Australia). Given subsequent revelations of fraud by banking officers ("BSP Loses K16m in Fraudulent Activities by Its Employees—Report"; *Post-Courier* 2010), this is perhaps not an unreasonable fear. Nevertheless, JRopex111 moves very quickly from the experience of poor customer service (familiar to me whenever I have tried to access BSP services) to the application of a moral lament about wantokism within a key national institution.

Banks then are national institutions that reconfirm negative nationalist views within the PNG financescape. Banks reflect and reproduce sinful national character and failed development (cf. R. Lawrence 2008). The next chapter explores how the practices of personal investment in international shares offered a pathway by which middle-class Papua New Guineans could imagine themselves escaping the constraints of their flawed local and national institutions, enjoying a prosperous future by tapping into global sources of wealth and its reproduction.

Notes

1. "Bell Rings on Loan Sharks, Gambling," *Post-Courier*, October 28, 2008. Also, Palme 2007.

2. Goddard (2005, 128 and 133) describes village magistrates advising a moneylender to assume a different line of business as his clients borrow too much and provoke disputes over defaults.

3. "Lose week" is an Anglicization of *lus wik*, meaning the week in a fortnightly pay cycle when one is not paid. The letter has been edited for brevity.

4. La Hasse (1992, 484), writing about South African cooperative schemes of the 1940s, notes similarities between savings schemes and pyramid schemes. Some pyramid schemes were known as "banks," while others had names suggestive of economic and political emancipation.

5. Papua New Guinea Banking Corporation, the historic provider of banking services to the majority of PNG's population. In 2002, PNGBC merged with Bank South Pacific (BSP).

6. Michael French Smith (1994, 135) mentions difficulties of one of his informants in conceptualizing large numbers.

7. Cf. Lattas on "full price" in a West New Britain cargo cult (2005, 52).

8. Compare Rebecca Lawrence's 2008 arguments about secrecy in investment banks.

9. This recalls the Pomio Kivung explanation of banks having no money because the Rabaul Chinese withdrew their savings to fund the ancestor figure Akun's visit to Australia (Lattas 2006, 144).

10. Bosco, Liu, and West (2009, 55) offer a similar example in relation to players of an underground lottery in China. For them, government opposition to their gambling on lottery results is evidence that the legitimate lottery is corrupt and that officials keep the winnings for themselves.

11. Blaming banks for the failure of pyramid schemes has parallels in Verdery's (1995, 641) account of Caritas and, closer to home, in riots against the commercial banks of Honiara orchestrated by the Family Charity Fund (chap. 2).

12. LiPuma (1999, 210–211) notes that money is easier to conceal than traditional valuables and extends this association with secrecy to Maring experiences of banks.

13. Compare Mosse's (2005, 118) comments on the moral discipline of savings in relation to development projects in India.

14. Compare the entrepreneurial development envisaged in the new strategy for national development: "The future development focus under Vision 2050 will shift from a poverty reduction mentality to a positive wealth creation mind-set" (Independent State of Papua New Guinea 2010, 51).

10 Nationals Investing in the Global

Papua New Guineans imagine the world as a collection of nations. Through the negative nationalist lens, they compare their own nation unfavorably to more prosperous and virtuous "white" nations such as Australia, England, and America. However, while Papua New Guinean imaginings of the global scale draw on feelings of inferiority and inequality, these negative sentiments exist alongside aspirations for belonging within a transnational Christian community (see chap. 7). In addition to the prospect of being responsible Christian citizens and beneficent Christian patrons within their own country, U-Vistract also offered participation in a broader global scale of finance, prosperity, and Christian community.

Middle-class Papua New Guineans are highly attracted to the cosmopolitan promises of global society and consumption, even if they lack the financial means or international mobility by which they might participate in a wider world outside the nation (Spark 2014, 2015). These constraints then mean that Papua New Guineans experience the global as "nationals" (Gewertz and Errington 1999), a term referring originally to Melanesians who replaced white Australian colonial officials within the PNG public service in the lead up to independence and in subsequent years. Nationals are often judged as not quite the equals of their white predecessors, as lacking in the required professional and worldly knowledge or in the work disciplines that elsewhere are believed to make society function properly. Nationals have unique problems in dealing with *wantoks* in the workplace, where cultural obligations undermine and override professional standards (Errington and Gewertz 2004, 138ff). Nationals then are "not quite white" (Bhabha 1990) subalterns in their own country and when traveling abroad.

This chapter explores how middle-class Papua New Guineans invested themselves as "nationals" in the scale-making project of global finance. The focus is on their aspirations around the personal financial discipline of investing. I therefore explore how U-Vistract shaped those aspirations and created a convincing narrative of itself as a credible means whereby Papua New Guineans could position themselves in an advantageous position within the flows of global finance. In doing so, they hoped to participate in cosmopolitan global society not as nationals but as investors.

The argument moves through three steps. First, I establish the contemporary shift in disciplines of personal finance from slow and steady accumulation based on thrift and saving to more ambitious aspirations for wealth based on risk and investment. Drawing on an interview with Pastor Paul, I show how normalized the idea of investment in shares has become to the point where U-Vistract was simply able to index very thin references to the New York Stock Exchange as a means of explaining how its returns to investors were to be generated.

The second step expands out from this point to show how narratives of global finance and e-commerce are used in a scale-making project that abstracts finance from the means of production and dazzles investors with its imagery of circulation and multiplication. In doing so, investors are made to feel that they are joining a global community. Yet the global can only be assembled from the national; therefore I explore the national scale-making that is implied in narratives of global investment.

In the final step, I explore the ambivalences that contemporary Papua New Guineans feel when contemplating practices of investment in the global. I discuss the moral dilemmas and fear of risks through the voice of Anna, a schoolteacher from Madang, who worries about the environmental risks of investing in mining. This section then goes on to explore another strand of U-Vistract's propaganda, namely its hostility to globalization as promoted by the PNG government and its development partners including the World Bank. The global is threatening and needs to be reformed by Christian leadership if it is to benefit the people of PNG.

From Saving to Investing

Certain consumption practices take on values of modernity assumed by the national state and can even be seen as signs of national progress. Foster (2002a) emphasises the importance of money in forming national and transnational identities. Saving money responsibly has been central to the formation of the nation of PNG since the Reserve Bank of Australia's 1960s attempts at educating "natives" about money and how to save it (Foster 2002a, chap. 2; LiPuma 1999, 204). Similar attempts at improving "financial literacy" underpin microfinance programs in PNG and beyond where a vision of national development based on grassroots enterprise informs saving and lending practices (cf. Mosse 2005, 118).

If the colonial state introduced disciplines of saving money, the postcolonial PNG state enjoins its citizens to become investors, particularly in share floats when state-owned enterprises are privatized (Curtin 2011, 356).[1] The 1999 launch of the Port Moresby Stock Exchange (POMSoX) encouraged Papua New Guineans to invest their savings in commercial enterprises in their own country. The POMSoX website presents its "major aim" in explicit nation-making terms: "The major aim of POMSoX is to provide a medium for mobilization and raising of national and international capital for the long-term benefit of the citizens of Papua New Guinea. POMSoX is important to ordinary people because they can buy a small number of shares in a company and they can be part of a launching of new companies in PNG and overseas. *It is an investment option that they can use their savings in productively rather than holding them in a savings account*" [Author's italics] (POMSoX, 2010). The national interest as the "long-term benefit of the citizens of PNG" financializes collective well-being and places it in the hands of individual investors. The presence of a national means of savings and investment through POMSoX expressly appeals to ideas of individuals using their savings "productively" and even contrasts this with the normal use of bank accounts, which are by implication unproductive.

This program by the POMSoX recalls Peebles's (2008) discussion of "barbaric hoarders" and "civilized savers"—productive members of the body politic. Rather than hoarding money as individuals or families, for the nation to be productive, its citizens must also be productive through financial investment, trusting in expert institutions such as banks and allowing money to flow for the national benefit. Peebles makes the case that the introduction of paper money in the nineteenth century nationalized money and forced people to join a national community as particular kinds of productive subjects. POMSoX too reimagines the PNG citizenry as moving from hoarding money to a project of productive investment that "gets more money flowing within PNG and creates growth and wealth." However, rather than encouraging the financial citizens of PNG to practice saving by embracing banking systems, as was the project in late nineteenth-century Europe (Peebles 2008, 242f), the new financial disciplines promoted by POMSoX are about investment in shares. Saving thus becomes equivalent to hoarding, a backward and unprofitable practice that is also antisocial.

As Peebles (2008, 252) observes, "hoarding is eminently rational not only if one does not trust one's social institutions, but also if one suspects that no one else does either." As was illustrated in the previous chapter, this is the very situation that characterizes contemporary PNG. People's distrust of banks and saturation with ideologies of entrepreneurial business and personal finance encouraged people to experiment with forms of investment. Many were unfamiliar with stockbrokers and other parts of the formal financial system. Therefore, being introduced to U-Vistract through family, church, friends, or colleagues made the scheme accessible and had the advantage of coming through a trusted source. Trust in abstract systems was mediated through these face-to-face social networks.

As we saw in the last chapter, many fast money scheme investors speak of their dissatisfaction with banks either in paying low rates of interest on their savings or in having very restrictive lending practices. Pauline regarded the banks as only benefiting the wealthy. She shifted from disappointment with low bank interest to the idea of "investing":

> Well, in my experience with the bank, I wanted to make money to pay the bank. And then of course, if it was for real, I could achieve a lot of things. So investing in that, yes, I think people were for the idea of investing and some of them, because of their experiences with the commercial banks. Because nowadays you don't get any interest, ah? You just put it there as safekeeping but forget about expecting interest, ah? You're not getting it! So this guy is paying interest—why not get engaged, you know? Be involved with, invest with him.
>
> So, you see, it is wanting to invest. That's the whole purpose for investing anyway. The whole purpose of investing is so that you can gain. So I think that was the big idea: invest to gain. OK, knowing full well that commercial banks don't give you anything anymore, unless you're one of these millionaires. So reaching that point you know that you can gain some interest (from U-Vistract) because your account there is just for safekeeping because it's safer in the bank. That's what we all know, we don't expect anything [from the banks].
>
> So I think the big idea was investing so that you can achieve. So that also drove them to that. And it blinded any thoughts about the possibility that this is a scam. Now, when you reflect, you know, "Oh you are so stupid." You are so silly to not have, ah, spotted that, the obvious. You know, the obvious things like getting profit, 100 percent profit or more than 100 percent profit, you know, within a week or two. How could you not have spotted that one? You were blinded to that from the eagerness to, the urge to be able to be successful. What's being successful? Successful comes from the, ah, investment.

Pauline was drawn into U-Vistract by the idea of financial investment and, like Geraldine (chap. 5), suspended her disbelief at the promises of high interest. Pauline emphasised the influence of ideas of achieving one's goals and being "successful" through financial investment. This represented not simply a new means to access money but implied a new entrepreneurial demeanor of success that also incorporated proactive management of money; the cultivation of a financial self as a properly disciplined and so productive citizen–investor.

Rather than investing in national institutions in which they had little trust in, working-class Papua New Guineans were attracted by the prospect of being able to invest in a global financescape. Pastor Paul reported that he "liked the idea of the New York Stock Exchange" and saw U-Vistract as "normal business deal—the way it's done all over the world;" "normal" because of the normativity of global finance as it is imagined to work outside of PNG. If national currency and financial institutions create communities of financial citizens as argued by Peebles, then in PNG these have been overridden to a degree by a negative nationalist suspicion of the "government system." Like transnational Christian citizenship, investing in global financial products provides a vehicle for "spatial-temporal extension" (Munn 1986) into a greater, more moral, and more productive scale than the fallen corrupted nation of PNG is able to accommodate.

As if a direct shadow of the newly launched POMSoX, a nationwide scam known as Hosava Stock Exchange emerged concurrently. The Director of Hosava, Eddie Aruba Mai, was jailed for fraud. According to the National, Mai extracted sufficient profits to purchase a rubber plantation in Central Province, registering the company on a Singaporean or Malaysian stock exchange at the same time (National 2003).

Hosava claimed to invest in small local (PNG) companies. These included a chain of regionally named "finance companies." "Karkar Finance" established an office in Madang town and took money from investors, promising high returns. Other centers had similarly named finance companies. These regional companies were designed to appeal to local or provincial identities and in doing so created a performance of PNG as a nation made up of its component regional parts (cf. Errington and Gewertz 2004).

Investors were told that Hosava borrowed money on their behalf to leverage returns, accessing finance from international sources in order to get money flowing within PNG. However, profits and economic growth were not the only objectives. Like U-Vistract, Karkar Finance forms had a semblance of Christian moral legitimacy with deductions shown for "taxes, interest and church tights[2] [sic]"—a vision of productive Christian investor citizenship.

"We Knew God Must Have Opened the Door for Noah"

As noted in earlier chapters, U-Vistract's construction of a global scale rested on a foundation of Pentecostal prosperity theology. Within this framework, global capitalism is seen as a means for Christians to realize promises of prosperity and to fulfill God's work. It is a world where the "invisible hand of the market" turns out to be God "opening the door." While prosperity theology is often regarded as magical in its approach to the generation of wealth, in practice many business or market mechanisms are indexed as the means by which Christians attain this wealth. These include investment in shares. Pastor Paul's testimony below illustrates the central of investment as a practice that connects individual Christians to global flows of wealth.

> If God tells us it's genuine, then we invest. I was introduced by a Christian friend. At first I didn't believe him but he said, "I've given K200 and every fortnight I'm getting K100." So when I saw the money, I thought, "It's real." We went down to someone in the city. He said, "Come and see me after two weeks. So after two weeks, I got K1,000 and then the following fortnight, K1,000. It was more than my usual pay!
>
> They told us Noah went to New York and invested in the stock market. He had contacts in the New York Stock Exchange. Because I was getting my

money, I didn't question where it came from. To me, I like the idea of the New York Stock Exchange. So it was just a normal business deal—the way it's done all over the world.

Only today people talk about pyramid schemes. Back then we thought it was a good investment. I didn't know what a pyramid scheme was then. Now I've been educated. It started off very nicely. We were experiencing problems only after two or three years and then people started complaining.

We knew God must have opened the door for Noah. So we thought, he's trying to bring in as many Papua New Guineans as possible to share the blessings. At that time, he was a very simple man. His wife was very simple. He didn't move around, he just stayed in a simple house, not getting rich. Even today people are saying, "Noah's going to pay." We don't know when.

Pastor Paul's narrative of investment is framed as something that happens within a Christian community. From this trusted introduction to his Christian friend, he experiments with the scheme and finds it immediately rewarding. When explaining the source of this extraordinary windfall, Paul does not reference God directly. Rather, he sees the returns as the outcome of investments in international share markets. Hitherto the wealth of the New York Stock Exchange has been inaccessible to ordinary Papua New Guineans, and Paul believes Noah Musingku to have been the face-to-face access point through which this gap can now be bridged. Pastor Paul had the evidence of payment before him but this was corroborated by the plausibility of sharing the benefits of global investment. Moreover, the scheme claimed divine inspiration, and Noah Musingku's exemplary humility demonstrated U-Vistract's Christian character (Kenema 2015). As with much Pentecostal thinking on evangelism, U-Vistract shared a divine vision to bring blessings to the nation of Papua New Guinea. Why would Pastor Paul think that the abundant blessings of the scheme could come from anywhere but God?

For someone who believes in an interventionist God, the absence of a magical or, rather, miraculous cause in U-Vistract's ability to generate money is striking. God may have opened the door for Noah, but it was the door to the New York Stock Exchange. Now Noah has access to this exogenous source of profit, he is able to assist other Papua New Guineans so that they too may benefit.

As a "normal business deal," the global origins of U-Vistract's putative wealth confirm the ease with which prosperity teachings bless and naturalize business activities and values, particularly from a Christian country like America, as well as a broader acceptance of the day-to-day activities of the secular world. As Maxwell (1998, 362) describes Zimbabwean Pentecostals: "a business culture seeps down into the main body of the movement." Nevertheless, the understanding of how the New York Stock Exchange might be a great source of wealth is still very thin, based on financial patter and a broader imaginary of the global economy as a somewhat immaterial network of financial transactions occurring in the electronic ether at breakneck pace.

"E-commerce—The Money Is Invested Overseas"

For working-class Papua New Guineans, money is not simply a local or national currency (Foster 1999b) but is frequently imagined as circulating rapidly through the investment systems of global finance. Global finance offers possibilities for generating and mobilizing wealth, not least through the internet and the current buzzword *e-commerce*, used to indicate that U-Vistract is up with the latest technology. Many investors were impressed by the computers and internet access in U-Vistract offices and use of other communications technology, particularly in Bougainville (Regan 2010, 117). The (now-defunct) International Bank of Meekamui (IBOM) website (www.ibom.biz) has the visual appearance typical of commercial bank websites. The language successfully recalls the self-managing patter of customer service: "Our internet banking service is a convenient, secure yet flexible way to manage your IBOM bank accounts." (IBOM 2006a) IBOM now offers online accounts where (supposedly) investors can log in to check their "e-commerce" accounts, balances of which are denominated in (fictitious) "Bougainville Kina," raising questions of what goods or services could possibly be purchased through e-commerce.

A printed version of one of these e-commerce accounts bears the logo, "Our Bank is God," a curious motto that brings together the scheme's Christian architecture with its technological and financial fetish expressed in its access to and mastery of the internet. Were this rephrased as "God is Our Bank," that might give a better sense of the divine source of abundance intended, but "Our Bank is God" points to the transcendence and immateriality of both the divine and the ubiquitous circulating world of electronic particle finance.

U-Vistract is not alone in mystifying technology or finance. These are intrinsic features of millennial neoliberal capitalism (Comaroff and Comaroff 1999, 2000). Thrift and Leyshon (1994, 323–324) draw on Habermas's (1992) distinctions between different types of power to argue that the erosion of the bureaucratic power of the state has given rise to a global electronic phantom state driven by money power and communicative power. This phantom state is not a nation-state but is a representation of the power of discourses of global finance. Thrift and Leyshon (1994, 324) see the phantom state as located in "world cities." Their analysis seems a useful way of viewing U-Vistract as the Kingdom of Papala: a phantom state without bureaucratic power but claiming money power through its more real (and devious) communicative power, expressed through its newsletters and other propaganda. Indeed, Musingku initially explained the Kingdom of Papala, using a technological metaphor, as the "software" to Meekamui's "hardware."

Through the internet, U-Vistract will subvert the constraints placed on it by the old physically located cash system. Ho (2005, 82), drawing on Tsing's work (2000b), characterizes the global economy as encouraging "spectacular financial accumulation as opposed to steady reproduction, [rewarding] the divestment of labour in favour of financial schemes, and [being] driven by the production, marketing, and circulation of brands and images." This is the same immaterial global economy conjured by U-Vistract and appearing in other guises across PNG. For example, Bank South Pacific (BSP) is currently promoting internet and SMS banking through mobile phones, so U-Vistract needs to be able to match this type of narrative of technical progress and mastery of the latest electronic financial technologies.

Identifying the source of wealth as e-commerce is not merely a technical matter but allows U-Vistract to explain how they have the money but it is not yet available, tangible, or visible. Coronil (2001, 79) describes the "ever more abstract commodification of (wealth's) elements across time and space." The transmogrification of the promised money from once-invested banknotes still materially kept at hand in bank vaults into the swirling virtual circulations of electronic global finance provides an answer to the question of "where is the money?" It is in a realm of international intangibility, perpetual electronic circulation, and rapid reproduction. Significantly, it is not stored in a bank where it is safe but does not multiply.

This is not an ideology peculiar to U-Vistract but is also represented on the Port Moresby Stock Exchange website where bank deposit savings are seen as unproductive compared to share ownership. The imagery of global finance makes the desirable feasible through conjuring an immaterial global scale of wealth creation and circulation.

Balthasar:

The system now has gone to e-commerce. Before, when the director was in Port Moresby, he paid in cash. Now, with e-commerce, he will be able to pay everyone through the internet.

[You must deal with disillusioned investors coming and asking for their money?]

Those people are desperate people. We are patient because we're not only waiting for U-Vistract. We don't just put our money in there and wait for it to come but we do other things, we go to work.

Most of them are not educated, that's why they think it will come just like that. We educated people understand that to set up a system takes a long time. It's gone out to the whole world, so that it will take time to establish. At the same time, it's not only Papua New Guineans who invested but other people: white men. John Green, he's from America and he works with U-Vistract to set up an internet electronic system.[3] He's the one who went to Singapore and printed the K40 billion. We heard the transaction from overseas is happening but it hasn't come yet.

We used to tell them, "You invested K10, K20 but we invested K2,000, so we're waiting patiently, so you have to wait too!"

All the police officers and public servants, they have a similar problem, even some MPs. They put a large amount of money in. They're hiding it, but, when the time comes, they'll get it. The police officers, they joined when Susie was still here. People here are quiet because they're aware that U-Vistract is setting up the system to make payments. It's like any other financial systems to make payments electronically. There was one case of a pastor who put in money, a small amount, to expand his church.

I don't know where that money comes from because I haven't been paid. All I know is they know what they're doing. They know where they've put my money. We just hope because we saw them getting paid 100 percent, not only in Madang but also in Port Moresby—working-class people in Port Moresby....

We can't compare U-Vistract with the banks. If I deposit money in the bank, they don't tell me where they put it. You only get a small interest. But U-Vistract they give 100 percent, they pay! The situation now is that they could continue paying but the bank stopped them. Maybe they invested the money somewhere. Who knows? For us they said the system is in the internet. It's global so they have invested the money somewhere and they will bring it out. It's invested overseas. Maybe we don't know— we're not told where but we think it's overseas because they've gone to e-commerce. It's global, so we're thinking it's overseas around the world.

Notwithstanding the imagery of money circulating rapidly across the globe through e-commerce, U-Vistract members are still waiting for their payments. In talking about the disillusionment of many U-Vistract investors, Balthasar comes close to the elite view of the "cargo cult mentality" (chap. 4) as he explains that uneducated investors expect money to come immediately. Educated investors, however, understand how long it takes to establish a new financial system. Patience, again, is a virtue, but this is not simply about hopeful waiting—they get on with work and other aspects of their lives in the meantime. Educated people work not only to a different temporal frame but also to a different moral economy of employment where their day-to-day duties continue despite the promise of a windfall that will eventually liberate everyone from work. Balthasar does not speak of his work with the same sense of vocation as Jackson, Victor, or Jack, but it may be that this sense of calling also informs his belief that people should continue working until the payments are finally made.

Balthasar's condescension is tempered by his expansiveness: it is not only the gullible poor who are waiting but the whole society, including "working-class people" in positions of responsibility. "Even MPs," included despite their independent access to money by virtue of their position, are quietly waiting for the new system to come into operation. This minimization of class differences caps off the vision of U-Vistract as a project of reforming the nation to the ideal of an inclusive and egalitarian community. This project of inclusion goes beyond PNG, so foreigners, including white men, are also incorporated into the U-Vistract system as it goes out redemptively to the whole world.

The appeal of global share markets as credible sources of prosperity lies in the conjuring of new types of wealth. Financial markets in particular have accelerated in their application of abstract quantification to creating new financial products that are invested with value, even as that value rises and falls with the great rapidly of electronic commerce and new forms of abstracted and quantified risk (LiPuma and Lee 2004). U-Vistract also took up these ideas of trading and even new products, such as Treasury bills for its investors (Sapan 2005d).

Ideas of money and, by extension, the economy and finance are not self-evident (Errington and Gewertz 2004, 6), nor does money circulate in such abstraction, immateriality, and fluidity that it transcends the influence of the actual people who produce, invest, and spend it (Hart 2000, 2007; Ho 2009; Thrift and Leyshon 1994; Zaloom 2006). Rather, money and finance always require reembedding by particular people in particular circumstances. As Ho (2009) argues, finance is not a universal abstraction but the product of local cultural habitus. Financial fraud, like all imaginings of money, will take a distinctive local character as it is embedded within a particular cultural context. That said, there are often competing cosmologies of commerce within cultures, not least in times of rapid economic change (Verdery 1996).

Individuals can and do exercise discernment as to whether they should invest in something too good to be true, and sometimes, like Geraldine in chapter 5, they change their minds, not least in the face of apparent payouts to friends and colleagues. For U-Vistract, the cultural embeddedness of global finance occurs primarily at the national scale, at least for the middle-class investors considered here.[4] Local moral concerns with commensurability are also voiced, but in the idiom of either national grassroots development or Christian duty.

Traditional cosmologies, such as those documented by Lattas (1998), are all but absent from U-Vistract's public statements, the exception being Musingku's invention of a Bougainvillean traditional pedigree for the Kingdom of Papala (chap. 2; Cox 2013). Kenema (2015) argues that for Musingku and his followers at Tonu, the scheme's traditional pedigree has great cultural and historical resonance. However, this appears to me to be a recent development within the scheme and one that primarily describes the most loyal of U-Vistract supporters in Bougainville. Claims of a traditional origin for the scheme have not translated across to its followers elsewhere. Rather, banks become a focus as the institutional form of money and a central symbol of (failed) national development and its attendant inequalities. As IBOM, U-Vistract displaced these disillusioning experiences of national financial institutions with the hope of transformation, redress, and prosperity.

As images of wealth become more abstract, they also become more transferrable. Although U-Vistract claims that its wealth is anchored in tangible and locally situated Bougainvillean gold assets, the scheme's appeal to investors centers on the higher world of global finance that few Papua New Guineans understand. This is not unlike populations of developed countries who leave the workings of share markets to financial experts or vote for conservative parties in the mistaken belief that they are better at "managing the economy." Indeed the global financial crisis exposed the hollowness of this expert knowledge as powerful financial institutions fell for their own sleights of hand in creating highly risky investment products and then revaluing them through convoluted processes that few understood the implications of (Cooper 2013).

Many Papua New Guineans believe that PNG is a "rich country," a view based on the idea that the nation is home to great natural resources. Nevertheless, this richness is not realized. As noted in earlier chapters, middle-class PNG is deeply troubled by poverty and underdevelopment. There is a sense that other countries have mastered ways of making money and building a prosperous nation. Clearly white people do know how to access these benefits, as evidenced by their more affluent lifestyles and more prosperous and functional countries (Bashkow 2006; Cox 2015). U-Vistract offers the promise of making this prosperity accessible to ordinary Papua New Guineans by connecting them to the circuits of global wealth production and distribution. Indeed it appeared to do so in Balthasar and Rebecca's experience and would have continued were it not for the interference of the PNG government and BPNG, both committed to the existing system of global dependency and foreign exploitation under the guidance of the World Bank.

A Nation of Shareholders

Foster (2008, 187ff) offers an intriguing juxtaposition of consumer citizenship and corporate citizenship. Taking up critiques of neoliberal market-based societies, Foster explores how the retreat of the state from society globally has created new domains of public action and expression of identities. On the one hand, citizenship of individuals has become closely linked to their identities and practices as consumers, including moral engagement through Christian associations (Dundon 2004), consumer boycotts and "ethical consumption" (Carrier 2008). On the other hand, corporations are increasingly defining themselves as corporate citizens and seeking to enhance their reputations through measuring and promoting their philanthropic activities.

Parallel to these appropriations of citizenship by corporations is the rise of shareholder activism, which offers the possibility of ethically empowered shareholders being able to rein in corporate practices that exploit workers or the natural environment. This involves a shift from lobbying politicians to direct engagement with corporate executives from within corporate governance mechanisms. It therefore represents an exercise of citizenship within the corporatized private sector (Foster 2008, 189). Such activities may seem remote from PNG, but Foster provides examples of how Coca-Cola has changed its environmental and labor practices in response to campaigns that involve links between metropolitan shareholder activists and, for example, Colombian trade unionists.[5] Shareholder activism provides an additional incentive for companies to act ethically as "good corporate citizens," mirroring the good shareholder citizenship of their investors. Aware of this kind of thinking, Anna (above) decided that she did not want to invest in Lihir Gold because she was concerned about the impact of the mine's tailings disposal on the ocean.

It is also worth considering the idea of a "nation of shareholders" as a development from earlier British reappropriations of Napoleon's famous insult, describing England as a "nation of shopkeepers" (Carrington 1968; Thatcher 1976; Benson and Ugolini 2003). Berdahl (2010, 89) draws on Comaroff and Comaroff's (2000, 304) argument that neoliberalism reconstitutes people as "consumers in a planetary marketplace." Berdahl also introduces the phrase a "nation of shoppers," pointing to the civic duty implicit in mass consumption that transforms both citizens and states. The shift from the nation of shopkeepers to the nation of shoppers embodies a move from work and production to consumption. The consumption-based aspirations of the global middle class include the consumption of financial products, such as shares (R. Martin 2002). These offer a surer pathway to wealth than petty entrepreneurialism and do so as a practice of consumption that reestablishes the shareholder as a consumer citizen who also embodies entrepreneurial virtues—a further leap to the nation of shareholders.[6]

In the PNG context, Bainton's (2010, 2011) account of Personal Viability (PV) on Lihir focuses on the development of an entrepreneurial discipline that will allegedly ensure prosperity (also Gewertz and Errington 1998). At the same time, though, many landowners prefer to act as rentiers, receiving royalties and compensation payments from the mine and often spending their gains in the pursuit of competitive cultural activities that PV teachings regard as unproductive. If PV was trying to cultivate a habitus of thrift, hard work, and entrepreneurialism, U-Vistract was appealing to the widespread desire for windfall profits and for a lifestyle of consumption decoupled from the necessity of labor. The Western retirement ideal of living off income from shares, once thought by Keynes (1936, 375–376) to be "parasitic" and in need of "euthanasia," also promises this dream of consumption without labor. Consumer citizens of a nation of shareholders can feel independent of social security systems while imagining themselves as wise and provident investors: entrepreneurial producers by proxy.

McMichael (1998, 111–112) argues that shareholder citizenship is part of a broader neoliberal restructuring of economies and governments. This aims to minimize state responsibility for services and privatize state-owned utilities and implies a shift away from the developmental state. The market becomes the chief provider of services and the state takes a regulatory role, leaving disadvantaged citizens, who are already poorly positioned in the market, to fend for themselves, trusting that welfare services will be unnecessary because of the supposed economic benefits that will "trickle down" from the wealthy to reach everyone. This represents a shift away from ideals of common good based on a social contract enacted through government services to the "fetish of individualism" (1998, 122). McMichael uses this term to encompass both shareholder citizenship and broader notions of voluntarism, including community organizations and programs based on individualized self-help, not state-provided services.

In a similar vein, Thomas (1997, 219) laments "the withering away of the state" and the implications for "societies in need of health services, education, welfare, and the police." While U-Vistract critiques neoliberal economic restructuring as represented by the World Bank, it does so only by accepting much of the neoliberal project, including core elements of its value system that undermine the vision of egalitarian national development. In place of the failing PNG state, U-Vistract offers the pseudo-state of Papala and the prospect of enough personal wealth to meet all development needs through individual patronage or through payments by various ministries of the Royal Government (Sapan 2005f). Unfortunately, PNG's current services provide no model of egalitarian development, so dissatisfaction with the state has not led to widespread demand for improvements to the system (Cox and Phillips 2015). Rather, people have given up on the efficacy of the state and tend to see access to money for individuals as a sufficient answer to the nation's profound developmental challenges. In this context, U-Vistract's pitch is consistent with current expectations and so appears both desirable and feasible.

Corporations engage in the public realm in ways that transform institutions such as public schools into sites of consumption dependent on commercial revenue as state funding is scaled back. This ongoing transformation of the public realm is more profound than is often acknowledged in much of the weak states literature as it changes the very terms on which citizens and states relate to each other. The state is not merely weak in its presence, but the responsibilities that might previously have been expected of the state and its citizens migrate to a consumer relationship to corporations that can even encompass national identities through consumption.

Papua New Guinea has numerous examples of the state having abrogated to mining companies its developmental responsibilities for providing services to remote communities (Ballard and Banks 2003), preferring to act more as a shareholder in the mining project and cobeneficiary of the revenues rather than a sovereign nation safeguarding the rights of its citizens and representing their long-term interests. It is fair to say that most communities welcome the additional resources offered by large resource development projects (Macintyre and Foale 2002, 2004; Minnegal and Dwyer 2017). Mostly the state has done little to create an enduring sense of loyalty among its notional citizens, and new corporate patrons offer possibilities of realizing hopes for more development at the same time as new identities of landowners emerge (Filer 1998; Golub 2014; Weiner and Glaskin 2007).

These broad ideas of corporate social responsibility have relevance to U-Vistract when raising the question of why U-Vistract portrayed its wealth as coming from global share markets, not a more familiar source of wealth to Papua New Guineans such as mining. Mining, logging, and fishery developments are all widely associated with corruption and environmental degradation (Greenpeace 2004), not to mention more localized vices such as drinking, gambling, and prostitution that reflect poorly on the moral caliber of the nation's male leaders. Mining, currently enjoying an unprecedented boom in PNG, is a known source of conflict and of inequitable distribution of royalties to small cliques of landowners, some with dubious claims (Weiner and Glaskin 2007). There are a number of landowner millionaires whose political maneuvering has granted them control over mining or gas revenues. They are known across the country for their extravagant expenditure on hotel accommodation, women, football teams, and so forth. The consumption behavior of these wealthy men serves as a marker of national inequity and the social evils that accompany large-scale resource developments. The pervasive view is that secrecy and venality constitute the real economy in PNG. By contrast, propriety and transparency characterize the idealized image of share markets of imagined wealthy and well-governed places, such as London and New York.

The fantasy of the share market, then, offers fair and rational distribution of profits according to the size of one's investment. This idealized vision of a shareholding democracy is inherently more egalitarian and transparent, with each shareholder citizen having the same rights as the next. Notwithstanding the mystifications of finance, shares offer the promise of multiplying wealth that is also accessible to anyone willing to invest, regardless of the level of their savings, their social standing, or their ethnicity. Ownership of shares brings into being new forms of participation in a global ecumene, an imagined community of shared prosperity. U-Vistract was able to sell itself to Papua New Guineans as a way of joining in this community of global shareholders, bypassing the pitfalls of investing nationally where investment vehicles have been vulnerable to the corruption that characterizes the nation for so many. The National Provident Fund provides a very public example of how a national savings and investment scheme has been systematically undermined to the extent that a national inquiry was called to investigate corrupt and illegal practices.

In joining other international investors as shareholders, U-Vistract investors also gain membership in a wider polity of global citizenship that takes them into the same realm as citizens of rich and white countries, offering Papua New Guineans the same benefits and prosperity as others already enjoy and on the same basis. Particularly in the PNG context, the immateriality of shares and particle finance has an important role in envisioning wealth as abstracted from the known this-worldly impacts of mining and other resource projects. The vision of a nation of shareholders through U-Vistract conjures a new type of wealth that will smooth out these inequalities and avoid environmental degradation. In the process, it will also create a new international polity where Papua New Guineans can take their proper place as prosperous global citizens.

Sharp (2013, 2016) has demonstrated the importance of social relationships among betel nut traders in PNG. While in the business to make money, traders also invest themselves in the relationships that facilitate the movement of goods and cash. They thus create an extended community stretching along the betel nut supply lines, linking coastal producers with Highlands resellers and consumers. U-Vistract investors similarly invested themselves in relationships with other investors and, as Christian patrons, with their rural relatives. However, these networks of face-to-face contacts were extended even further such that they imagined themselves joining a transnational community of Christian investors from around the word.

Anna—"Money in itself is a mystifying concept"

An interview that I conducted with Anna, the middle-aged teacher from Madang mentioned in chapter 5, brings together the themes of this chapter. Anna often contemplates making financial investments for her future well-being but has very mixed feelings about this on religious and moral grounds. She made an interesting observation on faith and money schemes after talking about the way U-Vistract was able to regenerate hope in their followers with new "updates":

> I think the details of all that new global finances, global community is remote. They, in their mind, what hangs like a carrot before them is the riches they will receive if and when it comes to them to benefit them directly that global economic system is quite remote. They only think they will have a lot of Kina in their hands.

> Money in itself is a mystifying concept. A lot of people don't know how money is made and where it comes from, how banks charge interest and so on. That is a concept that it is not at home with our society. But turning K100 into K1,000—they will immediately look at the physical money that's there. To go beyond that it is a mystery, so only faith can bring us to that mystery we don't understand. If they have assets, they see that's all right but if they turn to money, it is a mystery.

Here the mysteries of faith and the mysterious nature of money are joined in ways that would not surprise Keith Hart with his (2005, 167) quip, "If Durkheim ([1912] 1965) said we worship society and call it God, then money is the God of capitalist society." For Anna, the tangible nature of money paid to early investors assumes a higher evidential value because of the mysterious and foreign qualities of money itself. Unlike Victor's moral condemnation of Christian investors, the mystery of money makes it difficult to judge others and difficult to judge competing claims about where money comes from, particularly in relation to the abstracted forms of money intrinsic to global financial markets.

Money's incomprehensible otherness levels out competing explanations of how it is generated, such that all are reduced to acts of faith (Guyer 2007a; Miyazaki 2007). Official warnings against money schemes cannot be distinguished from the "updates" and bogus documents from U-Vistract agents by any critical means. Rather, the truth becomes a question of faith and is placed in the realm of mystery. In a context of such mystery, stories of early payments and personal connections take on heavier weighting as evidence because of their immediacy and the trust involved in known individuals. Guyer's rendering of economic and evangelical time expects the rational domain of the "near future" to give way to faith in more distant utopias. Yet evidence of payment and the suspicion of government are both imminent near-future domains of rationality that U-Vistract gave substance to. They thus allowed explanations of why the government is to blame or how the money is about to be paid to seem credible.

Anna reproduces a commonplace assessment of how the uneducated rural poor misunderstand the uses and origins of money and how it can be generated (LiPuma 1999, 208). Yet Anna also includes herself when talking about the mysterious nature of money and moral dilemmas of investment. She is highly educated and has studied abroad (subsequently realizing her dream of travel without the help of fast money schemes). It is unclear to her what she should do with her modest savings. She is unsatisfied with returns from her bank deposit but fears entering into a loan and regards share ownership with suspicion.

The investment options available to her seem foreclosed. She considered investing in Lihir Gold but rejected this option because of environmental and ethical concerns about the mine: "I think of investing in something worthwhile but I don't know how to do it. If I have money in a bank account it doesn't earn much interest. To invest takes money away from my control. I've considered investing in the stock market. I thought of Lihir Gold, but I was discouraged by the idea of the tailings going into the ocean, so I didn't want to invest. It might make me money but not at the expense of the environment."

In the end, improvements to her land are the only investments she considers trustworthy and controllable, as well as morally and environmentally sound. At a different stage of life, quiet retirement has taken the place of her earlier desires for money and international travel. Working Papua New Guineans across the country anticipate returning to the village on finishing work (Schram 2010) and often begin building a "permanent house" (cement floored and with roofing iron) years in advance. However, Anna's vision of retiring to her mother's land is modernized with facilities such as power and sanitation, ecotourism, and even academic tourism. Her desire to make a lot of money from U-Vistract has been replaced by something more like the grassroots vision of self-sufficient national development embodied in the PNG National Constitution:

> I wouldn't take a loan. I don't like the idea of paying interest. I'll save up enough money to build a house. I have already bought some tools and I want to build a toilet and good water supply. They already have electricity there, but I bought a 1,200-watt generator for a fridge. I'd like to retire to my mother's land and set up a guesthouse for tourists. Anthropologists could come and do research. There are a lot of oral stories that could be collected from my culture and tourists could also come and do nature walks and bird-watching.

Anna's concerns echo Foster's (1999b, 230–231) observations about the indeterminacy and risk of money forms. They also reflect the central themes developed in this book: Christianity, middle-class aspirations as they interact with global and local economies, making sense of financialized money, and practices of investment. In relation to the latter, Anna clearly sees investment in shares as a potential vehicle for her savings but does not embrace ideas of risk as Geraldine did. Anna's interest in investment is tempered by a cosmopolitan ethical concern for the environment, much as we would expect of shareholder activists (Foster 2008) or ethical consumers (Carrier 2008). Similarly, her vision of retiring to the village owes much to a cosmopolitan environmentalist imagination, particularly when counterposed against her (rejected) alternative of investing in mining shares.

Critiques of Globalization from the Periphery

Globalization and its accompanying financial practices are experienced as both promise and threat in PNG. The promises of prosperity are set against a legacy of colonial capitalist development that is always suspected to be expropriating profits from the exploitation of PNG's (national) natural resources, leaving poverty and environmental damage behind. Further, globalization as westernization destabilizes cultural norms, particularly around the rights and freedoms of women and sexual morality. This poses an ongoing dilemma of how to modernize without losing national cultural and moral bearings (Cox 2015). Middle-class Papua New Guineans tend to embrace economic development as a way forward, but they are also aware of its pitfalls, and their hopes for the future are selectively tempered by an underlying suspicion of global capital and a fear of losing their cultural moorings.

Neoliberal internationalism was the setting for Musingku's construction of a global scale for his scam, but not only in the millennial capitalist promises of more and more wealth from financial abstractions such as e-commerce. Musingku offered a critique of the World Bank and globalization that was already familiar to urban Papua New Guineans. Indeed, during his time in the public eye (although after he had served as president of the National Union of Students) Musingku witnessed large-scale student demonstrations against the World Bank's structural adjustment program (SAP) for PNG, particularly its proposals for land mobilization. In June 2001, three University of Papua New Guinea (UPNG) students were shot by police and lost their lives in these protests as a result of overreaction from PNG authorities (Kavanamur 2002). More recently, in June 2016, student protests against Prime Minister O'Neill at UPNG have been met with armed police violence.

Musingku's 2001 critique of globalism provides an example of his construction of the global scale. It includes hostility to the World Bank as a global engineer of the neoliberal project, particularly in developing countries. Musingku is free to identify the vested interests embedded in constructions of the neoliberal global market (cf. McMichael 1998, 105). Musingku sees elite financial interests as intentionally inimical to the well-being of the world's poor, both through ruthless exploitation and through the imposition of structural adjustment programs that coerce Third World governments into loan conditions that entail the destruction of basic services.

Musingku's accusation that PNG politicians have collaborated with the World Bank voices much disappointment and frustration with politicians. It also recalls McMichael's statement that, "Structural Adjustment Programmes allowed the multilateral institutions, in alliance with state managers and financial classes, to redefine development by reformulating the role of the state" (McMichael 1998, 109). In taking up these themes, U-Vistract has been able to deliver a thoughtful critique of the PNG state and the failure of the national development project and to insert itself credibly into this narrative. At the same time, U-Vistract's opponents, particularly Prime Minister Mekere Morauta (1999–2001), were instrumental in bringing in World Bank–initiated reforms, including the new Financial Institutions Act (2000), which contained specific provisions targeting fast money schemes at the urging of international financial institutions.

U-Vistract promised the riches of the immaterial world of global finance but at the same time decried this world as an oppressor. Musingku promised to replace the World Bank and its cronies (such as the PNG government and even PNG's mainline churches) with a new system of global finance aimed at meeting the basic needs of the people and founded on Christian rather than freemarket principles. However, the organizations that would oversee this transition sound familiar, echoing World Bank and other international and national financial institutions: the Royal Reserve Bank of Papala, the Royal International Bank of Meekamui (RIBM or IBOM), the Royal Central Bank of Meekamui, and so forth. This proliferation of banking institutions and agencies parallels Van Fossen's (2002) account of the pseudo-state of Melchizedek, which concocted over 300 fake banks and insurance companies, utilizing many of these fictional entities in pyramid schemes and other frauds targeting separatist groups in the Pacific Islands.

As Lattas (2006b, 130) notes of Pomio Kivung "cargo cult" followers, "They do not reject government and mission. They especially value their moral ordering and civilizing projects; they just want those projects more effectively realized in terms of their transformative processes." U-Vistract also appropriates the "moral ordering and civilising" project of development and so engages the visions of both grassroots national self-sufficiency and neoliberal global development agencies. U-Vistract's success in linking the two scales draws on broader Papua New Guinean discontent with the lack of progress in advancing the transformative processes promised in both national and global development projects. Unlike the secretive alternative mirror world of the underground dead in Pomio Kivung, however, U-Vistract initially operated in the open "real world" and made a spectacle of disbursing funds to successful investors, albeit through spectacles of deception such as opening the Royal Reserve Bank of Papala in Port Moresby.

Not only did U-Vistract adopt names and acronyms typical of development banks, it mimicked the methods of international development agencies, based on self-sufficiency achieved through income-generating projects (albeit with promises of endowments of K10,000 per family per month that surely constitute substantial income rather than "income generation"). A major shortcoming of the World Bank is its failure "to provide citizens of nations that implement the SAP with income to promote self-reliance and economic growth for the nation." Rather than treating Papua New Guineans as deserving global citizens, the World Bank aims "to keep third world nations as economic slaves." In this appeal to the rights of citizenship and its promises to deliver what is denied by the World Bank, U-Vistract reinvigorates the program of national development. This egalitarian vision has been imperiled by the long-term decline in state services and endemic corruption, as well as the more immediate influence of the World Bank's structural adjustment program for PNG. Balthasar's statement below indicates that this critique resonated with investors:

> So the whole system now in the world is drawn up by the World Bank. It's a corrupt system, so U-Vistract is building a new system. The World Bank, IMF, they have ripped the people. You see Africans they are suffering! Just the shell left behind. We don't want that to happen here in PNG.
>
> We are patient because the system in PNG, if you want to start something new, it takes a long time. So we are praying and patient. Because PNG, when it got independence, it was so used to the World Bank way of doing things, we are politically independent but not economically independent. Australia is economically independent.

The U-Vistract critique of PNG does not stop at the national scale: PNG's problems originate in the global financial system, headed by the World Bank and acting against the interests of people in poor countries by creating dependency. "Africans" are seen as the victims of these policies. It is imperative that PNG avoid their fate. As a rich country, endowed with natural resources, PNG should be able to meet its citizens' needs, but poverty and disadvantage are rife because of dependency.[7] In PNG and the Pacific Islands, there has been a reluctance to admit the persistence of poverty (Abbott and Pollard 2004). Africa often functions as an antitype that allows Papua New Guineans to make a favorable contrast with their own situation, where nobody is starving and everyone has enough food. The quotation from Somare at the beginning of this chapter is one of many examples. If Australia provides the model of a functional nation based on economic independence, then Africa represents poverty, victimhood, corruption, and dependency.

As mentioned in chapter 7, dependency is a troubling indication of national failure. In 2005, U-Vistract published an article in the *Papala Chronicles*, "Love Offering to PNG," in which it claimed to be offering "a massive K100 billion financial assistance package to PAPUA NEW GUINEA" (R. Brown 2005b). This article claimed that most of the money would go to the provinces, in an echo of routine complaints that government money never leaves Port Moresby and fails to address the needs of the people. Here U-Vistract positioned itself as a donor to PNG, reversing dependency on foreign donors and reinvigorating local development in what they called "an unprecedented act of Love and Friendship," again reiterating the Christian character of the scheme.

While this may seem fanciful, it has echoes in current events: the PNG government has recently taken on the role of donor to neighboring Solomon Islands, promising a K100 million program of support over five years (Pangkatana 2011). U-Vistract's appropriation of the national development project is not isolationist, nor does it try to engender a parochial nationalism. Musingku rejects the World Bank and criticizes other donors to PNG, including Australia, but nevertheless manages to retain an internationalist vision by replacing the structures of the world order with an alternative (virtual) global architecture. New development banks and international associations (the Royal Association of Nations and Kingdoms [RAONK]) have already been established to act in the interests of the poor, a mission the World Bank now professes.[8]

At the same time, U-Vistract positions itself as a patron of other nations in much the same way as individual investors can expect to be empowered as Christian patrons through the scheme. This Christian reform of the global financial architecture will release Papua New Guineans from their dependency and poverty and will make the wealth of global share-markets and banks available to faithful Christian investors so that they can deliver development themselves.

Notes

1. Curtin (2011, 356) notes the success of the Orogen Minerals float in 1996, which was oversubscribed and had high levels of investment from thousands of individual Papua New Guineans.

2. A misspelling of "tithes."

3. An American citizen by the name of John Green was arrested but then released only to continue working for U-Vistract in Bougainville ("Green Back in Bougainville," *Post-Courier*, September 19, 2008).

4. Large numbers of rural Bougainvilleans embraced the scheme with its early rhetoric about redeveloping Bougainville after the war.

5. Rebecca Lawrence (2008) discusses the relationships of investment banks and NGOs with reference to several campaigns in PNG.

6. In 1999, then Australian Prime Minister John Howard gave a number of speeches expressing pride in how his right-wing government had created a nation of shareholders through privatization (e.g., Howard 1999).

7. Compare also the discussion of "neoliberal negative nationalism" above. This viewpoint also underlies the wealth creation pillar of the Vision 2050 development strategy (Independent State of PNG 2010, 21, 30).

8. "Our mission is to fight poverty with passion and professionalism for lasting results and to help people help themselves and their environment by providing resources, sharing knowledge, building capacity and forging partnerships in the public and private sectors. "http://web.worldbank.org/WBSITE/EXTERNAL/EXTABOUTUS/0,,pagePK:50004410~piP K:36602~theSitePK:29708,00.html. Accessed October 6, 2011.

Conclusion: Disillusionment

THIS BOOK HAS examined how hundreds of thousands of Papua New Guineans were drawn into U-Vistract and related fast money schemes. In Melanesia, these Ponzi schemes are often seen as yet another instance of "cargo cult mentality," that is, as narratives of sloth, greed, and gullibility based on the fundamental credulousness of Papua New Guineans, which in turn is attributable to cultural or economic backwardness. However, this account is difficult to sustain in the face of evidence of widespread involvement of "elite" Papua New Guineans: modern, urban, educated, and salaried people. Interviews with middle-class Papua New Guineans complicate the popular account as they reveal a range of concerns with prosperity, citizenship, morality, and society that move well beyond greed and gullibility.

Indeed, these "dupes," deceived by an elaborate scam, also emerge as "investors": active participants in the global economy and consumers of its ideas and promises. For many Papua New Guineans, the U-Vistract scam acted as a mediating agent, providing a local embodiment of the globally circulating economy that would allow investors to access its promised benefits. Here the global scale is not merely composed of international finance and economic activities, or goals of egalitarian national development. It is also constituted by transnational Christian identities that cut across local, national, and global scales and provide an ethical grounding at each level. U-Vistract successfully coopted Christian leaders, institutions, and networks, as well as Christian ideas, language, and practices, particularly those already provided by Pentecostal prosperity theology.

The argument is not that U-Vistract succeeded because it mimicked Pentecostalism. Rather, U-Vistract constructed a parallel framework for making sense of already circulating images and ideas of money, wealth, and prosperity. These global images are bewildering, not least because of their possible moral implications. Like Pentecostalism, U-Vistract provided a Christian moral system that enabled such images to be appropriated and domesticated for a broad Papua New Guinean audience. Neo-Pentecostalism and U-Vistract both provided organizational and ideological structures through which individuals could selectively appropriate global imaginings of wealth and prosperity. U-Vistract and Pentecostalism were both scale-making projects that simultaneously created both global and nation scales and mediated the position of individuals within each of these intersecting scales.

U-Vistract's success in mediating global images of prosperity lay in its ability to locate them convincingly within PNG. This required a critique that addressed popular narratives of the failure of development due to corruption and greed and because of the influence of foreign economic interests. To these national debates, U-Vistract also brought Christian moral censure of individual investors and then marshaled them as Christian investor–citizens ready to renew the nation and help its people. U-Vistract imagined a transnational Christian community and financial system that would restore hopes for egalitarian development. At each scale, U-Vistract offered resolution of the moral dilemmas that accompany troubling inequalities between the middle class and the *grasruts*, or between the cosmopolitan global rich and those destined to live as "nationals" in developing countries. This articulation of scale-making projects reembedded Papua New Guineans in a new Christian ecumene connected to global flows of wealth. In this way it not only addressed individuals' immediate desires for money but also appealed to the common good and altruism as much as to personal greed. Investors invested not simply in financial products but also invested themselves in a vision of a new Christian moral economy.

U-Vistract drew on the weakness of the PNG state and the accompanying disillusionment, sense of injustice, and awareness of inequality. As providers of new resources, U-Vistract promoters were welcome to present their programs and their claims to offer an alternative source of patronage to the failing and increasingly personalized state systems (Foster 2002b, 242). Indeed, given the perceptions of pervasive corruption and *wantokism*, U-Vistract's appeal to Christian universalism offered new pathways to accessing resources that the (imagined or actual) capture of state systems by hostile cliques has closed off for many.

U-Vistract took up the unfulfilled promises of global capitalism and replaced them with a postcolonial vision of prosperity and equality. However, whereas notionally egalitarian practices of mass consumerism may offer "individuals the sort of agency and equality manifestly denied them in the realm of capital and labor" (Foster 2002a, 118), investors consuming U-Vistract as a financial product hoped to restore their lost egalitarian standing by becoming capitalists themselves. This was not simply a matter of benefiting directly from the scheme's promises of wealth to individuals but allowed investors the opportunity to embrace the virtues of entrepreneurialism that would free them from the burden of labor and the troubling matter of the dependency of relatives and wantoks. Investors like Isaac reimagined themselves as Christian patrons disbursing abundance and in the process retaining or enhancing the privileges of their class position. In Graeber's (2001, 105) words, "The object of desire becomes an illusory mirror of the desirer's own manipulated intentions."

In a predominantly Christian country, U-Vistract envisioned Christian prosperity that made the local appropriation of the global economy morally feasible.

This was not a simple blessing of accumulation for personal consumption. Rather, U-Vistract developed an elaborate imagining of new social roles and responsibilities that would resolve painful inequalities and the failure of corrupt governments to fulfil the modern vision of egalitarian national development.

The national scale that emerges from this study is more vital, more morally engaging, and more immanent than previously imagined within anthropologies of Melanesia. The nation may be troubling, even failing and in need of Christian critique and reinvigoration, but it is not a distant, dimly recognized, or irrelevant entity. The Papua New Guinean working class represented here live within the national scale and interpret international images of wealth through national visions, alongside more local concerns for kin and the transnational Christian critique of the nation and the moral subject (LiPuma 2000).

U-Vistract combined visions of global finance with neo-Pentecostal prosperity teachings and disillusionment with Papua New Guinea's national development. In Tsing's (2005) terms, this was a powerful "scale-making project" that goes some of the way to explaining the spread and longevity of the scam. The scheme succeeded not only because it was able to appear as a credible conduit for people's desire for money but also because it could also make this desire morally credible. In the useful terminology of Errington and Gewertz (2004), U-Vistract presented a vision of the "desirable and the feasible," but not only was its notional source of money seen as feasible, it also made its investors' desires morally feasible.

Tsing (2000a) warns against trying to fit scales neatly within a vertical hierarchy. In U-Vistract we see people experiencing the world through a distinctively Papua New Guinean conjunction of scale-making projects. U-Vistract's success in mimicking these scales, exploiting (or "arbitraging," to follow Guyer 2004) the tensions between and contradictions within them and shaping a moral narrative of person, nation, and globe gave it immense persuasive power. That said, it is also important not to lose sight of the diverse positionings of investors, not all of whom swallowed all of the U-Vistract patter, and of how apparent evidence of payments can be very convincing to those with doubts. This is a story of desire, but it is a socially and ethically mediated desire, not the unbounded grasping danger of the cargo cult narrative (nor the voracious emptiness that is often imagined of individualism and consumerism).

With one or two exceptions, the voices that guide this study are "elite" only in relation to the great majority of underserviced Papua New Guineans who have no mobility out of the subsistence economy or to the ever-increasing numbers of those who prefer to live at the margins of the cash economy in peri-urban settlements. Most of the people I spoke with had very humble material aspirations and none of the feeling of power that the true "elites" of the country take for granted. Middle-class U-Vistract investors may not have particularly close ties to the village and place less value on attempts to replicate village patterns of sociality in town (Sahlins's *developman*) but they do inhabit a moral universe that includes a critique of selfishness and greed. If their models for living are not so much shaped by tradition and kinship, global ideas of finance and consumerism are clearly apparent and indicate that there are many urban Papua New Guineans who see themselves as part of a global middle-class ecumene. When transposed to the village social context, rather than attempting to delimit realms of *kastom* and *bisnis* (K. Martin 2007), U-Vistract investors imagine themselves as proprietors of development, as Christian patrons.

Rather than greedy and gullible, U-Vistract investors emerge from this study as morally engaged members of a transnational Christian civil society. This is a surprising conclusion to draw from studying fraud, but it is all the more surprising in Papua New Guinea where anthropological interest has historically constructed the village as the central place where social meanings are generated. Here, urban Melanesians demonstrate moral and relational sensibilities that combine global aspirations for prosperity with Papua New Guinean disillusionment with the nation. In doing so, perhaps a more individualistic rendering of Melanesia emerges, but these are individuals who are also more cosmopolitan in sentiment and whose Christian values lead them to seek to avoid charges of selfishness, even as they mark out class distinctions (Macintyre 2011; cf. Gewertz and Errington 1999).

This study, then, offers another distinct account of the "possessive individual" of recent anthropological discussion (Sykes 2007b, 258), drawing attention to new modes of proprietorship of the self, of money, and, through Christian citizenship, of the nation. Middle-class investors in U-Vistract were embarking on a project of possessing an economically desirable and morally feasible place for themselves and their national community within a global ecumene (Macintyre 2011; cf. Were 2007, 250). Indeed, for the true believers possessing this vision became so morally desirable that the ridiculous promises of a Ponzi scam were rendered economically feasible.

U-Vistract financialized people's hopes for themselves, the nation, and the world, bringing these scale-making projects into a compelling vision of a new abundant moral economy.

Disillusionment

For all of the convincing power of this new moral economy, U-Vistract has not actually delivered on its promises. A decade and longer after the fast money scheme boom and bust in Port Moresby, investors are giving up on the hope of receiving their money. While U-Vistract has done an extraordinary job of maintaining these hopes and even extending them abroad through the internet and international networks of scammers, its efforts at rebranding (Cox 2016) are failing. As we have seen in the chapters of this book, some investors realized this more readily than others. The cognitive dissonance literature (Stone 2000) provides a range of psychological explanations for how people sustain their beliefs in the face of events that would seem to disprove them. U-Vistract's moral rigor, blaming of authorities, expansion, institutional reform, and renewal of its leadership hierarchy all have precedents in such studies. There is still a core of loyal followers at Tonu who remain adamant that the system is nearly in place and that U-Vistract will have the last word (Kenema 2015). However, the meetings elsewhere are less frequent and poorly attended as members accept that they have been duped and that they have lost their money. Fast money schemes are regarded by many as a folly and as a moral lesson that requires modern Papua New Guineans to be vigilant against any resurgence of cargoistic beliefs.

Nancy—Doubt and Dystopia

I close with an interview I conducted with Nancy, a Bougainvillean living in Madang. Her sister was involved in U-Vistract in Madang for several years and was also very active in the United Church, particularly its women's fellowship. Nancy promoted Money Rain for several years, but she now has serious doubts and feels guilty about taking people's money.

Nancy:

> There was no pressure, we just used nice words to attract people into the scheme, but I feel guilty because I led others into Money Rain. I was happy when Money Rain stopped. Some of the investors, I gave their money back to them when it stopped.
>
> But I did tell people to think twice before they invested. But some people accused me that I was not telling people sooner because I was greedy and I was keeping it a secret just for myself. From 1999, I started to hold back.
>
> I feel guilty because some of them have lost their money. They had belief in the scheme because I was a Christian but that hasn't helped them. What is going to happen to my sister? I'm very worried for her. When things don't go right, she is upset. I told her to stop collecting money because if it's not from God, then [it must be from the Devil].

Nancy knew she had led others into losing their money using her reputation as a Christian. Her sister did the same but on a larger scale and fears reprisals from disgruntled investors and even divine judgement. However, Nancy also indicated the intensity of people's desire to invest in Money Rain, including returning her warnings about the risk of the scheme with accusations that she was greedy and keeping the benefits for herself.

Nancy presented me with a file of web pages she had printed out. The websites were for various (bogus) international banks and were given to her by U-Vistract as proof that there was money invested overseas. She asked me to check whether they were real or not, as she could not verify them herself.

I explained that were I to take the websites and look them up, then I would most likely report back that the sites no longer existed or that they were all fake banks and so forth. I explained that if she reported this to U-Vistract, they would probably tell her I was lying or was working for the government against the scheme, or perhaps they would confirm that the websites she had been given were now out of date because those banks had been subsumed by a much larger financial institution that would soon ensure that U-Vistract would get an even bigger return for its investors. My response seemed to confirm Nancy's growing doubts and made sense of her experience with money scheme promoters. She replied as follows:

> Sometimes I wonder if it's true and I ask myself, "What's going to happen if it's all true?" If all that money comes, nobody will work: nurses, doctors, shops, road workers— all of them invested. All of the business houses too, all of them put money in, so all the businesses will be closed. So therefore maybe this isn't real. Everyone will have new vehicles, so there will be lots of accidents. Everyone says they will eat in the hotels when their money comes but who will cook for them? Because all the hotel workers, they invested too. Everyone will build a new house but all the builders they won't be working because they'll be millionaires too. How can it continue for life? They tell us, "You'll have to withdraw money too quickly because you have make room for the next payment." How can there be so much money? Who will do the work?

Without access to external means to check whether U-Vistract's overseas banks were real, Nancy used an interesting logical process. She asked herself what would happen if the promises were true and millions of Kina were actually paid. Nancy conjured a vision of the future, critiquing fast money promises by turning them back on themselves. Knowing how many Madang people had joined U-Vistract and who would therefore become millionaires overnight, she began to doubt whether their dreams of big houses, cars, hotel meals, and overseas travel would be possible, as she imagined that everyone in Madang would quit their jobs to enjoy their newfound wealth. Who would be left to do the work, and how would society continue to function?[1] Reaching this reductio ad absurdum was a way of disproving U-Vistract's promises for Nancy where other reference points (e.g., warnings from the Bank of Papua New Guinea) failed to provide adequate grounds for assessing the money scheme's claims.

Nancy's nonworking dystopia echoed some of the claims of money scheme promoters. Not only did U-Vistract threaten the conventional banking system, but, as Balthasar (from U-Vistract's Madang organizing committee) put it, "I think they don't want us to be rich, so we can work." Conjuring a future free from work appealed as a utopia, but when this vision was subjected to scrutiny, a dysfunctional countervision emerged of a nonproductive society that doesn't work. U-Vistract's promises of wealth for all were unreconcilable with the imagination of what this would mean in practice. Because being wealthy implied not working and having others to work for you, dreams of egalitarian amity dissolved into a capitalist labor hierarchy. If society was unworkable without work, then the scheme's ability to produce money without work was in doubt. Indeed, if money represents the value of labor (as indeed it is for many, including Victor (chap. 5): "A man who does not work shall not eat" or Lindsay (also chap. 5): "you must sweat work") and not merely the means for realizing dreams of consumption, then a future without work also becomes an absurd future where money itself makes no sense.

This example illuminates the "this-worldly" scale of U-Vistract: its promises of abundance may seem millenarian but are understood as real wealth in the same real (but greatly improved) world investors already inhabit: a world of school fees, *tinpis*, and rice (Dundon 2004). This scale becomes clearer when contrasted with the vision of life without work depicted by Biersack (1996, 105ff). Biersack's Paiela informants regard heaven as a place without work or suffering and characterized by leisure and feasting. This is entirely feasible as a millenarian vision of the future and gains credence from the lifestyles of white people who already embody the lack of work, good health, and immortality. U-Vistract, however, is not a transformation of the future on a cosmological scale but is a reform of the present, or perhaps the "near future" (Guyer 2007a) on a this-worldly, even national, economic scale; hence Nancy is able to reason to herself that its promises cannot possibly be true. While the utopian vision of a world without work characterizes Paiela and (other) millenarian hopes, for Nancy the implications of such a vision relocate U-Vistract in the realm of fancy, dispelling its purchase on the "real" world.[2]

Having reasoned that promises of life without work must be false, Nancy had little alternative but to abandon hopes of prosperity, falling back on more traditional Christian ideas of humble toil. But even here there was little comfort for her because she knew she had used her standing as a Christian to defraud people. She therefore sought reconciliation with some investors in repaying as many as she could. Her sister seemed to lack the same insights and risks danger. Since we met, the sister has fled to Buka where she is said to still be working for U-Vistract.

Nancy's predicament exemplifies many of the contradictions of hope in an age of global finance. It is good to hope, but our hopes are most compelling when they answer the questions of scalar friction. Hope must articulate a vision of how we think the world should work, but in order to be convincing, it can only do this in terms of how we think the world does work. There is much financial patter circulating in the world today, and it is very difficult not to be drawn into its cosmology. Progressive political parties release policies that are "fully costed," a responsibility that rarely falls on the shoulders of conservatives who are believed by the public to be naturally financially responsible. Activists buy shares in corporations in order to move motions in favor of labor rights or environmental protection (Foster 2008). The divestment movement has had very public success at using financial levers against fossil fuel interests (350.org). Ethical consumers buy products from companies they believe to have less exploitative practices (Dolan 2008). And microfinance websites like Kiva.org promise donors the opportunity to connect with people living in poverty and to "make a difference" by enabling them to start a microenterprise. All of these examples of hopeful ethical engagements with capitalism have their parallels with the hopes of the middle-class Papua New Guineans who invested in U-Vistract. All of these alternatives are indexed to the very systems they try to escape or critique (Maurer 2005).

Where U-Vistract envisioned its investors as benign Christian patrons dispensing development to the grassroots, Nancy followed the logic through an extra step to reach an absurdity where even the grassroots are so rich that they no longer have to work. In doing so, she intuited that capitalism requires hierarchies of labor that are inequitable. Yet the scale of the financialized economy magnifies these inequities and devalues labor, not least in the ways that global corporations seek to reduce production costs by basing their operations in countries with extremely low wages and poor protection of workers' rights.

Nancy's doubtful dystopia where society falls apart because no one works cuts through the financial patter to a more concrete imagining of economic relations. For Nancy, "the economy" is no longer a mystified domain only accessible through the mediation of certified experts or the heroic exercise of entrepreneurial risk-taking. Rather, she imagines how things work as the result of the labors of people. In doing so, she echoes many of the conclusions of contemporary anthropologies of finance that reveal the social construction of finance as a discourse and social field. The production and distribution of global finance discourse has often been rendered as the privilege of a "pinnacle elite" (Ho 2009), yet it has also spread around the world, taking root even among those at the bottom of the pyramid (Elyachar 2005) and for Wall St financiers and microfinance participants alike, this has collateralized their social relationships (Schuster 2015). As this book has shown, PNG is well and truly within this network.

Hope, it seems, is now profoundly financialized in PNG and beyond. However, the abstractions of global finance contain, conceal, and perpetuate inequalities that undermine the very social relations that are necessary for hope to be grounded in a new moral economy. Like middle-class investors in U-Vistract, none of us are immune to the appeal of a more ethical economic system, but, like Nancy, our efforts to imagine alternatives often arrive back at a contradictory logic where the hoped-for alternative seems unworkable or impractical.

U-Vistract mobilized thousands of people, some as simple opportunists but many as Christian citizens, ready to use the scheme's new resources to redeem their fallen nation. However, the fundamental flaw in this project was that, in embracing the promises of finance capital, they hoped to overcome the very inequalities that the financial system inexorably produces. Captured by the scheme's scale-making, they repeated the patter and even engaged with it morally, but in doing so simply normalized the financial relations they had set out to reform. Moreover, the moralistic Christian disciplines of the self often nurture a sense of entitlement among middle-class actors that hinders the building of more effective political alliances. Again, these challenges of turning a critique into a political movement play out in PNG in particular ways (not only through a born-again Christian scam), but they are common wherever a moral middle class attempts to effect change.

As this book has argued, the middle classes of PNG, as elsewhere, are pained by corruption and poor service delivery. They find inequality troubling, even if their hopes for rectifying the situation often reproduce the logics of patronage politics or the condescension of Christian charity. Even promoters of an elaborate scam such as U-Vistract are motivated by a "heart for the people." U-Vistract was an empty deception that manipulated people, and I see no emancipatory potential in fraud. Nevertheless, as a vantage point for observing articulations of middle-class moral and financial aspirations, the U-Vistract experience confirms that even relatively privileged Papua New Guineans still hold on to the vision of egalitarian grassroots development that their nation was founded on in 1975. This vision is yet to find a convincing political expression. However, as the middle class becomes aware of its growing economic precarity, I hope that it will increasingly judge its plutocratic national leaders by this yardstick and find ways of building greater solidarity with the grassroots that can articulate a shared commitment to equitable development.

Notes

1. Nancy would reject Adam Smith's idea that the lure of riches, although an elaborate deception on the part of Providence, is fundamental to the functioning of society (Davis 1990).

2. Andrew Strathern's (1980) "chief skeptic" Ongka argued that the Red Box Cult was false because their money was simply old banknotes, not newly minted cash produced by the "wind people." Ongka's this-wordly expectations disproved the millenarian claims.

Glossary of Foreign Language Terms

Tok Pisin	English
Bikhet	Arrogant, insolent, willful
Bilas	Decoration; traditional costume
Bilum	Net bag or woven bag
Bisnis	Business; clan
Buai	Betel nut
Fotnait	Payday; fortnight
Gavman	Government
Giaman (im)	Fraud; defraud
Grasrut	Grassroots, poor, rural class
Gristok	Lies, deception
Haus sik	Hospital, clinic
Isi money	Easy money
Kago	Cargo, consumer goods
Kastom	Custom, culture, tradition
Kiap	Colonial officer
Kwik moni	Fast money
Lo	Law
Lotu	Faith, religion
Lus wik	Alternate week in a pay cycle
Papagraun	Landowner
Pe de	Payday
Sande	Rotating credit system; Sunday
Susokman	Office worker, middle-class person
Tambu	In-law, affine
Tinpis	Canned fish
Traiim tasol	Just try it
Wantok	Relative, kinsman or kinswoman
Winmoni	Windfall gain
Wok	Work; ritual
Wokmoni	Money earned through labor

References

Abbott, David, and Steve Pollard. 2004. *Hardship and Poverty in the Pacific: Strengthening Poverty Analysis and Strategies in the Pacific*. Pacific Studies Series. Manila: Asian Development Bank.

Akin, David, and Joel Robbins, eds. 1999. *Money and Modernity: State and Local Currencies in Melanesia*. ASAO Monograph. Pittsburgh: University of Pittsburgh Press.

Alexeyeff, Kalissa. 2011. "Bingo and Budgets: Gambling with Global Capital in the Cook Islands." In Patterson and Macintyre 2011b, 201–230.

Allen, Bryant, R. Michael Bourke, and John Gibson. 2005. "Poor Rural Places in Papua New Guinea." *Asia Pacific Viewpoint* 46 (2): 201–217.

Amarshi, Azeem, Kenneth Good, and Rex Mortimer. 1979. *Development and Dependency: The Political Economy of Papua New Guinea*. Melbourne: Oxford University Press.

Ambassador to Bougainville. 2012. "The Real Story of the Sovereign Nation of Bougainville Islands & the Twin Kingdom of Papa'ala and Me'ekamui."

Anderson, Benedict. 1983. *Imagined Communities: Reflections on the Origin and Spread of Nationalism*. London: Verso.

Anderson, Tim. 2008. "Women Roadside Sellers in Madang." *Pacific Economic Bulletin* 23 (1): 59–73.

Apami, John. 2001. "PNG Should Not Be Poor: Dollar." *National*, December 10.

Appadurai, Arjun. 1996. *Modernity at Large: Cultural Dimensions of Globalization*. Minneapolis: University of Minnesota Press.

Apter, Andrew. 1999. "IBB = 419: Nigerian Democracy and the Politics of Illusion." In *Civil Society and the Political Imagination in Africa*, edited by John Comaroff and Jean Comaroff, 267–307. Chicago: University of Chicago Press.

———. 2005. *The Pan-African Nation: Oil and the Spectacle of Culture in Nigeria*. Chicago: University of Chicago Press.

Arvedlund, Erin. 2009. *Madoff: the Man Who Stole $65 Billion*. Melbourne: Penguin.

ASIC (Australian Securities and Investments Commission). 1999. "High Risk Investment Stopped by ASIC." Media Release. October 29.

Ayius, Albert. 2006. Unpublished interview notes.

Bailey, Frederick George. 1991. *The Prevalence of Deceit*. Ithaca, NY: Cornell University Press.

Bainton, Nicholas. 2006. "Virtuous Sociality and Other Fantasies: Pursuing Mining, Capital and Cultural Continuity in Lihir, Papua New Guinea." PhD diss, University of Melbourne.

———. 2009. "Keeping the Network Out of View: Mining, Distinctions and Exclusion in Melanesia." *Oceania* 79 (1): 18–33.

———. 2010. *The Lihir Destiny: Cultural Responses to Mining in Melanesia*. Asia-Pacific Environment Monograph 5. Canberra: ANU E-Press.

———. 2011. "Are you viable?' Personal Avarice, Collective Antagonism and Grassroots Development in Papua New Guinea." In Patterson and Macintyre 2011b, 231–259.

Bainton, Nicholas, and John Cox. 2009. "Parallel States, Parallel Economies: Legitimacy and Prosperity in Papua New Guinea." State, Society and Governance in Melanesia, Discussion Paper 2009/5. Canberra: Research School of Pacific and Asian Studies, Australian National University.

Ballard, Chris, and Glenn Banks. 2002. "Resource Wars: The Anthropology of Mining." *Annual Review of Anthropology* 32: 287–313.

Bank of Papua New Guinea. 2005. "Illegal Deposit Taking (Fast Money) Schemes." Public Notice, May 28.

Barbara, Julien, John Cox, and Michael Leach. 2015. "The Emergent Middle Classes in Timor-Leste and Melanesia: Conceptual Relevance and Identification." SSGM Discussion Paper 2015/4. Canberra: Australian National University.

Barber, Karin. 1995. "Money, Self-Realization and the Person in Yoruba Texts." In *Money Matters: Instability, Values and Social Payments in the Modern History of West African Communities*, edited by Jane Guyer, 205–224. Portsmouth, NH: Heinemann.

Barker, John. 1990a. "Introduction: Ethnographic Perspectives on Christianity in Oceania." In *Christianity in Oceania: Ethnographic Perspectives*, edited by John Barker, 1–24. Lanham, MD: University Press of America.

———. 2007a. "Introduction: The Anthropological Study of Morality in Melanesia." In *The Anthropology of Morality in Melanesia and Beyond*, edited by John Barker, 1–21. Aldershot, UK: Ashgate.

———. 2007b. "All Sides Now: The Postcolonial Triangle in Uiaku." In *The Anthropology of Morality in Melanesia and Beyond*, edited by John Barker, 75–91. Aldershot, UK: Ashgate.

———. 2013. "Anthropology and the Politics of Christianity in Papua New Guinea." In *Christian Politics in Oceania*, edited by Matt Tomlinson and Debra McDougall, 146–170. London: Berghahn.

Bashkow, Ira. 2000a. "Confusion, Native Scepticism, and Recurring Questions about the Year 2000: 'Soft' Beliefs and Preparations for the Millennium in the Arapesh Region, Papua New Guinea." *Ethnohistory* 47 (1): 133–169.

———. 2000b. "'Whitemen' Are Good to Think With: How Orokaiva Morality Is Reflected on Whitemen's Skin." *Identities* 7 (3): 281–332.

———. 2006. *The Meaning of Whitemen: Race and Modernity in the Orokaiva Cultural World*. Chicago: University of Chicago Press.

Bayart, Jean-Francois, and Stephen Ellis. 2000. "Africa in the World: A History of Extraversion." *African Affairs* 99 (395): 217–267.

Benson, John, and Laura Ugolini, eds. 2003. *A Nation of Shopkeepers: Five Centuries of British Retailing*. New York: Palgrave Macmillan.

Berdahl, Daphne. 2010. "Local Hero, National Crook: 'Doc' Schneider and the Spectacle of Finance Capital." In Daphne Berdahl, *On the Social Life of Postsocialism: Memory, Consumption, Germany*, 101–111. Edited by Matti Bunzl; foreword by Michael Herzfeld. Bloomington: Indiana University Press.

Berman, Bruce. 1998. "Ethnicity, Patronage and the African State: The Politics of Uncivil Nationalism." *African Affairs* 97 (3): 305–341.

Bernard, Harvey Russell. 2011. *Research Methods in Anthropology: Qualitative and Quantitative Approaches*. 5th ed. Lanham, MD: Altamira.

Besnier, Niko. 2009. "Modernity, Cosmopolitanism and the Emergence of Middle Classes in Tonga." *Contemporary Pacific* 21 (2): 215–262.

Bezemer, Daniel J. 2001. "Post-Socialist Financial Fragility: The Case of Albania." *Cambridge Journal of Economics* 25: 1–23.

Bhabha, Homi. 1994. The *Location of Culture*. New York: Routledge.

Bhattacharya, Utpal. 1998. "On the Possibility of Ponzi Schemes in Transition Economies." Accessed December 5, 2008. http://www1.fee.uva.nl/fm/Conference/cifra1999/ponzi.pdf.

Bielo, James. 2007 "The Mind of Christ: Financial Success, Born-Again Personhood, and the Anthropology of Christianity." *Ethnos* 72 (3): 316–338.

Biersack, Aletta. 1996. "Word Made Flesh: Religion, the Economy, and the Body in the Papua New Guinea Highlands." *History of Religions* 36 (2): 85–111.

———. 2005. "On the Life and Times of the Ipili Imagination." In Robbins and Wardlow 2005, 135–162.

Binde, Per. 2005. "Gambling, Exchange Systems, and Moralities." *Journal of Gambling Studies* 21 (4): 445–479.

Black, Shameem. 2009. "Microloans and Micronarratives: Sentiment for a Small World." *Public Culture* 21 (2): 269–292.

Blum, Susan. 2005. "Five Approaches to Explaining 'Truth' and 'Deception' in Human Communication." *Journal of Anthropological Research* 61 (3): 289–315.

Borenstein, Eliot. 1999. "Public Offerings: MMM and the Marketing of Melodrama." In *Consuming Russia: Popular Culture, Sex and Society since Gorbachev*, edited by Adele M. Barker. Durham, NC: Duke University Press.

Bornstein, Erica. 2006. "Rituals without Final Acts: Prayer and Success in World Vision Zimbabwe's Humanitarian Work." In Engelke and Tomlinson 2006, 85–103.

Bosco, Joseph, Lucia Huwy-Min Liu, and Matthew West. 2009. "Underground Lotteries in China: The Occult Economy and Capitalist Culture." *Research in Economic Anthropology* 29: 31–62.

Brenneis, Don. 2006. "Reforming Promise." In *Documents: Artifacts of Modern Knowledge*, edited by Annelise Riles, 41–70. Ann Arbor: University of Michigan Press.

Brison, Karen. 1996. "Becoming Savage: Western Representations and Cultural Identity in a Sepik Society." *Anthropology and Humanism* 21 (1): 5–18.

Brown, Bruce. 1998. *Scams and Swindlers: Investment Disasters and How to Avoid Them; True Stories from ASIC*. Melbourne: Centre for Professional Development, Australian Securities and Investments Commission.

Brown, Robin. 2005a. "Meekamui vs Autonomy." *Papala Chronicles* 3, April 15.

———. 2005b. "Love Offering to PNG." *Papala Chronicles* 6, May 7.

Buck, Pem Davidson. 1989. "Cargo-Cult Discourse: Myth and the Rationalization of Labor Relations in Papua New Guinea." *Dialectical Anthropology* 13: 157–171.

Burridge, Kenelm. (1960) 1995. *Mambu: A Melanesian Millennium*. Princeton, NJ: Princeton University Press.

———.1969. *New Heaven, New Earth: A Study of Millenarian Activities*. Oxford: Blackwell.

Cahn, Peter S. 2006. "Building Down and Dreaming Up: Finding Faith in a Mexican Multilevel Marketer." *American Ethnologist* 33 (1): 126–142.

———. 2008. "Consuming Class: Multilevel Marketers in Neoliberal Mexico." *Cultural Anthropology* 23 (3): 429–452.

Callick, Rowan. 2000. "New Guinea Martyrs Day Observance." *St Peter's Eastern Hill Views*.

Callon, Michael. 1998. *The Laws of the Markets*. Oxford: Blackwell.

Cammack, Diana. 2008. "Chronic Poverty in Papua New Guinea." Background paper for the *Chronic Poverty Report*. Manchester: Poverty Research Centre.

Carrier, James. 1994. *Gifts and Commodities: Exchange and Western Capitalism since 1700*. London: Routledge.

———. 1997a. "Introduction." In *Meanings of the Market: The Free Market in Western Culture*, edited by James Carrier, 1–67. New York: Berg.

———. 1997b. "Mr Smith, Meet Mr Hawken." In *Meanings of the Market: The Free Market in Western Culture*, edited by James Carrier, 129–157. New York: Berg.

———. 1998a. "Introduction." In Carrier and Miller 1998, 1–24.

———. 1998b. "Abstraction in Western Economic Practice." In Carrier and Miller 1998, 25–48.

———. 2008. "Think Locally, Act Globally: The Political Economy of Ethical Consumption." *Research in Economic Anthropology* 28: 31–51.

Carrier, James, and Daniel Miller, eds. 1998. *Virtualism: A New Political Economy*. New York: Berg.

Carrington, Charles E. 1968. *The British Overseas: A Nation of Shopkeepers*. 2nd ed. London: Cambridge University Press.

Carvajal, Ana, Hunter Monroe, Catherine Pattillo, and Brian Wynter. 2009. "Ponzi Schemes in the Caribbean." IMF Working Paper, WP/05/95.

Chin, James. 2008. "Contemporary Chinese Community in Papua New Guinea: Old Money versus New Migrants." *Chinese Southern Diaspora Studies* 2: 117–126.

Chu, Julie. 2010. *Cosmologies of Credit: Transnational Mobility and the Politics of Destination in China*. Durham, NC: Duke University Press.

Clark, Jeffrey. 1997. "Imagining the State, or Tribalism and the Arts of Memory in the Highlands of Papua New Guinea." In *Narratives of Nation in the South Pacific*, edited by Ton Otto and Nicholas Thomas, 65–91. Amsterdam: Harwood Academic.

Coleman, Simon. 2000. *The Globalisation of Charismatic Christianity: Spreading the Gospel of Prosperity*. Cambridge: Cambridge University Press.

———. 2006. "When Silence Isn't Golden: Charismatic Speech and the Limits of Literalism." In Engelke and Tomlinson 2006, 39–61.

Comaroff, Jean, and John Comaroff. 1999. "Occult Economies and the Violence of Abstraction: Notes from the South African Post-Colony." *American Ethnologist* 26 (2): 279–303.

———. 2000. "Millennial Capitalism: First Thoughts on a Second Coming." *Public Culture* 12 (2): 291–343.

———, eds. 2001. *Millennial Capitalism and the Culture of Neoliberalism*. Durham, NC: Duke University Press.

Commonwealth of Australia. 2010. Official Committee Hansard, House of Representatives Standing Committee on Communications, Reference: Cybercrime, Wednesday, March 17.

Conroy, John. 2000. "Papua New Guinea." In *The Role of Central Banks in Microfinance in Asia and the Pacific*, edited by Asian Development Bank, 213–245. Vol. 2. Country Studies. Manila: Asian Development Bank.

Cooper, Melinda. 2013. "The Strategy of Default: Liquid Foundations in the House of Finance." *Polygraph* 23/24: 79–96.

Coronil, Fernando. 2001. "Toward a Critique of Globalcentrism: Speculations on Capitalism's Nature." In *Millennial Capitalism and the Culture of Neoliberalism*, edited by Jean Comaroff and John Comaroff, 63–87. Durham, NC: Duke University Press.

Corten, Andre, and Ruth Marshall-Fratani, eds. 2001. *Between Babel and Pentecost: Transnational Pentecostalism in Africa and Latin America*. Bloomington: Indiana University Press.

Cox, John. 2009. "Active Citizenship or Passive Clientelism: Accountability and Development in Solomon Islands." *Development in Practice* 19 (8): 964–980.

———. 2011. "Prosperity, Nation and Consumption: Fast Money Schemes in Papua New Guinea." In Patterson and Macintyre 2011b, 172–200.

———. 2013. "The Magic of Money and the Magic of the State: Fast Money Schemes in Papua New Guinea." *Oceania* 83 (3): 175–191.

———. 2014a. "Fast Money Schemes Are Risky Business: Gamblers and Investors in a Papua New Guinean Ponzi Scheme." *Oceania* 84 (3): 289–305.

———. 2014b. "Fake Money, Bougainville Politics and International Scammers." SSGM In Brief 2014/7. Canberra: Australian National University.

———. 2015. "Israeli Technicians and the Post-Colonial Racial Triangle in Papua New Guinea." *Oceania* 85 (3): 342–358.

———. 2016. "Value and the Art of Deception: Public Morality in a Papua New Guinean Ponzi Scheme." In *Anthropologies of Value: Cultures of Accumulation across the Global North and South*, edited by Luis Angosto-Ferrandez and Geir Henning Presterudstuen, 51–74. London: Pluto.

Cox, John, and Martha Macintyre. 2014. "Christian Marriage, Money Scams and Melanesian Social Imaginaries." *Oceania* 84 (2): 138–157.

Cox, John, and Georgina Phillips. 2015. "Sorcery, Christianity and the Decline of Medical Services." In *Talking It Through: Responses to Sorcery and Witchcraft Beliefs and Practices in Melanesia*, edited by Miranda Forsyth and Richard Eves, 37–54. Canberra: Australian National University Press.

Curtin, Timothy. 2011. "Privatisation Policy in Papua New Guinea." In *Policy Making and Implementation: Studies from Papua New Guinea*, edited by Ron May, 345–367. Studies from Papua New Guinea, SSGM Monograph No. 5. ANU E-Press.

———. 2000. "Cargo Cults and Discursive Madness." *Oceania* 70 (4): 345–361.

Davis, J. Ronnie. 1990. "Adam Smith on the Providential Reconciliation of Individual and Social Interests: Is Man Led by an Invisible Hand or Misled by a Sleight of Hand?" *History of Political Economy* 22 (2): 341–352.

Debord, Guy. 1994. *The Society of the Spectacle*. New York: Zone.

De Goede, Marieke. 2005. *Virtue, Fortune and Faith: A Genealogy of Finance*. Minneapolis: University of Minnesota Press.

Demian, Melissa. 2003. "Custom in the Courtroom, Law in the Village: Legal Transformations in Papua New Guinea." *Journal of the Royal Anthropological Institute* 9: 97–115.

———. 2017. "Making Women in the City: Notes from a Port Moresby Boarding House." *Signs: Journal of Women in Culture and Society* 42 (2): 403–425.

Dinnen, Sinclair. 1998. "Law, Order and State." In Zimmer-Tamakoshi 1998b, 333–350.

Dolan, Catherine. 2008. "Arbitraging Risk through Moral Values: The Case of Kenyan Freetrade." *Research in Economic Anthropology* 28: 271–296.

Donaghue, Kieran. 2004. "Microfinance in the Asia-Pacific." *Asian-Pacific Economic Literature* 18 (1): 41–61.

Douglas, Bronwen. 2000. "Weak States and Other Nationalisms: Emerging Melanesian Paradigms?" State, Society and Governance in Melanesia Discussion Paper 2000/3.

Canberra: Research School of Pacific and Asian Studies, Australian National University.

———. 2002. "Christian Citizens: Women and Negotiations of Modernity in Vanuatu." *Contemporary Pacific* 14 (1): 1–38.

———. 2003. "Christianity, Tradition, and Everyday Modernity: Towards an Anatomy of Women's Groupings in Melanesia." *Oceania* 74 (1/2): 6–23.

Dowa, Philip. 2005. "Supernatural Powers That Be." *National Weekender*, November 18.

Droogers, Andre. 2001. "Globalisation and Pentecostal Success." In Corten and Marshall-Frantani 2001, 41–61.

Dundon, Alison. 2004. "Tea and Tinned Fish: Christianity, Consumption and the Nation in Papua New Guinea." *Oceania* 75 (2): 73–88.

Dyrud, Marilyn. 2005. "'I brought you a good news': An Analysis of Nigerian 419 Letters." *Proceedings of the 2005 Association for Business Communication Annual Convention*, Irvine, CA.

Elyachar, Julia. 2005. *Markets of Dispossession: NGOs, Economic Development, and the State in Cairo.* Durham, NC: Duke University Press.

Engelke, Matthew, and Matt Tomlinson, eds. 2006. *The Limits of Meaning: Case Studies in the Anthropology of Christianity.* New York: Berghahn.

Epstein, T. S. 1964. Personal Capital Formation among the Tolai of New Britain. In *Capital Saving and Credit in Peasant Societies*, edited by Raymond Firth and Basil Selig Yamey. London: George Allen and Unwin.

Errington, Frederick. 1974. "Indigenous Ideas of Order, Time, and Transition in a New Guinea Cargo Movement." *American Ethnologist* 1 (2): 255–267.

Errington, Frederick, and Deborah Gewertz. 1997. "The Rotary Club of Wewak: The Middle Class in Papua New Guinea." *Journal of the Royal Anthropological Institute* 3 (2): 333–353.

———. 2004. *Yali's Question: Sugar, Culture and History.* Chicago: University of Chicago Press.

———. 2005. "On Humiliation and Class in Contemporary Papua New Guinea." In Robbins and Wardlow 2005, 163–170.

———. 2007. "Reconfiguring Amity at Ramu Sugar Limited." In *The Anthropology of Morality in Melanesia and Beyond*, edited by John Barker, 93–109. Aldershot, UK: Ashgate.

Evara, Rosalyn. 2010. "Bank Managers Warned against Lying." Post-Courier, February 25.

Eves, Richard. 2003. "Money, Mayhem and the Beast: Narratives of the World's End from New Ireland (Papua New Guinea)." *Journal of the Royal Anthropological Institute*, n.s, 9: 527–547.

Eves, Richard, Nicole Haley, Ron May, Phillip Gibbs, John Cox, and Francesca Merlan and Allan Rumsey. 2014. "Purging Parliament: A New Christian Politics in Papua New Guinea?" SSGM Discussion Paper 2014/1. Canberra: Australian National University.

Ewald, Francois. 1991. "Insurance and Risk." In *The Foucault Effect: Studies in Governmentality*, edited by Graham Birchill, Colin Gordon, and Peter Miller, 192–210. Chicago: University of Chicago Press.

Fairfax, Lisa M. 2001. "'With friends like these …': Toward a More Efficacious Response to Affinity-Based Securities and Investment Fraud." *Georgia Law Review* 36: 63–119.

Fassin, Didier. 2011. *Humanitarian Reason: A Moral History of the Present.* Berkeley: University of California Press.

Fife, Wayne. 1995. "The Look of Rationality and the Bureaucratization of Consciousness in Papua New Guinea." *Ethnology* 34 (2): 129–141.

Filer, Colin. 1985. "What Is This Thing Called Brideprice?" *Mankind* 15 (2): 163–183.

———. 1998. "The Melanesian Way of Menacing the Mining Industry." In Zimmer-Tamakoshi 1998b, 147–177.

———. 2006. "Custom, Law and Ideology in Papua New Guinea." *Asia Pacific Journal of Anthropology* 7 (1): 65–84.

———. 2007. "Local Custom and the Art of Land Group Boundary Maintenance in Papua New Guinea." In *Customary Land Tenure and Registration in Australia and Papua New Guinea: Anthropological Perspectives*, edited by James Weiner and Katie Glaskin, 135–173. Asia-Pacific Environment, Monograph 3. Canberra: Australian National University E-Press.

Foale, Simon. 2001. "Where's Our Development? Land-Owner Expectations and Environmentalist Agendas in Western Solomon Islands." *Asia Pacific Journal of Anthropology* 2 (2): 44–67.

Foster, Robert. 1991. "Making National Cultures in the Global Ecumene." *Annual Review of Anthropology* 20: 235–260.

———. 1992a. "Take Care of Public Telephones: Moral Education and Nation-State Formation in Papua New Guinea." *Public Culture* 4 (2): 31–45.

———. 1992b. "Commoditization and the Emergence of *kastam* as a Cultural Category: A New Ireland Case in Comparative Perspective." *Oceania* 62 (4): 284–294.

———, ed. 1995a. *Nation Making: Emergent Identities in Postcolonial Melanesia*. Ann Arbor: University of Michigan Press.

———. 1995b. "Introduction: The Work of Nation-Making." In Foster 1995a, 1–30.

———. 1995c. "Print Advertisements and Nation Making in Metropolitan Papua New Guinea." In *Nation Making: Emergent Identities in Postcolonial Melanesia*, edited by Robert Foster, 151–181. Ann Arbor: University of Michigan Press.

———. 1998. "Your Money, Our Money, the Government's Money: Finance and Fetishism in Melanesia." In *Border Fetishisms: Material Objects in Unstable Spaces*, edited by Patricia Spyer, 60–90. New York: Routledge.

———. 1999a. "Melanesianist Anthropology in the Era of Globalisation." *Contemporary Pacific* 11 (1): 140–159.

———. 1999b. "In God We Trust: The Legitimacy of Melanesian Currencies." In Akin and Robbins 1999, 214–231.

———. 2002a. *Materializing the Nation: Commodities, Consumption and Media in Papua New Guinea*. Bloomington: Indiana University Press.

———. 2002b. "Bargains with Modernity in Melanesia and Elsewhere." *Anthropological Theory* 2 (2): 233–251.

———. 2008. *Coca-Globalisation: Following Soft Drinks from New York to New Guinea*. New York: Palgrave Macmillan.

Fraenkel, Jon. 2004. *The Manipulation of Custom: From Uprising to Intervention in Solomon Islands*. Canberra: Pandanus.

Gell, Alfred. 1992. "The Technology of Enchantment and the Enchantment of Technology." In *Anthropology, Art and Aesthetics*, edited by J. Coote and A. Shelton. 40–63. Oxford: Clarendon.

Gesch, Patrick. 2007. "Working Out of Two Mindsets." *Contemporary Papua New Guinea Studies* 7: 17–34.

Gewertz, Deborah, and Frederick Errington. 1991. *Twisted Histories, Altered Contexts: Representing the Chambri in a World System*. Cambridge: Cambridge University Press.

———. 1993. "First Contact with God: Individualism, Agency and Revivalism in the Duke of York Islands." *Cultural Anthropology* 8 (3): 279–305.

———. 1996. "On PepsiCo and Piety in a Papua New Guinea 'Modernity.'" *American Ethnologist* 23 (3): 476–493.

———. 1998. "Sleights of Hand and the Construction of Desire in a Papua New Guinea Modernity." *Contemporary Pacific* 10 (2): 345–368.

———. 1999. *Emerging Class in Papua New Guinea: The Telling of Difference*. Cambridge: Cambridge University Press.

———. 2004. "Toward an Ethnographically Grounded Study of Modernity in Papua New Guinea." In *Globalization and Culture Change in the Pacific Islands*, edited by Victoria Lockwood, 273–289. Saddle River, NJ: Pearson Education.

———. 2010. *Cheap Meat: Flap Food Nations in the Pacific Islands*. Berkeley: University of California Press.

Ghai, Yash, and Anthony Regan. 2000. "Bougainville and the Dialectics of Ethnicity, Autonomy and Separation." In *Autonomy and Ethnicity: Negotiating Competing Claims in Multi-Ethnic States*, edited by Yash Ghai, 242–261. Cambridge: Cambridge University Press.

Gibbs, Philip. 2004. "Growth, Decline and Confusion: Church Affiliation in Papua New Guinea." *Catalyst* 34 (2): 164–184. Accessed March 11, 2011. http://www.philipgibbs.org /pdfs/Growth%20decline.pdf.

———. 2005a. "Political Discourse and Religious Narratives of Church and State in Papua New Guinea." SSGM Working Paper 2005/1. Canberra: Research School of Pacific and Asian Studies, Australian National University.

———. 2005b. "Finding Faith in the City: Inculturation and the Urban Experience of Engan Catholics." In *Urbanization and Mission in Asia and the Pacific*, edited by Robert Kisala, 211–245. Manila: Logos. Accessed March 11, 2011. http://www.philipgibbs.org /pdfs/Faithcity.pdf.

———. 2006. "Papua New Guinea." In *Globalisation and the Re-shaping of Christianity in the Pacific Islands*, edited by Manfred Ernst, 81–158. Suva, Fiji: Pacific Theological College.

Giddens, Anthony. 1990. *The Consequences of Modernity*. Cambridge: Polity.

Gifford, Paul. 2001. "The Complex Provenance of Some Elements of African Pentecostal Theology." In Corten and Marshall-Fratani 2001, 62–79.

———. 2004. *Ghana's New Christianity: Pentecostalism in a Globalizing African Economy*. Bloomington: Indiana University Press.

Goddard, Michael. 2005. *The Unseen City: Anthropological Perspectives on Port Moresby, Papua New Guinea*. Canberra: Pandanus, Australian National University.

Godelier, Maurice and Andrew Strathern, eds. 1991. *Big Men and Great Men: Personifications of Power in Melanesia*. Cambridge: Cambridge University Press.

Goffman, Erving. 1962. *Asylums: Essays on the Social Situation of Mental Patients and Other Inmates*. Chicago: Aldine.

Golub, Alex. 2014. *Leviathans at the Gold Mine: Creating Indigenous and Corporate Actors in Papua New Guinea*. Durham, NC: Duke University Press.

———. 2016. "Crisis and Identity in Contemporary Papua New Guinea." Hot Spots, *Cultural Anthropology* website, October 27. Accessed December 12, 2017. https://culanth.org/fieldsights/987-crisis-and-identity-in-contemporary-papua-new-guinea.

Gomez, Brian. 2004. "Plane May Have Left Weapons on Bougainville." *National*, October 19.

Government of Papua New Guinea. 2000. Memorandum of Economic and Financial Policies. Accessed December 6, 2008. http://www.imf.org/external/np/loi/2000/png/01/index.htm.

Graeber, David. 2001. *Toward an Anthropological Theory of Value: The False Coin of Our Own Dreams*. New York: Palgrave.

Greenpeace. 2004. *The Untouchables:Rimbunan Hijau's World of Forest Crime and Political Patronage*. Amsterdam: Greenpeace International.

Gregoriou, Greg, and Francois-Serge L'Habitant 2009. "Madoff: A Riot of Red Flags." EDHEC Business School.

Gregory, Christopher. 1999. "South Asian Economic Models for the Pacific? The Case of Microfinance." *Pacific Economic Bulletin* 14 (2): 82–92.

Gridneff, Ilya. 2009. "U-Vistract Conman Offers 'Jesus Money.'" *Sydney Morning Herald*, July 8.

Guyer, Jane. 1995a. "The Currency Interface and Its Dynamics." In *Money Matters: Instability, Values and Social Payments in the Modern History of West African Communities*, edited by Jane Guyer, 1–33. Portsmouth, NH: Heinemann.

———, ed. 1995b. *Money Matters: Instability, Values and Social Payments in the Modern History of West African Communities*. Portsmouth, NH: Heinemann.

———. 2004. *Marginal Gains: Monetary Transactions in Atlantic Africa*. Chicago: University of Chicago Press.

———. 2007. "Prophecy and the Near Future: Thoughts on Macroeconomic, Evangelical, and Punctuated Time." *American Ethnologist* 34 (3): 409–421.

Habermas, Jurgen. 1992. "Further Reflections on the Public Sphere." In *Habermas and the Public Sphere*, edited by Craig Calhoun, 422–461. Cambridge: MIT Press.

Halvaksz, Jamon. 2007. "Cannabis and Fantasies of Development: Revaluing Relations through Land in Rural Papua New Guinea." *Australian Journal of Anthropology* 18 (1): 56–71.

Hameiri, Shahar. 2007. "The Trouble with RAMSI: Reexamining the Roots of Conflict in Solomon Islands." *Contemporary Pacific* 19 (2): 409–441.

Hart, Keith. 1986. "Heads or Tails? Two Sides of the Coin." *Man*, n.s, 21 (4): 637–656.

———. 2000. *The Memory Bank: Money in an Unequal World*. London: Profile.

———. 2007. "Money Is Always Personal and Impersonal." *Anthropology Today* 23 (5): 12–16.

Hart, Keith, and Horacio Ortiz. 2008. "Anthropology in the Financial Crisis." *Anthropology Today* 24 (6): 1–3.

Hauck, Volker, Angela Mandie-Filer, and Joe Bolger. 2005. "Ringing the Church Bell: The Role of Churches and Public Performance in Papua New Guinea." Discussion Paper 57E. Maastricht, The Netherlands: European Centre for Development Policy Research.

Hau'ofa, Epeli. 1987. "The New South Pacific Society: Integration and Independence." In *Class and Culture in the South Pacific*, edited by Antony Hooper, Steve Britton, Ron Crocombe, Judith Huntsman, and Cluny Macpherson, 1–15. Auckland and Suva: University of Auckland and University of the South Pacific.

Hayano, David M. 1989. "Like Eating Money: Card Gambling in a Papua New Guinea Highlands Village." *Journal of Gambling Studies* 5 (3): 231–245.

Hemry, Melanie. 2009. "Life without Regret." *Believer's Voice of Victory* 37 (6): 8–11.

Hermann, Elfriede. 1992. "The Yali Movement in Retrospect: Rewriting History, Redefining 'Cargo Cult.'" *Oceania* 63 (1): 55–71.

Hermkens, A. -K. 2013. "Like Moses Who Led His People to the Promised Land: Nation- and State-Building in Bougainville." *Oceania* 83 (3): 192–207.

Herzfeld, Michael. 2005. *Cultural Intimacy: Social Poetics in the Nation-State*. New York: Routledge.

Hinn, Benny. n.d. "Your Supernatural Wealth Transfer Is Coming." Accessed September 12, 2014. http://www.bennyhinn.org/articles/7574/your-supernatural-wealth-transfer-is -coming.

Hirsch, Eric. 1990. "From Bones to Betelnuts: Processes of Ritual Transformation and the Development of 'National Culture' in Papua New Guinea." *Man*, n.s, 25 (1): 18–34.

———. 1994. "Between Mission and Market: Events and Images in a Melanesian Society." *Man*, n.s, 29 (3): 689–711.

———. 1995. "Local Persons, Metropolitan Names: Contending Forms of Simultaneity among the Fuguye, Papua New Guinea." In Foster 1995a, 185–206.

———. 2007. "Looking Like a Culture." *Anthropological Forum* 17 (3): 225–238.

Ho, Karen. 2005. "Situating Global Capitalisms: A View from Wall St Banks." *Cultural Anthropology* 20 (1): 68–96.

———. 2009. *Liquidated: An Ethnography of Wall Street*. Durham, NC: Duke University Press.

Holmes, Douglas, and George Marcus. 2005. "Cultures of Expertise and the Management of Globalization: Toward the Re-Functioning of Ethnography." In *Global Assemblages: Technology, Politics, and Ethics as Anthropological Problems*, edited by Aihwa Ong and Stephen J. Collier, 235–252. Oxford: Blackwell.

Hooper, Antony, Steve Britton, Ron Crocombe, Judith Huntsman, and Cluny Macpherson, eds. 1987. *Class and Culture in the South Pacific*. Auckland and Suva: University of Auckland and University of the South Pacific.

Howard, John. 1999. "The 1999 Corporate Public Affairs Oration." Speech presented to the Centre for Corporate Public Affairs by the Prime Minister the Hon. John Howard, MP. Melbourne, March 26. Accessed October 30, 2011. http://www.parlinfo.aph.gov.au /parlInfo.

Howes, Stephen, Andrew Anton Mako, Anthony Swan, Grant Walton, Thomas Webster, and Colin Wiltshire. 2014. *A Lost Decade? Service Delivery and Reforms in Papua New Guinea 2002–2012*. Canberra: The National Research Institute and the Development Policy Centre.

Hukula, Fiona. 2012. "Conversations with Convicted Rapists." In *Engendering Violence in Papua New Guinea*, edited by Margaret Jolly, Christine Stewart and Caroline Brewer, 197–212. Canberra: ANU E-Press.

Hunt, Stephen. 2000. "'Winning Ways': Globalisation and the Impact of the Health and Wealth Gospel." *Journal of Contemporary Religion* 15 (3): 331–347.

———. 2002. "The 'Health and Wealth' Gospel in the UK: Variations on a Theme." *Culture and Religion* 3 (1): 89–104.

IBOM (International Bank of Meekamui). 2006a. Accessed June 10, 2013. www.ibom.biz home page.

———. 2006b. "Satisfaction Guaranteed!" Accessed June 10, 2013. www.ibom.biz/testimonials .aspx.

Independent State of Papua New Guinea. 2011. *Papua New Guinea Vision 2050.* Waigani, PNG: National Strategic Task Force.

Jackson, Kevin, ed. 1995. *The Oxford Book of Money.* Oxford: Oxford University Press.

Jacobsen, Michael. 1995. "Vanishing Nations and the Infiltration of Nationalism: The Case of Papua New Guinea." In *Nation Making: Emergent Identities in Postcolonial Melanesia,* edited by Robert Foster, 227–249. Ann Arbor: University of Michigan Press.

Jafas, James. 2007. "Legitimate Payouts Must Not Be Cancelled." *Post-Courier,* September 12.

Jagui, Michael. 2005a. "Money Will Either Make or Break You." *Papala Chronicles* 14, September 16.

———. 2005b. "Fees First in History." *Papala Chronicles* 16, October 7.

———. 2005c. "Straight Forward Percentage: No Deductions like Conventional Banks." *Papala Chronicles* 18, October 21.

———. 2005d. "Fijian Security Force Arrive." *Papala Chronicles* 19, November 4.

Jarvis, Chris. 2000. "The Rise and Fall of Pyramid Schemes in Albania." *IMF Staff Papers* 47 (1): 1–29.

Jay Pee Gee. 2007. "Handout Mentality Aids Dependency." *National,* February 5.

Jebens, Holger. 2000. "Signs of the Second Coming: On Eschatological Expectation and Disappointment in Highland and Seaboard Papua New Guinea." *Ethnohistory* 47 (1): 171–204.

———, ed. 2004. *Cargo, Cult and Culture Critique.* Honolulu: University of Hawaii Press.

———. 2005. *Pathways to Heaven: Contesting Mainline and Fundamentalist Christianity in Papua New Guinea.* Oxford: Berghahn.

Johnson, Patricia Lyons. 1993. "Education and the 'New' Inequality in Papua New Guinea." *Anthropology and Education Quarterly* 24 (3): 183–204.

Jolly, Margaret. 1992a. "Specters of Inauthenticity." *Contemporary Pacific* 4 (1): 49–72.

———. 1992b. "Custom and the Way of the Land: Past and Present in Vanuatu and Fiji." *Oceania* 62 (4): 330–354.

———. 1996. "Devils, Holy Spirits, and the Swollen God: Translation, Conversion, and Colonial Power in the Marist Mission, Vanuatu, 1887–1934." In *Conversion to Modernities: The Globalization of Christianity,* edited by Peter van der Veer, 231–262. New York: Routledge.

———. 2012. "Introduction—Engendering Violence in Papua New Guinea: Persons, Power and Perilous Transformations." In *Engendering Violence in Papua New Guinea,* edited by Margaret Jolly, Christine Stewart, and Caroline Brewer, 1–46. Canberra: ANU E-Press.

———. 2013. "Agreeing to Disagree about Kago." In *Kago, Kastom and Kalja: The Study of Indigenous Movements in Melanesia Today,* edited by Marc Tabani and Marcellin Abong, 187–212. Marseilles: Pacific-CREDO.

Jolly, Margaret, and Nicholas Thomas. 1992. "Introduction." *Oceania* 62 (4): 241–248.

Jorgensen, Dan. 2005. "Third Wave Evangelism and the Politics of the Global in Papua New Guinea: Spiritual Warfare and the Recreation of Place in Telefolmin." *Oceania* 75 (4): 444–460.

———. 2007a. "Changing Minds: Hysteria and the History of Spirit Mediumship in Telefolmin." In *The Anthropology of Morality in Melanesia and Beyond,* edited by John Barker, 113–130. Aldershot, UK: Ashgate.

———. 2007b. "Clan Finding, Clan-Making and the Politics of Identity in a Papua New Guinea Mining Project." In *Customary Land Tenure and Registration in Australia and Papua New Guinea: Anthropological Perspectives*, edited by James F. Weiner and Katie Glaskin, 57–72. Asia-Pacific Environment, Monograph 3. Canberra: Australian National University E-Press.

Josephides, Lisette. 2005. "Moral and Practical Frameworks for the Self in Conditions of Social Change." In Robbins and Wardlow 2005, 115–124.

Jourdan, Christine. 1995. "Stepping-Stones to National Consciousness: The Solomon Islands Case." In Foster 1995a, 127–149.

JRopex 111. 2007. "Too Much Nepotism in the Bank." *Post-Courier*, August 6.

Kahn, Joel. 1997. "Demons, Commodities and the History of Anthropology." In *Meanings of the Market: The Free Market in Western Culture*, edited by James Carrier, 69–98. New York: Berg.

Kaima, Sam. 2004. "Politics of 'Payback': Villager Perception of Elections in the Markham Open." Paper presented at the Political Culture, Representation and Electoral Systems in the Pacific Conference, University of the South Pacific, Emalus Campus, Port Vila, Vanuatu, July 10–12.

Kamit, L. Wilson. 2006. "Speech by the Governor of the Bank of Papua New Guinea Mr L. Wilson Kamit, CBE on the Occasion of the Presentation of Certificate of Registration of Alekano Savings and Loan Society Limited."

Kaplan, Michael. 2003. "Iconomics: The Rhetoric of Speculation." *Public Culture* 15 (3): 477–493.

Karim, Lamia. 2011. *Microfinance and Its Discontents: Women in Debt in Bangladesh*. Minneapolis: University of Minnesota Press.

Karp, Ivan. 2002. "Development and Personhood: Tracing the Contours of a Moral Discourse." In *Critically Modern: Alternatives, Alterities, Anthropologies*, edited by Bruce Knauft, 82–104. Bloomington: Indiana University Press.

Kavanamur, David. 2002. "Melanesia in Review: Papua New Guinea." *Contemporary Pacific* 14 (2): 456–461.

Kavanamur, David, and Robert Turare. 1999. "Sustainable Credit Schemes for Rural Development in Papua New Guinea." *Development Bulletin* 50: 11–14.

Kavanamur, David, Charles Yala, and Quinton Clements. 2003a. "A Mixed Inheritance." In *Building a Nation in PNG: Views of the Post-Independence Generation*, edited by David Kavanamur, Charles Yala, and Quinton Clements, 1–8. Canberra: Pandanus.

Keane, Webb. 1996. "Materialism, Missionaries, and Modern Subjects in Colonial Indonesia." In *Conversion to Modernities: The Globalization of Christianity*, edited by Peter van der Veer, 137–170. New York: Routledge.

———. 2002. "Sincerity, 'Modernity,' and the Protestants." *Cultural Anthropology* 17 (1): 65–92.

———. 2007. *Christian Moderns: Freedom and Fetish in the Mission Encounter*. Berkeley: University of California Press.

Keesing, Roger M. 1978. "Politico-Religious Movements and Anticolonialism on Malaita: Maasina Rule in Historical Perspective (Part I)." *Oceania* 48 (4): 241–261.

———. 1979. "Politico-Religious Movements and Anticolonialism on Malaita: Maasina Rule in Historical Perspective (Part II)." *Oceania* 49 (1): 46–73.

Kenema, Simon. 2015. "Bougainville Revisited: Understanding the Crisis and U-Vistract through an Ethnography of Everyday Life in Nagovisi." PhD diss, University of St. Andrews.

Kenneth, Gorethy. 2003. "PM Warns against PNG Money Scams." *Post-Courier*, September 25.

———. 2005a. "U-Vistract Broke!" *Post-Courier*, October 5.

———. 2005b "U-Vistract Targets 21M Collection!" *Post-Courier*, October 10.

———. 2010a. "No Money Back Guarantee." *Weekend Courier*, May 22.

———. 2010b. "'I have lost trust in banks.'" *Post-Courier*, September 2.

Kewa, Christina. 2003. "Prayers for U-Vistract Loss." *Post-Courier*, October 15.

Keynes, John Maynard. 1936. *The General Theory of Employment, Interest, and Money*. London: Macmillan.

Kich, Martin. 2005. "A Rhetorical Analysis of Fund-Transfer-Scam Solicitations." *Cercles* 14: 129–142.

King, David. 1998. "Elites, Suburban Commuters, and Squatters: The Emerging Urban Morphology of Papua New Guinea." In Zimmer-Tamkoshi 1998b, 183–194.

Kinna, Augustine. 2006a. "Food Crisis Descends upon U-Vistract Camp." *Post-Courier*, April 10.

———. 2006b. "Fijians Alive as ABG 'Targeted U-Vistract.'" *National*, November 24.

Kirtzman, Andrew. 2009. *Betrayal. The Life and Lies of Bernie Madoff*. New York: HarperCollins.

Knauft, Bruce, M. 1999. *From Primitive to Postcolonial in Melanesia and Anthropology*. Ann Arbor: University of Michigan Press.

———. 2002. *Exchanging the Past: A Rainforest World of Before and After*. Chicago: University of Chicago Press.

Koczberski, Gina. 2007. "Loose Fruit Mamas: Creating Incentives for Smallholder Women in Oil Palm Production in Papua New Guinea." *World Development* 35 (7): 1172–1185.

Koehn, Daryl. 2001. "Ethical Issues Connected with Multi-Level Marketing Schemes." *Journal of Business Ethics* 29: 153–160.

Koim, Sam. 2009. "What about the Rest of the Public Servants?" *Post-Courier*, April 1.

Kone, Eric. 2002. "U-Vistract Man Sets Up in SI." *Post-Courier*, August 7.

Korimbao, Daniel. 2000a. "Parliament in Funds Bungle: K300,000 'Invested' in Fast Cash Scheme." *National*, January 25.

———. 2000b. "Narokobi Denies Report on Fast Cash." *National*, January 26.

Korovilas, James. 1999. "The Albanian Economy in Transition: The Role of Remittances and Pyramid Investment Schemes." *Post-Communist Economies* 11 (3): 399–414.

Korovilas, Clarence L, Jr, Thomas R. Cox, and Robert J. Morad. 2010. "A Review of Recent Investor Issues in the Madoff, Stanford and Forte Ponzi Scheme Cases." *Journal of Business and Securities Law* 10: 113–122.

Kowa, Eric. 2011. "The Crippling State of the PNG Middle Class." PNG Blogs, November 9. Accessed January 30, 2015. http://www.pngblogs.com/2011/11/crippling-state-of-png-middle-class.html.

Krau, Dominic, and Julia Daia Bore. 2002. "BPNG Raids Illegal 'Bank.'" *National*, August 20.

Krige, Detlev. 2011. "'We are running for a living': Work, Leisure and Speculative Accumulation in an Underground Numbers Lottery in Johannesburg." *African Studies* 70 (1): 3–24.

———.2012. "Fields of Dreams, Fields of Schemes: Ponzi Finance and Multi-Level Marketing in South Africa." *Africa: The Journal of the International African Institute* 82 (1): 69–92.

Krugman, Paul. 2008. "The Madoff Economy." *New York Times*, December 19.

Kulick, Don, and Christopher Stroud. 1990. "Christianity, Cargo and Ideas of Self: Patterns of Literacy in a Papua New Guinea Village." *Man*, n.s. 25 (2): 286–304.

Kurer, Oscar. 2007. "Why Do Papua New Guinean Voters Opt for Clientelism? Democracy and Governance in a Fragile State." *Pacific Economic Bulletin* 22 (1): 39–53.

La Hausse, Paul. 1992. "Who Was Elias Kuzwayo? Nationalism, Collaboration and the Picaresque in Natal." *Cahiers d'etudes africaines* 32 (127): 469–507.

Lattas, Andrew. 1998. *Cultures of Secrecy: Reinventing Race in Bush Kaliai Cargo Cults.* Madison: University of Wisconsin Press.

———. 2005. "Capitalizing on Complicity: Cargo Cults and the Spirit of Modernity on Bali Island (West New Britain)." *Ethnohistory* 52 (1): 47–80.

———. 2006a. "Technologies of Visibility: The Utopian Politics of Cameras, Television, Videos and Dreams in New Britain." *Australian Journal of Anthropology* 17 (1): 15–31.

———. 2006b. "The Utopian Promise of Government." *Journal of the Royal Anthropological Institute* 12 (1): 129–150.

———. 2007. "Cargo Cults and the Politics of Alterity: A Review Article." *Anthropological Forum*, 17 (2): 149–161.

———. 2010. *Dreams, Madness and Fairy Tales in New Britain.* Durham, NC: Carolina Academic Press.

———. 2011. "Logging, Violence and Pleasure: Neoliberalism, Civil Society and Corporate Governance in West New Britain." *Oceania* 81 (1): 88–107.

Lawrence, Peter. 1964. *Road Belong Cargo: A Study of the Cargo Movement in the Southern Madang District, New Guinea.* Melbourne: Melbourne University Press.

Lawrence, Rebecca. 2008. "NGO Campaigns and Banks: Constituting Risk and Uncertainty." *Research in Economic Anthropology* 28: 241–269.

Leal, Pablo Alejandro. 2007. "Participation: The Ascendancy of a Buzzword in the Neo-Liberal Era." *Development in Practice* 17 (4): 539–548.

Leavitt, Stephen. 1995. "Political Domination and the Absent Oppressor: Images of Europeans in Bumbita Arapesh Narratives." *Ethnology* 34 (3): 177–189.

———. 2000. "The Apotheosis of White Men?" *Oceania* 70 (4): 304–323.

———. 2005. "'We are not straight': Bumbita Arapesh Strategies for Self-Reflection in the Face of Images of Western Superiority." In Robbins and Holly Wardlow 2005, 73–84.

Lindstrom, Lamont. 1993. *Cargo Cult: Strange Stories of Desire from Melanesia and Beyond.* Honolulu: University of Hawaii Press.

Lipset, David, and Jamon Halvaksz. 2009. "Smoke as Mirror: Marijuana, the State, and Representations of the Nation in Pacific Newspapers." *Ethnology* 48 (2): 119–138.

LiPuma, Edward. 1998. "Modernity and Forms of Personhood in Melanesia." In *Bodies and Persons: Comparative Perspectives from Africa and Melanesia*, edited by Michael Lambek and Andrew Strathern, 53–79. Cambridge: Cambridge University Press.

———. 1999. "The Meaning of Money in the Age of Modernity." In Akin and Robbins 1999, 192–213.

———. 2000. *Encompassing Others: The Magic of Modernity in Melanesia.* Ann Arbor: University of Michigan Press.

LiPuma, Edward, and Benjamin Lee. 2004. *Financial Derivatives and the Globalization of Risk.* Durham, NC: Duke University Press.

Lockwood, Victoria, ed. 2004. *Globalization and Culture Change in the Pacific Islands.* Upper Saddle River, NJ: Pearson Education.

Logan, Sarah. 2012. "Rausim! Digital Politics in Papua New Guinea." State, Society and Governance in Melanesia Discussion Paper 2013/9. Canberra: Australian National University.

Lutu, Bob. 2000. "Reference Letter for Mr Noah Musingku." Affidavit in Support. M.P. No. 62 of 2000. In the Matter of U-Vistract Finance Corporation Limited. National Court of Justice at Waigani, Papua New Guinea.

Macintyre, Martha. 1998. "The Persistence of Inequality: Women in Papua New Guinea since Independence." In Zimmer-Tamakoshi 1998b, 211–231.

———. 2003. "Petztorme Women: Responding to Change in Lihir, Papua New Guinea." *Oceania* 74: 120–133.

———. 2008. "Police and Thieves, Gunmen and Drunks: Problems with Men and Problems with Society in Papua New Guinea." *Australian Journal of Anthropology* 19 (2): 179–193.

———. 2011. "Money Changes Everything: Papua New Guinean Women in the Modern Economy." In Patterson and Macintyre 2011b, 90–120.

———. 2013. "Instant Wealth: Visions of the Future on Lihir, New Ireland, Papua New Guinea." In *Kago, Kastom and Kalja: The Study of Indigenous Movements in Melanesia Today*, edited by Marc Tabani and Marcellin Abong, 123–146. Marseilles: Pacific-CREDO.

Macintyre, Martha, and Simon Foale. 2002. "Politicised Ecology: Local Responses to Mining in Papua New Guinea." Resource Management in Asia-Pacific, Working Paper 33. Canberra: Research School of Pacific and Asian Studies, Australian National University.

———. 2004. "Global Imperatives and Local Desires: Competing Economic and Environmental Interests in Melanesian Communities." In *Globalization and Culture Change in the Pacific Islands*, edited by Victoria Lockwood, 149–164. Saddle River, NJ: Pearson Education.

Maclean, Neil. 1984. "Is Gambling *'bisnis'*? The Economic and Political Functions of Gambling in the Jimi Valley." *Social Analysis* 16, 44–59.

———. 1994. "Freedom or Autonomy: A Modern Melanesian Dilemma." *Man*, n.s, 29 (3): 667–688.

Maclellan, Nic. 2007. "Fiji, Iraq, and Pacific Island Security." *Race and Class* 48 (3): 47–62.

Macpherson, Crawford Brough. 1962. *The Political Theory of Possessive Individualism: Hobbes to Locke*. Oxford: Clarendon.

Marcus, George. 1995. "Ethnography in/of the World System: The Emergence of Multi-Sited Ethnography." *Annual Review of Anthropology* 24: 95–117.

Marshall, Ruth. 2009. *Political Spiritualities: The Pentecostal Revolution in Nigeria*. Chicago: University of Chicago Press.

Marshall-Fratani, Ruth. 1996. "Mediating the Global and Local in Nigerian Pentecostalism." *Journal of Religion in Africa* 28 (3): 278–315.

———. 2001. "The Global and Local in Nigerian Pentecostalism." In Corten and Marshall-Fratani 2001, 80–105.

Martin, Bernice. 1995. "New Mutations of the Protestant Ethic among Latin American Pentecostals." *Religion* 25 (2): 101–117.

Martin, Keir. 2007. "Your Own *Buai* You Must Buy: The Ideology of Possessive Individualism in Papua New Guinea." *Anthropological Forum* 17 (3): 285–298.

———. 2010. "The Death of the Big Man: Depreciation of Elites in New Guinea." *Ethnos* 75 (1): 1–22.

———. 2013. *The Death of the Big Men and the Rise of the Big Shots.* Oxford: Berghahn.

Martin, Randy. 2002. *The Financialization of Daily Life.* Philadelphia: Temple University Press.

Masiu, Romulus. 2006. "U-Vistract Plots War." *Post-Courier*, March 9.

Masono. Raymond. 2006. "Government Capacity and Citizen Expectations in Bougainville: The Impact of Political Autonomy." Crawford School of Economics and Government. Policy and Governance, Discussion Paper 06-08. Canberra: Australian National University.

Matbob, Patrick. 2010. "Banking: Inculcating the Culture of Saving; Bringing Hope to Rural Dwellers." *Islands Business.* February.

Maurer, Bill. 2005. Mutual Life, Limited: Islamic Banking, Alternative Currencies, Lateral Reason. Princeton, NJ: Princeton University Press.

———. 2006. "The Anthropology of Money." *Annual Review of Anthropology* 35: 15–36.

Mauss, Marcel. 1990 [1950]. *The Gift: The Form and Reason for Exchange in Archaic Societies.* London: Routledge.

Maxwell, David. 1998. "'Delivered from the Spirit of Poverty?' Pentecostalism, Prosperity and Modernity in Zimbabwe." *Journal of Religion in Africa* 28 (3): 350–373.

McDougall, Debra. 2003. "Fellowship and Citizenship as Models of National Community: United Church Women's Fellowship in Ranongga, Solomon Islands." *Oceania* 74 (1/2): 61–80.

———. 2013. "Evangelical Public Culture: Making Stranger-Citizens in Solomon Islands." In *Christian Politics in Oceania*, edited by Matt Tomlinson and Debra McDougall, 122–145. London: Berghahn.

McDowell, Nancy. 1988. "A Note on Cargo Cults and Cultural Constructions of Change." *Pacific Studies* 11 (2): 121–134.

McKeown, Eamonn. 2006. "Modernity, Prestige, and Self-Promotion: Literacy in a Papua New Guinean Community." *Anthropology and Education Quarterly* 37 (4): 366–380.

McLeod, Shane. 2004. "Pyramid Scams Thrive in PNG." *ABC—The World Today*, May 24.

McMichael, Philip. 1998. "Development and Structural Adjustment." In Carrier and Miller 1998, 95–116.

Media Council of Papua New Guinea. 2007. *State of the Media Report, March 2007: Baseline Data on Media Content, Organisational Profiles and Distribution Networks to be Used to Measure the Progress and Impact of MDI.* Media for Development Initiative. Madang, PNG: Diwai Pacific.

Memoinenu, Adam. 2005. "Code of Work Ethics." *Papala Chronicles* 2, April 8.

Memsup, Jacklynne, and Martha Macintyre. 2000. "Petztorme: A Women's Organisation in the Context of a PNG Mining Project." In "Women and Governance from the Grassroots." State Society and Governance in Melanesia Discussion Paper 2000/2, edited by Bronwen Douglas, 24–26. Canberra: Research School of Pacific and Asian Studies, Australian National University.

Metta, Jack. 2000. "Musingku Moves on to Rabaul after Kavieng." *National*, May 23.

Meyer, Birgit. 1998. "The Power of Money: Politics, Occult Forces and Pentecostalism in Ghana." *African Studies Review* 41: 15–37.

———. 1999. "Commodities and the Power of Prayer: Pentecostalist Attitudes towards Consumption in Contemporary Ghana." In *Globalization and Identity: Dialectics of Flow and Closure*, edited by Brigit Meyer and Peter Geschiere, 151–176. Oxford: Blackwell.

——. 2004. "Christianity in Africa: From African Independent to Pentecostal-Charismatic Churches." *Annual Review of Anthropology* 33: 447–474.

Miikaii, Samuel. 2005. "Success Story of Royal International Banking System." *Papala Chronicles*, March 26.

Minikula, Damaris. 2005. "Hundreds Conned into Buying Gold." *National*, November 24.

Minnegal, Monica, and Peter Dwyer. 2017. *Navigating the Future: An Ethnography of Change in Papua New Guinea*. Canberra: ANU Press.

Mitchell, Timothy. 1999. "Society, Economy and the State Effect." In *State/Culture. State-Formation after the Cultural Turn*, edited by George Steinmetz, 76–97. Ithaca, NY: Cornell University Press.

——. 2002. *Rule of Experts: Egypt, Techno-Politics, Modernity*. Berkeley: University of California Press.

Miyazaki, Hirokazu. 2000. "Faith and Its Fulfilment: Agency, Exchange, and the Fijian Aesthetics of Completion." *American Ethnologist* 27 (1): 31–51.

——. 2004. *The Method of Hope: Anthropology, Philosophy and Fijian Knowledge*. Stanford, CA: Stanford University Press.

——. 2006. "Economy of Dreams: Hope in Global Capitalism and Its Critiques." *Cultural Anthropology* 21 (2): 147–172.

——. 2007. "Arbitraging Faith and Reason." *American Ethnologist* 34 (3): 430–432.

——. 2013. *Arbitraging Japan: Dreams of Capitalism at the End of Finance*. Berkeley: University of California Press.

Momis, John. 2006. "Mediating Peace and Autonomy through Consultation and Consensus: The Bougainville Experience." Paper presented to the Third Asia Pacific Mediation Forum Conference, University of the South Pacific, Suva, June 26–30, 2006. Pacific Islands Governance Portal Digital Library. *Conference Papers* 7. Suva, Fiji: University of the South Pacific. Accessed January 18, 2010. http://www.governance.usp.ac.fj.

Monsell-Davis, Michael. 1993. "Urban Exchange: Safety-Net or Disincentive?" *Canberra Anthropology* 16 (2): 45–66.

Morauta, Louise. 1974. *Beyond the Village: Local Politics in Madang, Papua New Guinea*. Canberra: Australian National University Press.

Morris, Rosalind. 2001. "Modernity's Media and the End of Mediumship? On the Aesthetic Economy of Transparency in Thailand." In *Millennial Capitalism and the Culture of Neoliberalism*, edited by Jean Comaroff and John Comaroff, 192–214. Durham, NC: Duke University Press.

Mosko, Mark. 2012. "Laki Charms: 'Luck' and Personal Agency in North Mekeo Social Change." *Social Analysis* 56 (2): 19–38.

——. 2014. "Cards on Kiriwina: Magic, Cosmology, and the 'Divine Dividual' in Trobriand Gambling." *Oceania* 83 (3): 239–255.

Mosse, David. 2005. *Cultivating Development: An Ethnography of Aid Policy and Practice*. London: Pluto.

Mount Hagen Interdenominational Pastors Fellowship. 2003. "A Call to National Repentance." Advertisement. *Post-Courier*, October 15.

Munn, Nancy. 1986. *The Fame of Gawa: A Symbolic Study of Value Transformation in a Massim (Papua New Guinea) Society*. Cambridge: Cambridge University Press.

Musaraj, Smoki. 2011. "Tales from Albarado: The Materiality of Pyramid Schemes in Postsocialist Albania." *Cultural Anthropology* 26 (1): 84–110.

Musingku, Noah. 1999. "Circular Number Jul2799." Unpublished memorandum dated July 27.

———. 2009. "Most Wanted Man." Accessed May 21, 2010. http://nmusingku.blogspot
.com/2009/06/hidden-treasure.html.

———. 2011a. "Opening Speech—14th U-Vistract Anniversary." Accessed November 7, 2011.
http://papaala-chronicles.blogspot.com/20110701archive.html.

———. 2011b. "Closing Speech—14th U-Vistract Anniversary." Accessed November 7, 2011.
http://papaala-chronicles.blogspot.com/2011/08/closing-speech-14th-uv-anniversary
.html.

Nachman, Stephen. 1984. "Lies My Informants Told Me." *Journal of Anthropological Research*
40 (4): 536–555.

———. 1986. "Discomfiting Laughter: 'Schadenfreude' among Melanesians." *Journal of
Anthropological Research* 42 (1): 53–67.

Nash, Jill, and Eugene Ogan. 1990. "The Red and the Black: Bougainvillean Perceptions of
Other Papua New Guineans." *Pacific Studies* 13 (2): 1–17.

(The) National. 1999a. "Vele 'Pressured' to Allow Money Schemes." August 5.

———. 1999b. "Praying for Reprieve." September 23.

———. 2000a. "U-Vistract Calls for More Time." March 28.

———. 2000b. "Court Deals Blow to U-Vistract." June 15.

———. 2002. "Musingku Faces Arrest after Breaching Order." September 12.

———. 2003. "Hosava Boss in Ruau Estate Deal." *National*, January 13.

———. 2004a. "B'ville Leaders Slam Musingku's 'Promises.'" May 23.

———. 2004b. "Once upon a Time There Was U-Vistract." Editorial. May 25.

———. 2005. "Modern Shylocks." Editorial. November 10.

———. 2006. "Scam Probe at City Hall." August 14.

———. 2009. "Musingku Must Be Reined In." Editorial. July 10.

Nelson, Diane. 2012a. "Banal, Familiar, and Enrapturing: Financial Enchantment after
Guatemala's Genocide." *Women's Studies Quarterly* 40 (3&4): 205–225.

———. 2012b. "Pirates, Robbers, and Mayan Shamans: The Terrible and Fine Allure of the
Spirits of Capital." *Science Fiction Studies* 39 (3): 437–458.

Newsom, John. 2002. "Bougainville Microfinance: Rebuilding Rural Communities after the
Crisis." *Development Bulletin* 57: 85–88.

Newland, Lynda. 2010. "Miracle Workers and Nationhood: Reinhard Bonnke and Benny
Hinn in Fiji." *Contemporary Pacific* 22 (1): 74–99.

O'Callaghan, Mary-Louise. 2000a. "Sinking Noah's Ark of Funny Money." *The Australian*,
May 6.

———. 2000b. "Only My Cash in Pyramid Deal, Says Watchdog." *The Australian*, May 13.

Okole, Henry. 2003. "Enhancing Nation Building through the Provincial Government
System in Papua New Guinea." In *Building a Nation in PNG: Views of the Post-
Independence Generation*, edited by David Kavanamur, Charles Yala, and Quinton
Clements, 51–67. Canberra: Pandanus

O'Neill, Kevin. 2010. *City of God: Christian Citizenship in Postwar Guatemala.* Berkeley:
University of California Press.

Opperman, Thiago Cintra. 2011. "Tsuhana: Processes of Disorder and Order in Halia." PhD
diss, University of Sydney.

———. 2015. "Fake It until You Make It: Searching for Mimesis in Buka Village Politics."
Oceania 85 (2): 199–218.

Ortiz, Horacio. 2013. "Financial Value: Economic, Moral, Political, Global." *Hau Journal of Ethnographic Theory* 3 (1): 64–79.

Otto, Ton. 1992. "The Ways of *kastom*: Tradition as Category and Practice in a Manus Village." *Oceania* 62 (4): 264–283.

———. 2009. "What Happened to Cargo Cults? Material Religions in Melanesia and the West." *Social Analysis* 53 (1): 82–102.

Palme, Robert. 2007. "60,000 Live on Loan Cash." *Post-Courier*. September 20.

Pamba, Kevin. 1999. "Money Rain Boss Wants to Fly Out and Get Cash." *National*, October 29.

Pangkatana, John. 2011. "PNG Gives K100million to Solomon Islands." *Post-Courier*, October 7.

Papala Chronicles 8. 2005a. "Businessman Gerald Kukui Showing Off His ID Card and Bank Statement while Two Bankers and a Chief Look On." May 21.

———.18. 2005b. "Liberating Wealth to God's Kingdom," October 21.

———.18. 2005c. "U-V Not a Finance Company," October 21.

Parenteau, Robert W. 2005. "The Late 1990s' US Bubble: Financialization in the Extreme." In *Financialization and the World Economy*, edited by Gerald Epstein, 111–148. Northampton, MA: Edward Elgar.

Parkop, Powes. 2009. "Fast Money Schemes Deceiving." *Post-Courier*, July 2, 2009.

Patterson, Mary. 2011. "Enchanted Economies in the Pacific and Beyond." In Patterson and Macintyre 2011b, 59–89.

Patterson, Mary, and Martha Macintyre. 2011a. "Introduction: Capitalism, Cosmology and Globalisation in the Pacific." In Patterson and Macintyre 2011b, 1–29.

———, eds. 2011b. *Managing Modernity in the Western Pacific*. St. Lucia: University of Queensland Press.

Peebles, Gustav. 2008. "Inverting the Pan-Opticon: Money and the Nationalization of the Future." *Public Culture* 20 (2): 233–265.

———. 2010. "The Anthropology of Credit and Debt." *Annual Review of Anthropology* 39: 225–240.

Pickles, Anthony. 2013a. "Pocket Calculator: A Humdrum 'Obviator' in Papua New Guinea? *Journal of the Royal Anthropological Institute* (n.s.) 19: 510–526.

———. 2013b. "'One-Man One-Man': How Slot-machines Facilitate Papua New Guineans' Shifting Relations to Each Other." In *Qualitative Research in Gambling: Exploring the Production and Consumption of Risk*, edited by Rebecca Cassidy, Claire Loussouarn, and Andrea Pisac, 171–184 Oxford: Routledge.

———. 2014a. "Introduction: Gambling as Analytic in Melanesia." *Oceania* 84 (3): 207–221.

———. 2014b. "'Bom Bombed Kwin': How Two Card Games Model Kula, Moka, and Goroka." *Oceania* 84 (1): 272–288.

Piot, Charles. 2010. *Nostalgia for the Future: West Africa after the Cold War*. Chicago: University of Chicago Press.

Pomponio, Alice, and David Lancy. 1986. "A Pen or a Bushknife? School, Work and 'Personal Investment' in Papua New Guinea." *Anthropology and Education Quarterly* 17 (1): 40–61.

(POMSoX) Port Moresby Stock Exchange. 2010. "History." Accessed June 28. www.pomsox.com.pg/history.php.

Post-Courier. 1999a. "Help 'Fast Money' Men—MPs." August 13.

———. 1999b. "Our Window of Hope—Kabui." August 26.

———. 2000a. "U-Vistract Takes Steps to File Afresh." April 25.

———. 2000b. "Judge Bangs Table over 'Fast Money.'" June 13.

———. 2001a. "U-Vistract—Change and Get Paid." May 31.

———. 2001b. "Skate Urges Christians to Rise." September 25.

———. 2010. "BSP Loses K16m in Fraudulent Activities by Its Employees—Report." March 26.

Pozza, Clarence L, Jr, Thomas R. Cox, and Robert J. Morad. 2010. "A Review of Recent Investor Issues in the Madoff, Stanford and Forte Ponzi Scheme Cases." *Journal of Business and Securities Law* 10: 113–122.

Presterudstuen, Geir Henning. 2014. "Horse Race Gambling and the Economy of 'Bad Money' in Contemporary Fiji." *Oceania* 84 (3): 256–271.

Prime Minister of Australia. 2009. "Kevin Rudd-Joint Press Conference with the Right Honorable Grand Chief Sir Michael Somare Prime Minister of Papua New Guinea, Parliament House," Parliament House, April 28. Accessed March 15, 2010. http://www .pm.gov.au/node/5207.

Reed, Adam. 2003. *Papua New Guinea's Last Place: Experiences of Constraint in a Postcolonial Prison*. New York: Berghahn.

Regan, Anthony. 2009. "Bougainville's Bernie Madoff: Noah Musingku, U-Vistract, and the Kingdom of Papala, 1996–2009; Fraud, Alternative Explanations, and Shadow States and Economies." Unpublished draft manuscript provided courtesy of the author.

———. 2010. *Light Intervention: Lessons from Bougainville*. Washington, DC: United States Institute of Peace.

Reith, Gerda. 1999. *The Age of Chance: Gambling in Western Culture*. London: Routledge.

———. 2007. "Gambling and the Contradiction of Consumption: A Genealogy of the 'Pathological' Subject." *American Behavioral Scientist* 51(1): 33–55.

Riles, Annelise. 2001. *The Network Inside Out*. Ann Arbor: University of Michigan Press.

———. 2006a. "Introduction: In Response." In *Documents: Artifacts of Modern Knowledge*, edited by Annelise Riles, 1–40. Ann Arbor: University of Michigan Press.

———. 2006b. "[Deadlines]: Removing the Brackets on Politics in Bureaucratic and Anthropological Analysis." In *Documents: Artifacts of Modern Knowledge*, edited by Annelise Riles, 71–94. Ann Arbor: University of Michigan Press.

———. 2008. "The Anti-Network: Private Global Governance, Legal Knowledge and the Legitimacy of the State." *American Journal of Comparative Law* 56 (3): 605–630.

Robbins, Joel. 1998. "On Reading 'World News': Apocalyptic Narrative, Negative Nationalism and Trans-National Christianity in a Papua New Guinea Society." *Social Analysis* 42 (2): 103–130.

———. 2004a. *Becoming Sinners: Christianity and Moral Torment in a Papua New Guinea Society*. Berkeley: University of California Press.

———. 2004b. "The Globalisation of Pentecostal and Charismatic Christianity." *Annual Review of Anthropology* 33: 117–143.

Robbins, Joel, and David Akin. 1999. "An Introduction to Melanesian Currencies: Agency, Identity, and Social Reproduction." In Akin and Robbins 1999, 1–40.

Robbins, Joel, and Holly Wardlow, eds. 2005. *The Making of Global and Local Modernities in Melanesia: Humiliation, Transformation and the Nature of Cultural Change*. Aldershot, UK: Ashgate.

Robinson, Kathryn. 2007. "Introduction: Asian and Pacific Cosmopolitans; Self and Subject in Motion." In *Asian and Pacific Cosmopolitans: Self and Subject in Motion*, edited by Kathryn Robinson, 1–15. New York: Palgrave Macmillan.

Roca, Roger Sansi. 2007. "'Dinheiro Vivo' Money and Religion in Brazil." *Critique of Anthropology* 27 (3): 319–339.

Roeber, Carter. 1999. "Middle Class Criminals: The Romance of the Ether and the City in Zambia." *City and Society* 11 (1–2): 99–116.

Roitman, Janet. 2003. "Unsanctioned Wealth; Or the Productivity of Debt in Northern Cameroon." *Public Culture* 15 (2): 211–237.

———. 2006. "The Ethics of Illegality in the Chad Basin." In *Law and Disorder in the Postcolony*, edited by Jean Comaroff and John Comaroff, 247–272. Chicago: University of Chicago Press.

Rosi, Pamela, and Laura Zimmer-Tamakoshi. 1993. "Love and Marriage among the Educated Elite." In *The Business of Marriage: Transformations in Oceanic Matrimony*. edited by Richard Marksbury, 175–204. Pittsburg: University of Pittsburgh Press.

Rousseau, Benedicta. 2015. "Finding the Diamond: Prosperity, Secrecy, and Labour in Vanuatu." *Oceania* 85 (1): 24–37.

Sahlins, Marshall. (1992) 2005. "The Economics of Develop-Man in the Pacific." Reprinted in Robbins and Wardlow 2005, 23–41.

Sai, Anastasia. 2007. "Tamot: Masculinities in Transition in Papua New Guinea." PhD diss, Victoria University, Melbourne.

Sapan, Tony. 2005a. "Women Helpers at Equal Par with Spouses (sic)." *Papala Chronicles* 9, May 28.

———. 2005b. "UK & Global Spiritual Get RKP Recognition." *Papala Chronicles* 13, June 25.

———. 2005c. "PNG Urged to Check Its Conscience." *Papala Chronicles* 15, September 23.

———. 2005d. "Millions Transacted on the First Day." *Papala Chronicles* 16, October 7.

———. 2005e. "Fees First in History." *Papala Chronicles* 16, October 7.

———. 2005f. "Take Care with Cash." *Papala Chronicles* 18, October 21.

———. 2005g. "Priscilla's Christmas Gift." *Papala Chronicles* 22, December 9.

———. 2005h. "Siwai Greater Roles in Implementation." *Papala Chronicles* 20, December 2.

Schoeffel, Penelope. 1997. "Myths of Community Management: Sustainability, the State and Rural Development in Papua New Guinea, Solomon Islands and Vanuatu." State Society and Governance in Melanesia Discussion Paper 1997/8. Canberra: Research School of Pacific and Asian Studies, Australian National University.

Schram, Ryan. 2010. "Finding Money: Business and Charity in Auhelawa, Papua New Guinea." *Ethnos* 75 (4): 447–470.

———. 2015. "Notes on the Sociology of Wantoks in Papua New Guinea." *Anthropological Forum* 25 (1): 3–20.

Schrauwers, Albert. 2003. "Through a Glass Darkly: Charity, Conspiracy and Power in New Order Indonesia." In *Transparency and Conspiracy: Ethnographies of Suspicion in the New World Order*, edited by Harry West and Todd Sanders, 125–147. Durham, NC: Duke University Press.

Schuster, Caroline. 2015. *Social Collateral: Women and Microfinance in Paraguay's Smuggling Economy*. Berkeley: University of California Press.

Sen, Amartya. 1999. *Development as Freedom*. Oxford: Oxford University Press.

Sexton, Lorraine. 1982. "*Wokmeri*: A Women's Savings and Exchange System in Highland Papua New Guinea." *Oceania* 52 (3): 167–198.

———. 1986. *Mothers of Money, Daughters of Coffee: The Wok Meri Movement*. Ann Arbor: University of Michigan Press.

Sharp, Tim, John Cox, Ceridwen Spark, Stephanie Lusby, and Michelle Rooney. 2015. "The Formal, the Informal and the Precarious: Making a Living in Urban Papua New Guinea." State Society and Governance in Melanesia Discussion Paper 2015/2. Canberra: ANU E-Press.

Sharp, Timothy. 2013. "Bais, Bisnis and Betel Nut: The Place of Traders in the Making of a Polynesian Market." In *Engaging with Capitalism: Cases from Oceania* (Research in Economic Anthropology, vol. 33), edited by Fiona McCormack and Kate Barclay, 227–256. Bingley, UK: Emerald.

———. 2016. "Trade's Value: Relational Transactions in the Papua New Guinea Betel Nut Trade." *Oceania* 86 (1): 75–91.

Shaw, Judith, and Matthew Clarke. 2004. "Risky Business in Bougainville: Implementing Microfinance in Post-Conflict Environments." Accessed February 26, 2010. Paper presented at https://www.microfinancegateway.org/sites/default/files/mfg-en -paper-risky-business-in-bougainville-implementing-microfinance-in-post-conflict -environments-2004_0.pdf Shipton, Parker. 1989. *Bitter Money: Cultural Economy and Some African Meanings of Forbidden Commodities*. American Ethnological Society, Monograph No. 1. Washington, DC: American Anthropological Society.

———. 1995. "How Gambians Save: Culture and Economic Strategy at an Ethnic Crossroads." In *Money Matters: Instability, Values and Social Payments in the Modern History of West African Communities*, edited by Jane Guyer, 245–276. Portsmouth, NH: Heinemann.

Silverman, Eric Kline. 2005. "Sepik River Selves in a Changing Modernity: From Sahlins to Psychodynamics." In Robbins and Wardlow 2005, 85–102.

Simmel, Georg. (1907) 1990. *The Philosophy of Money*. London: Routledge.

Sklair, Leslie. 1998. "The Transnational Capitalist Class." In Carrier and Miller 1998, 135–160.

Smith, Daniel Jordan. 2007. *A Culture of Corruption. Everyday Deception and Popular Discontent in Nigeria*. Princeton, NJ: Princeton University Press.

Smith, Felicia. 2010. "Madoff Ponzi Scheme Exposes 'The Myth of the Sophisticated Investor.'" *University of Baltimore Law Review* 40 (2): 215–284.

Smith, Graeme. 2012. "Chinese Reactions to Anti-Asian Riots in the Pacific." *Journal of Pacific History* 47: 93–109.

Smith, Michael French. 1994. *Hard Times on Kairiru Island: Poverty, Development, and Morality in a Papua New Guinea Village*. Honolulu: University of Hawaii Press.

Spark, Ceridwen. 2011. "Gender Trouble in Town: Educated Women Eluding Male Domination, Gender Violence and Marriage in Papua New Guinea." *Asia Pacific Journal of Anthropology* 12 (2): 164–179.

———. 2014. "An Oceanic Revolution? *Stella* and the Construction of New Femininities in Papua New Guinea and the Pacific." *Australian Journal of Anthropology* 25 (1): 54–72.

———. 2015. "Working Out What to Wear in Papua New Guinea: The Politics of Fashion in Stella Magazine." *Contemporary Pacific* 27 (1): 39–70.

Standish, Bill. 2007. "The Dynamics of Papua New Guinea's Democracy: An Essay." *Pacific Economic Bulletin* 22 (1): 135–157.

Stasch, Rupert. 2008. "Knowing Minds Is a Matter of Authority: Political Dimensions of Opacity Statements in Korowai Moral Psychology." *Anthropological Quarterly* 81 (2): 443–453.

Stead, Victoria. 2016. "Mobility and Emplacement in North Coast Papua New Guinea: Worlding the Pacific Marine Industrial Zone." *Australian Journal of Anthropology* 27 (1): 30–48.

Stent, William. 1977. "An Interpretation of a Cargo Cult." *Oceania* 47 (3): 187–219.

Stevenson, Michael. 1986. *Wokmani: Work, Money and Discontent in Melanesia.* Sydney: Oceania.

Stewart, Pamela, and Andrew Strathern 2004. *Witchcraft, Sorcery, Rumors and Gossip.* Cambridge: Cambridge University Press.

Stone, Jon, ed. 2000. *Expecting Armageddon: Essential Readings in Failed Prophecy.* New York: Routledge.

Stopim Pyramid Schemes & Scams Lo PNG. 2016. Facebook page. Accessed June 21, 2016. https://www.facebook.com/photo.php?fbid=1397239280292031&set=0.1007533789333120 &type=3&theater.

Strange, Susan. 1986. *Casino Capitalism.* Oxford: Blackwell.

——. 1998. *Mad Money: When Markets Outgrow Governments.* Ann Arbor: University of Michigan Press.

Strathern, Andrew. 1979. "The Red-Box Money Cult in Mount Hagen, 1968–71 (Part I)." *Oceania* 50 (2): 88–102.

——. 1980. "The Red-Box Money Cult in Mount Hagen, 1968–71 (Part II)." *Oceania* 50 (3): 161–175.

Strathern, Marilyn. 1975. *No Money on Our Skins: Hagen Migrants in Port Moresby.* New Guinea Research Bulletin 61. Canberra: Australian National University.

——. 1988. *The Gender of the Gift: Problems with Women and Problems with Society in Melanesia.* Berkeley: University of California Press.

——. 1992. "The Decomposition of an Event." *Cultural Anthropology* 7: 244–254.

——. 1999. *Property, Substance and Effect: Anthropological Essays on Persons and Things.* London: Athlone.

Street, Alice. 2014. *Biomedicine in an Unstable Place: Infrastructure and Personhood in a Papua New Guinean Hospital.* Durham, NC: Duke University Press.

Sutcliffe, Richard. 2011. "The Imaginary Excess of Reason: Critical Reflections on Magic and Modernity in the Context of Post-Millennial Capitalism." In Patterson and Macintyre 2011b, 30–58.

Sykes, Karen. 2001. "Paying School Fees Is a Father's Duty: Critical Citizenship in Central New Ireland." *American Ethnologist* 28 (1): 5–31.

——. 2005. "Turning to Violence: Hazarding Intent in Central New Ireland." In Robbins and Wardlow 2005, 171–182.

——. 2007a. "Introduction: Interrogating Individuals: The Theory of Possessive Individualism in the Western Pacific." *Anthropological Forum* 17 (3): 213–224.

——. 2007b "The Moral Grounds of Critique: Between Possessive Individuals, Entrepreneurs and Big Men in New Ireland." *Anthropological Forum* 17 (3): 255–268.

Sympathizer. 2003. "Money Schemes Are Satan's Snares." *National,* November 20, 2003.

Tabani, Marc. 2013. "What's the Matter with Cargo Cults Today?" In *Kago, Kastom and Kalja: the Study of Indigenous Movements in Melanesia Today,* edited by Marc Tabani and Marcellin Abong, 7–28. Marseilles: Pacific-CREDO.

Tanis, James. 2005. "Nagovisi Villages as a Window on Bougainville in 1998." In *Bougainville before the Conflict*, edited by Anthony Regan and Helga Griffin, 447–472. Canberra: Pandanus, ANU Press.

Taussig, Michael. 1980. *The Devil and Commodity Fetishism in South America*. Chapel Hill: University of North Carolina Press.

———. 1993. *Mimesis and Alterity: A Particular History of the Senses*. London: Routledge.

Taylor, Charles. 2004. *Modern Social Imaginaries*. Durham, NC: Duke University Press.

Tennant, David. 2011. "Why Do People Risk Exposure to Ponzi Schemes? Econometric Evidence from Jamaica." *Journal of International Financial Institutions, Markets and Money* 21: 328–246.

Thatcher, Margaret. 1976. "Speech to British Chamber of Commerce in the Hague." Accessed January 13, 2011. http://www.margaretthatcher.org/document/103165.

Thomas, Nicholas. 1997. "Nation's Endings: From Citizenship to Shopping?" In *Narratives of Nation in the South Pacific*, edited by Ton Otto and Nicholas Thomas, 211–219. Amsterdam: Harwood Academic.

Thrift, Nigel. 1998. "Virtual Capitalism: The Globalisation of Reflexive Business Knowledge." In Carrier and Miller 1998, 161–187.

———. 2001. "'It's the Romance Not the Finance That Makes the Business Worth Pursuing': Disclosing a New Market Culture." *Economy and Society* 30 (4): 412–32.

Thrift, Nigel, and Andrew Leyshon. 1994. "A Phantom State? The De-Traditionalization of Money, the International Financial System and International Financial Centres." *Political Geography* 13 (4), 299–327.

Tomlinson, Matt. 2011. "The True Me: Individualism and Biblical Types in Fijian Methodism." In Patterson and Macintyre 2011b, 147–171.

Tomlinson, Matt, and Matthew Engelke. 2006. "Meaning, Anthropology, Christianity." In Engelke and Tomlinson 2006, 1–37.

Tomlinson, Matt, and Debra McDougall, eds. 2013a. *Christian Politics in Oceania*. London: Berghahn.

———. 2013b. "Introduction." In *Christian Politics in Oceania*, edited by Matt Tomlinson and Debra McDougall, 1–21. London: Berghahn.

Tonkinson, Robert. 2007. "*Homo anthropologicus* in Aboriginal Australia: 'Secular Missionaries,' Christians and Morality in the Field." In *The Anthropology of Morality in Melanesia and Beyond*, edited by John Barker, 171–189. Aldershot, UK: Ashgate.

Toreas, Winterford. 2014. "Police Chief Tells Musingku Not to Mislead Public." *Post-Courier*, March 5, 13.

Trouillot, Michel-Rolph. 2001. "The Anthropology of the State in the Age of Globalization: Close Encounters of the Deceptive Kind." *Current Anthropology* 42 (1): 125–138.

Tsing, Anna Lowenhaupt. 2000a. "The Global Situation." *Cultural Anthropology* 15 (3): 327–360.

———. 2000b. "Inside the Economy of Appearances." *Public Culture* 12 (1): 115–144.

———. 2005. *Friction: An Ethnography of Global Connections*. Princeton, NJ: Princeton University Press.

Turner, Mark. 1990. *Papua New Guinea: The Challenge of Independence; A Nation in Turmoil*. Ringwood, Victoria: Penguin Australia.

Tuzin, Donald. 1997. *The Cassowary's Revenge*. Chicago: University of Chicago Press.

U-Vistract News. 2001a. "The U-Vistract Vision: 'Every Knee Shall Bow and Every Tongue Confess That Jesus Christ is Lord' Phil 2:9–11; Financiers of the End-Time Harvest."

———. 2001b. "Globalism: Economic Slavery of the Third World."

United States Embassy, Port Moresby. 2006. "Ponzi Politics." Diplomatic CableWe #06PORTMORESBY274. Accessed September 3, 2011. http://wikileaks.org /cable/2006/07/06PORTMORESBY274.html.

Van der Veer, Peter, ed. 1996. *Conversion to Modernities: The Globalization of Christianity*. New York: Routledge.

Van Fossen, Anthony B. 2002. "Financial Frauds and Pseudo-States in the Pacific Islands." *Crime, Law and Social Change*. 37 (4): 357–378.

———. 2003. "Money Laundering, Global Financial Instability and Tax Havens in the Pacific Islands." *Contemporary Pacific*. 15 (2): 237–275.

Verdery, Katherine. 1995. "Faith, Hope and Caritas in the Land of the Pyramids: Romania, 1990 to 1994." *Comparative Studies in Society and History* 37 (4): 625–699.

———. 1996. *What Was Socialism and What Comes Next?* Princeton, NJ: Princeton University Press.

Vulum, Sam. 2005. "The Rise and Rise of Money-Making Schemes." *Islands Business*, October.

Wardlow, Holly. 2002. "'Hands-up'-ing Buses and Harvesting Cheese-Pops: Gendered Mediation of Modern Disjuncture in Melanesia." In *Critically Modern: Alternatives, Alterities, Anthropologies*, edited by Bruce Knauft, 144–172. Bloomington: Indiana University Press.

———. 2006a. "All's Fair When Love Is War: Romantic Passion and Companionate Marriage among the Huli of Papua New Guinea." In *Modern Loves: The Anthropology of Romantic Courtship and Companionate Marriage*, edited by Jennifer Hirsch and Holly Wardlow, 51–77. Ann Arbor: University of Michigan Press.

———. 2006b. *Wayward Women: Sexuality and Agency in a Papua New Guinea Society*. Berkeley: University of California Press.

Weber, Max. (1920) 1976. *The Protestant Ethic and the Spirit of Capitalism*. 2nd ed. Translated by Talcott Parsons. London: Allen and Unwin.

———. (1927) 1999. *Essays in Economic Sociology*, edited by Richard Swedberg. Princeton, NJ: Princeton University Press.

Weiner, James F, and Katie Glaskin. 2007. *Customary Land Tenure and Registration in Australia and Papua New Guinea: Anthropological Perspectives*. Asia-Pacific Environment Monograph 3. Canberra: Australian National University E-Press.

Wendel, John P. 2007. "Making and Unmaking Possessive Individuals: 'Xavier Borrowing' at a Catholic Mission Pacific Islands Secondary School." *Anthropological Forum* 17 (3): 269–283.

Werbner, Richard. 2007. "Foreword." In *Asian and Pacific Cosmopolitans: Self and Subject in Motion*, edited by Kathryn Robinson, x–xvi. New York: Palgrave Macmillan.

Were, Graeme. 2007. "Fashioning Belief: The Base of the Baha'i Faith in Northern New Ireland." *Anthropological Forum* 17 (3): 239–253.

West, Harry, and Todd Sanders, eds. 2003. *Transparency and Conspiracy: Ethnographies of Suspicion in the New World Order*. Durham, NC: Duke University Press.

West, Paige. 2001. "Environmental Non-Governmental Organizations and the Nature of Ethnographic Inquiry." *Social Analysis* 45 (2): 55–77.

———. 2006. *Conservation Is Our Government Now: The Politics of Ecology in Papua New Guinea*. Durham, NC: Duke University Press.

———. 2012. *From Modern Production to Imagined Primitive: The Social World of Coffee from Papua New Guinea*. Durham, NC: Duke University Press.

White, Geoffrey, and Lamont Lindstrom, eds. 1997. *Chiefs Today: Traditional Pacific Leadership and the Postcolonial State*. Stanford, CA: Stanford University Press.

Wikipedia. 2011a. "Noah Musingku." Accessed January 28, 2011. http://en.wikipedia.org /wiki/NoahMusingku.

———. 2011b. "U-Vistract." http://en.wikipedia.org/wiki/U-Vistract. Accessed January 28, 2011.

Wolfers, Edward P. 2006. "International Peace Missions in Bougainville, Papua New Guinea, 1990–2005. Host State Perspectives." Paper presented at the Regional Forum on Reinventing Government, Exchange and Transfer of Innovations for Transparent Governance and State Capacity. Nadi, Fiji Islands, February 20–22.

Wood, Mike. 1995. "'White Skins,' 'Real People' and 'Chinese' in Some Spatial Transformations of the Western Province, PNG." *Oceania* 66 (1): 23–50.

World Bank. 2007. *Strategic Directions for Human Development in Papua New Guinea. Directions in Development*. Washington, DC: World Bank. Accessed December 20, 2017. http://documents.worldbank.org/curated/en/349761468287124426/Strategic -directions-for-human-development-in-Papua-New-Guinea.

Worsley, Peter. (1957) 1968. *The Trumpet Shall Sound: A Study of "Cargo Cults" in Melanesia*. 2nd, augmented ed. New York: Schocken.

Zaloom, Caitlin. 2003. "Ambiguous Numbers: Trading Technologies and Interpretation in Financial Markets." *American Ethnologist* 30 (2): 258–272.

———. 2006. *Out of the Pits: Traders and Technology from Chicago to London*. Chicago: University of Chicago Press.

———. 2009. "How to Read the Future: The Yield Curve, Affect and Financial Prediction." *Public Culture* 21 (2): 245–268.

Zelizer, Viviana. 1994. *The Social Meaning of Money*. New York: Basic.

———. 2011. *Economic Lives: How Culture Shapes the Economy*. Princeton, NJ: Princeton University Press.

Zimmer, Laura. 1986. "Card Playing among the Gende: A System for Keeping Money and Social Relationships Alive." *Oceania* 56 (4): 245–263.

Zimmer-Tamakoshi, Laura. 1993. "Nationalism and Sexuality in Papua New Guinea." *Pacific Studies* 16 (4): 61–97.

———. 1997. "The Last Big Man: Development and Men's Discontents in the Papua New Guinea Highlands." *Oceania* 68 (2): 107–122.

———. 1998a. "Introduction." In Zimmer-Tamakoshi 1998b, 1–16.

———, ed. 1998b. *Modern Papua New Guinea*. Kirksville, MO: Thomas Jefferson.

———. 2014. "'Our Good Work' or 'the Devil's Work'? Inequality, Exchange, and Card Playing among the Gende." *Oceania* 84 (3): 222–238.

Zorn, Jean. 2012. "Engendering Violence in the Papua New Guinea Courts: Sentencing in Rape Trials." In *Engendering Violence in Papua New Guinea*, edited by Margaret Jolly, Christine Stewart, and Caroline Brewer, 163–196. Canberra: ANU E-Press.

Zuckoff, Mitchell. 2005. *Ponzi's Scheme: The True Story of a Financial Legend*. New York: Random House.

Index

DR. JOHN COX is Research Fellow at the Institute for Human Security and Social Change at La Trobe University in Melbourne, Australia. He has more than twenty years of experience working in the Pacific region as a development practitioner and anthropologist.

Lightning Source UK Ltd.
Milton Keynes UK
UKHW020618091218
333620UK00012B/578/P